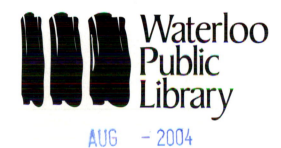

How It Works®

Science and Technology

Third Edition

Marshall Cavendish
99 White Plains Road
Tarrytown, NY 10591

Website: www.marshallcavendish.com

Third edition updated by Brown Reference Group plc.

Library of Congress Cataloging-in-Publication Data
How it works: science and technology.—3rd ed.
p. cm.
Includes index.
ISBN 0-7614-7314-9 (set)   ISBN 0-7614-7318-1 (Vol. 4)
1. Technology—Encyclopedias. 2. Science—Encyclopedias.
[1. Technology—Encyclopedias. 2. Science—Encyclopedias.]
T9 .H738 2003
603—dc21   2001028771

Consultant: Donald R. Franceschetti, Ph.D., University of Memphis

Brown Reference Group
Editor: Wendy Horobin
Associate Editors: Paul Thompson, Martin Clowes, Lis Stedman
Managing Editor: Tim Cooke
Design: Alison Gardner
Picture Research: Becky Cox
Illustrations: Mark Walker

Marshall Cavendish
Project Editor: Peter Mavrikis
Production Manager: Alan Tsai
Editorial Director: Paul Bernabeo

Printed in Malaysia
Bound in the United States of America
08 07 06 05 04   6 5 4 3 2

Title picture: Kismet, the baby robot, see *Computer*

How It Works®

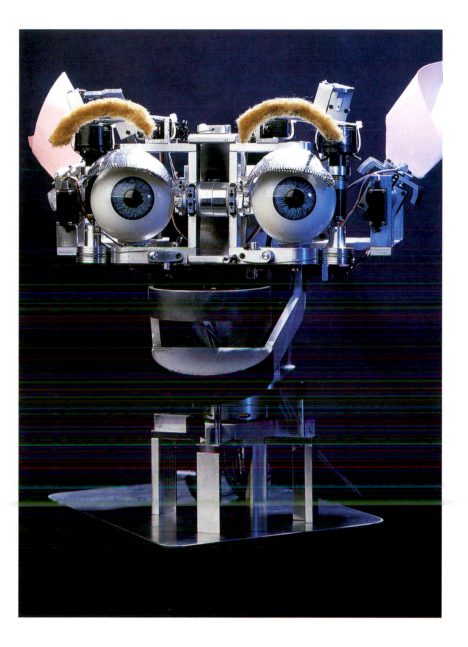

Science and Technology

Volume 4

Chemical and Biological Warfare

Cosmology

Marshall Cavendish

New York • London • Toronto • Sydney

Contents

Volume 4

Chemical and
    Biological Warfare 437
Chemical Bonding and Valency 442
Chemistry, Analytical 445
Chemistry, Inorganic 449
Chemistry, Organic 453
Chemistry, Organometallic 459
Chemistry, Physical 461
China and Porcelain 465
Chromatography 469
Chromium 472
Civil Engineering 474
Climatology 477
Clock 481
Clothing Manufacture 489
Clutch 491
Coal Mining 493
Coal Tar 498
Cocoa Manufacture 499
Coffee 501

Coffee-Making Equipment 504
Cog Railway 506
Coins and Minting 507
Colorimetry 510
Compact Disc, Audio 513
Compressor and Pump 518
Computer 523
Computer Graphics 532
Computer Network 537
Computer Printer 543
Concrete 546
Condensed-Matter Physics 550
Conduction, Electrical 554
Confectionery 557
Contact Lens 560
Conveyor 564
Copper 566
Corrosion Prevention 569
Cosmology 572

Chemical and Biological Warfare

Although the destructive power of chemical and biological weapons reached new heights in the 20th century, the use of such agents in warfare has a long history. The Greeks and Romans used human and animal corpses to poison drinking water, and the practice of throwing the corpses of plague victims over the walls of besieged cities brought many a conflict to a speedy end. In their war of attrition against the native tribes of North America, the settlers reportedly distributed infected blankets from smallpox hospitals as presents to mollify disaffected chiefs. In military terms, chemical and biological warfare has been seen as a means of rendering an opponent vulnerable by incapacitating troops, by affecting crops and livestock, and by spreading panic.

Today, chemical weapons are banned under the terms of the Chemical Weapons Convention (CWC), which came into force in 1997. The possession of biological weapons was also banned by a 1972 convention, but research proceeds under a number of guises; despite these international agreements a number of countries are suspected of having active programs to develop and test such weapons. Even with these conventions in place, there are large stockpiles of old weapons to be destroyed, and tests need to be developed to aid identification and verification of chemical and biological agents.

Chemical weapons

Thousands of different compounds have been tested as agents for killing or incapacitating people and for destroying vegetation, crops, and livestock. Casualty-producing agents include poison gas, nerve gas, and psychochemicals. Poisonous gases such as chlorine, phosgene, and mustard gas were developed for use in World War I. Chlorine and phosgene affect the air passages and promote massive secretion of fluid into the lungs. Mustard gas is a vesicant, producing blisters on exposed skin, and causing lung damage. The nerve gases are organophosphorus compounds similar to those used today as insecticides. It was the search for superior insecticides in Germany that led in 1936 to the discovery of tabun, the first nerve gas. Two related compounds (Sarin and Soman) were discovered soon afterward and together formed the basis of Germany's secret weapon during World War II (though they were never used). Work in Britain in the 1950s (at Imperial Chemical Industries) resulted in another group of nerve gases—the V agents. These are much more toxic than the poison gases and as little as

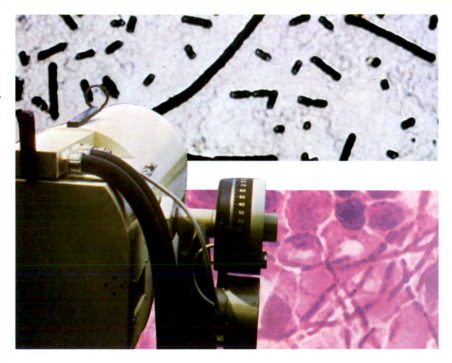

▲ Laser-beam monitoring equipment (far left) can detect particle clouds of biological agents. Typhoid bacilli (top) responsible for food poisoning can be spread by aerosol dust, which is inhaled, or by lice bites. Anthrax (bottom, shown in the pleural fluid that surrounds the lungs) is an animal disease that can cause fever, breathing difficulties, and even death among humans. The deadly effect of anthrax became apparent in the wake of the attacks in New York and Washington on September 11, 2001, when a number of letters containing anthrax spores were sent to prominent figures in the United States. Five people died as a result of handling the letters and many Senate buildings and mail-sorting offices had to be decontaminated with chlorine dioxide gas to remove any trace of anthrax spores.

one-thousandth of a gram could prove fatal. While termed gases, these agents are volatile liquids that vaporize to a greater or lesser extent depending on atmospheric conditions.

Nerve gases are highly toxic because they interfere with the passage of information in parts of the nervous system, particularly with the nervous control of muscle contraction, by inhibiting irreversibly a key enzyme—acetylcholinesterase. Initial symptoms of nerve gas exposure include sweating and vomiting. As muscular control is lost, there is tightness in the chest, convulsions, and finally death from asphyxiation. Exposure to a lethal dose results in death within minutes.

Psychochemicals were developed in the 1950s after discoveries in brain research had revealed that the passage of information between cells in the nervous system involved particular chemicals. A number of compounds, both natural and synthetic, can stimulate or block specific parts of the nervous system, for example, mescaline, lysergic acid diethylamide (LSD), and quinuclidinyl benzilate (BZ). BZ produces giddiness, disorientation, and amnesia when sprayed over troops.

Incapacitants, like the tear gases, are used by governments throughout the world. CS gas (2-chlorobenzal malonitrile), a British discovery of the 1950s, is dispersed as an aerosol (for example, from an exploding cartridge) or is dusted onto the ground as a powder. It causes a burning sensation when contacting the skin, difficulty in breathing, tears, and nausea. In confined spaces, tear gas has proved fatal.

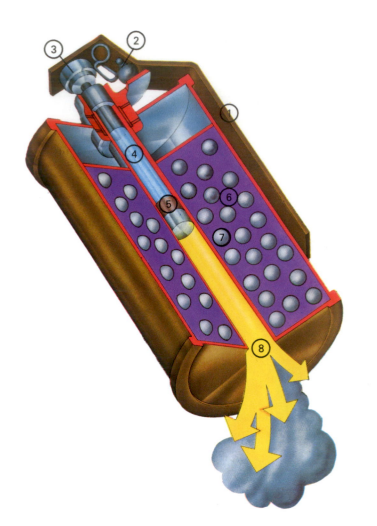

Venezuelan equine encephalomyelitis, and Q fever) and bacterial (tularemia and brucellosis). These agents were designed to be disseminated in aerosol form, or in the case of yellow fever (which has a death rate approaching 100 percent), mosquitoes were to be used as vectors of the disease.

A number of organisms (plant and animal) that normally do not infect human populations produce highly toxic substances. Saxitoxin, a product of a marine microorganism that forms part of the diet of some shellfish, was considered by the CIA as a potential agent. So too was ricin, a product of the castor bean, alleged to have been used to assassinate a Bulgarian exile in London in 1978.

Use of chemical and biological agents in warfare

The most persistent use of chemical weapons was between 1915 and 1918. Chlorine, phosgene, and mustard gas caused over one million casualties on all sides, 10 percent of them fatal. Since that time, chemical and biological agents have been used but in a different way—mainly by well-equipped armies against small, poorly defended groups.

Italian aircraft sprayed phosgene and mustard gas over parts of Ethiopia during their annexation of 1935–1936. The Japanese used mustard gas in their invasion of China in 1937, and they were also experimenting with biological agents (especially plague bacteria) in China at this time. The United States was accused of using poison gas in the Korean war (1951). The U.S. military did spread 17 million gallons of defoliants from spray bombers over southeast Asia between 1962 and 1971, causing the destruction of 36 percent of the mangrove forests and disrupting the ecology. The devastation produced remains to this day and continues to disrupt recovery.

Modern armies train in antigas suits, which are quite effective against gas, and they possess systems that give early warning of an attack. To be useful, nerve gas would need to be delivered suddenly, for example, in an attempt by an armored

Defoliating agents are herbicides based on compounds that mimic the action of plant growth hormones and cause plants to outgrow their strength. The defoliants 2,4-D and 2,4,5-T (di- and tri-chlorphenoxy acetic acid) were used in various proportions as Agents Blue, Orange, and White by the U.S. Army in the Vietnam War. These preparations were found to be contaminated with dioxin, a highly toxic carcinogen that resulted in many casualties.

▲ Releasing the lever (1) of a chemical grenade causes the primer mechanism (2) to make the prime (3) break the phial of delay mixture (4). The ignition mixture (5) triggers the fuel (6) to carry the active agent (7) out of the outlet port (8).

Biological weapons and toxins

A number of bacteria and viruses harmful to human, animal, and plant populations have been investigated for their potential in warfare. In some cases, the organism itself has been proposed as the agent to be dispersed, in other cases, the toxic products (toxins) of organisms. Largely through research at secret establishments at Porton Down (Britain) and Fort Detrick (Maryland) anthrax bomblets were designed in the 1940s for use against German cities. Though these were never used, the desolate Gruinard Island off the west coast of Scotland remains a grim warning of the devastating and persistent effects that anthrax can have. Between 1940 and 1968, the United States had developed various antipersonnel agents, both viral (yellow fever,

▶ A U.S. Air Force plane sprays a defoliant agent over forest during the Vietnam War in order to strip trees (to expose troop movements) and ruin crops.

division to break through front line troops. An army operating in antigas suits would be below maximal efficiency, and it is claimed that this would confer some advantage on the attacker. Of course, nerve gas, like the neutron bomb, does not destroy property, and an attack on important strategic targets (power stations, bridges, and air and seaports) would leave these intact. However, gas is a fickle weapon, dependent upon prevailing winds, humidity, and temperature for its effectiveness. Although troops may be protected, civilians could be caught downwind of any attack. While antidotes are available, these must be administered within minutes.

The most recent use of chemical weapons occurred during the Iran–Iraq war of 1983–1988, when Iraq launched extensive chemical attacks on its neighbor. Although the use of such weapons ran contrary to the 1925 Geneva Protocol, response to Iraq's flaunting of its conventions went largely unremarked, and a number of other countries saw it as an opportunity to arm themselves with similar weapons. This lack of censure rebounded when the allied forces were faced with the prospect of Iraq's arsenal of chemical and biological weapons during the 1991 Gulf War.

A more alarming use of a chemical agent occurred in 1995, when the nerve gas Sarin was introduced into the Tokyo subway by the Aum Shinrikyo cult. Twelve people died in the attack and 5,500 were affected by the gas.

International law

The 1925 Geneva Protocol outlawed the first use in war of asphyxiating, poisonous, or other gases. This treaty has now been superseded by the Chemical Weapons Convention (CWC), which came into force in 1997 after ratification by 135 countries. Under the terms of the treaty, member states are prohibited from developing, producing, stockpiling, selling, or using these weapons and are also committed to destroying any chemical weapons they may already have. Signatories to the 1972 Biological and Toxin Weapons Convention undertake never to develop, produce, stockpile, or retain biological agents or toxins other than for defense or for the treatment of disease. Signatories also agree never to use these weapons or variants of them in armed conflict.

Disposal of chemical weapons

Though countries are now banned from producing chemical weapons, there remains the problem of disposal of stockpiled chemicals and loaded munitions. Added to this is disposal of abandoned weapons left behind during earlier conflicts. The CWC forbids dumping in water, land burial, and open-pit burning as methods of disposal because of the possibility of environmental contamination. However, the convention permits weapons that were buried before 1977 to stay underground unless they are exposed by excavation. The state that abandoned them is then responsible for their

▲ NATO troops exercising under simulated chemical warfare conditions in specially designed all-enveloping battlefield protection suits.

safe disposal. Similarly, it is safer in many instances to let weapons dumped in deep water remain where they are. Many of the chemicals used break down or dissolve in water in a relatively short period of time, though mustard forms into insoluble globules and has caused injuries to fishermen and others when it has washed up on beaches.

Acceptable technologies under the CWC, therefore, restrict disposal to incineration or degradation. Incineration has been adopted by a number of countries, including the United States, Germany, and Canada. Only the United States and Russia have admitted having current stockpiles of chemical weapons of some 30,000 and 40,000 tons (27,000 and 36,000 tonnes), respectively, though the widespread nature of wars over the last century means that most countries need to have the ability to dispose of old and dumped weapons.

▼ A civil defense mask, consisting of a close-fitting helmet and hood, designed to exclude nuclear-fallout dusts, chemical agents, and biological aerosols. For maximum protection, it is worn with a body suit.

The Baseline incineration process used by the United States is designed to expose workers at the plant to minimum contact with the chemicals involved. The chemical is removed from the container by automated equipment, which separates it into four streams—chemical agents, explosive and propellant materials, contaminated containers, and potentially contaminated packing materials. The chemicals are burned first at 2700°F (1480°C) and then again in an afterburner, which eliminates any trace contamination. Gases and particulates from the effluent are removed by pollution-abatement techniques, leaving a product that is no more toxic than effluents from a chemical plant. The other materials are destroyed in furnaces and disposed of in an environmentally safe manner.

A number of methods have been put forward for chemical degradation of toxic agents. Some chemicals can be degraded quite easily with acids and alkalis, others may require various oxidation techniques such as biological or electrochemical oxidation, wet-air oxidation, and supercritical oxidation. Other techniques convert the chemicals into combustible gases using molten-metal or plasma-arc processes, which can then be burned and put through a pollution-abatement process. One method developed in the United Kingdom can break toxic chemicals down into carbon dioxide, water, and harmless salts by means of an electrochemical oxidation reaction that employs highly reactive silver ions.

Biological weapon defenses

While research into potential biological agents is banned, military research into vaccines against their effects proceeds. Biological agents can be cultured in a room the size of an average living room using little more than a beer fermenter, a gas mask, and a protective plastic overgarment, making biological weapons manufacture easy to hide from investigators and within the capabilities of terrorists. The only restraint on their use in terrorism may be the uncertainty of any long-term effects, which would have consequences for the terrorist as well as the target.

Realistically, even if vaccines can be developed for biological agents, unless the bacteria used in the weapon is known and their deployment predicted, it would be impossible to vaccinate an entire country's population against attack. Advances in genetic engineering, while useful in developing the means to combat known bacterial agents, can also be used to develop strains that are immune to vaccines and antibiotics. Highly infectious "superbugs" already exist in nature, such as the deadly Ebola virus, which can kill 90 percent

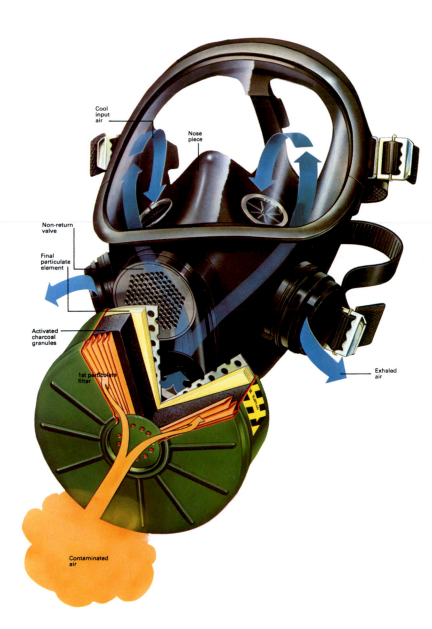

Cool input air

Nose piece

Non-return valve

Final particulate element

Activated charcoal granules

1st particulate filter

Exhaled air

Contaminated air

of its victims within a week of contracting the disease. There is no known treatment or cure for Ebola, and even the manner in which it spreads is uncertain.

Physical defenses against biological weapons are less complicated than those for chemical weapons, as most cannot penetrate intact skin. Some sort of gas mask and protective clothing would suffice, although wearing them for long periods in hot climates would prove difficult. Sunlight and ambient temperatures would do much to reduce the effectiveness of many organisms after only a few days or weeks. Physical defenses would prove impractical, however, against some bacteria. Anthrax can persist in the environment for more than 40 years.

Identifying biological attacks

A problem that persists despite the existence of treaties to ban biological weapons is detecting their presence in the event of a suspected attack. Unlike chemical agents, which may be colored or have a characteristic smell and can be easily detected, biological agents are invisible. The U.S. military is investigating the use of ion-trap mass spectrometry and laser-induced breakdown spectoscopy to identify biological agents in the air by pinpointing characteristic chemicals associated with them. The military is also developing its Biological Integrated Detection System (BIDS), which tries to identify agents through antibody-antigen combinations. The antibody will react to a specific biological agent in about 30 minutes. So

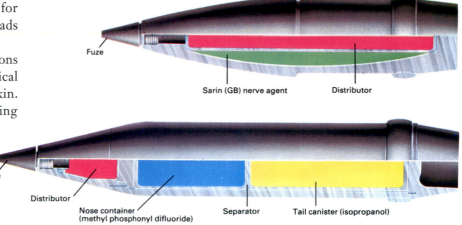

far, four agents can be detected by this method: *Bacillus anthracis* (anthrax), botulinum toxin, *Yersinia pestis* (bubonic plague), and staphylococcus enterotoxin B. However, the enormous range of biological toxins casts doubt on whether this method can be applied to all potential agents, or even if it can keep up with natural mutations.

Perhaps the most effective method of preventing use of biological weapons is increasing intelligence operations and monitoring the sale of pathogens from laboratories around the world, particularly to countries or organizations suspected of having secret development programs. Efforts are also being concentrated on identifying baseline data for endemic diseases around the world so as to pick up any unusual outbreaks.

▲ Traditional chemical shells (top) contain the nerve agent in its active, lethal form but are not immune to leaks. The binary chemical shell (bottom) contains the two harmless contents of the nerve agent (in this case, Sarin), and the separator keeps the two apart until the shell is fired—a safe distance from the troops that are dispatching it.

Other forms of biowarfare

Biological weapons are not just developed to attack humans—the damage that can be caused by biological attacks on animals and crops can be economically devastating to a country. It is also easier to spread disease among crops without being seen, and the agent used can be a natural pathogen of the crop, making it difficult to detect whether the outbreak was deliberate. Military uses of these pathogens aimed to deprive the enemy of food crops, but crop tampering could be used by "bioterrorists" to destabilize governments through food shortages, or even by a company to gain financial advantage over its rivals. By the time it abandoned its biowarfare program in 1968, the United States had amassed 33,000 tons (30,000 tonnes) of wheat-stem rust and 1.1 tons (1 tonne) of rice blast. Russia also had stockpiles of wheat-stem rust and rice and maize pathogens.

FACT FILE

- In 1979 in Sverdlosk, Russia, over 1,000 people died in an epidemic of anthrax. Reports indicated that they suffered an inhalation rather than a cutaneous or intestinal form of the disease. Many Western observers have suggested that spores released in the atmosphere by an accident at a biological warfare plant may have been to blame.

- Eight grams of aerosol spray containing anthrax spores would be sufficient to inflict the same level of casualties as a one-megaton nuclear weapon. An island in Scotland, Gruinard, where anthrax experiments were conducted in World War II, is still a prohibited area.

SEE ALSO: AMMUNITION • GAS AND DUST MASK • MICROBIOLOGY • NONLETHAL WEAPON • POISON • PROTECTIVE CLOTHING

Chemical Bonding and Valency

Almost all of the hundred or so chemical elements form chemical compounds. In these compounds, atoms of different elements are held together in fixed proportions by some form of chemical bonding. Moreover, many of the elements exist in bonded forms. Metals, for example, are held together by their own form of bonding, in which a pool of electrons are shared by all the atoms in the sample. Most nonmetallic elements exist as molecules; chlorine (Cl_2), phosphorus (P_4), and sulfur (S_8) are examples of this phenomenon.

Valency is the number of bonds that an atom can form with other atoms. Hydrogen has a valency of one, since an atom of hydrogen forms a single bond when it participates in molecules. Nitrogen has a valency of three, so an atom of nitrogen combines with three atoms of hydrogen in ammonia molecules (NH_3). The valency of an element is not necessarily equal to the number of atoms with which each atom of that element will bond. In a molecule of nitrogen (N_2), for example, each atom bonds with only one other, yet the valency of nitrogen is still three because a triple bond joins the two atoms in the molecule, so each atom participates in three bonds.

The noble-gas configuration

The noble gases of group 18 (or VIIIa) of the periodic table are extremely reluctant to react, yet the elements immediately before and after them in order of increasing atomic number are the most reactive of all elements. This discovery gave chemists a clue to a driving force of chemical reactions.

Consider fluorine, neon, and sodium—a series of elements whose atomic numbers increase in steps of one unit. Compounds of neon are unknown: it has no chemical reactivity. Fluorine, which has one less electron per atom than neon, is extremely reactive. When it reacts, it often forms compounds in which it is present as a negative fluoride ion (F^-)—its atoms acquire an electron from some other element of the compound. Sodium, too, is extremely reactive, but it forms positive ions (Na^+) by losing one electron. The common factor for these three elements is that their most stable forms—F^-, Ne, and Na^+—are isoelectronic: they all have the same number of electrons. The same effect happens around the other noble gases, so electron counts of 2 (helium), 10 (neon), 18 (argon), 36 (krypton), 54 (xenon), and 86 (radon) are unusually stable.

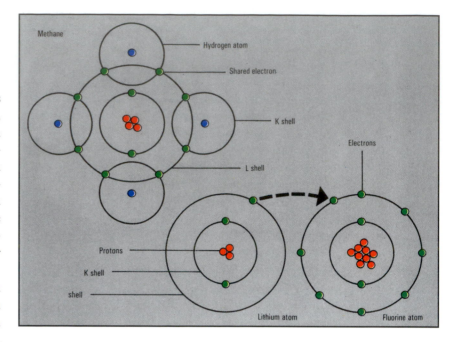

The valencies of the elements are largely accounted for by the number of electrons that an atom of that element must gain, lose, or share to make up a noble-gas configuration; sodium (11 electrons) has a valency of one, for example.

Electron shells and shielding

Quantum mechanics helps explain why the noble-gas configuration is so stable. Electrons arrange themselves in shells around the nucleus of an atom. In these shells, each electron experiences both an electrostatic attraction from the positively charged protons in the nucleus and a repulsion from the negative charges of the other electrons around the nucleus.

Each noble-gas configuration represents the completion of an electron shell. The first shell can hold two electrons, the second shell eight, and so on. Addition of an electron to a noble-gas configuration starts a new shell, which lies farther from the nucleus than the completed shells. Electrons in the inner shells effectively shield the outer electron from the attractive force of the nucleus.

Where an atom has a near-complete noble-gas configuration, an additional electron fits into the almost-full outer shell. The repulsive effect of the electrons alongside it in the same shell is weak. Because of the weak shielding effect, the electron experiences a relatively strong attraction to the nucleus, even if there are more electrons than protons, as is the case in a negative ion or an anion.

Ionic bonding

Sodium chloride (NaCl) is an example of a simple ionic compound. When such a compound forms, electrons transfer from atoms of one element to atoms of the other. Consequently, both types of

▲ A schematic representation of covalent and ionic bonding. In methane (CH_4, top left), a carbon atom and four hydrogen atoms complete their outer electron shells by sharing electrons in covalent bonds. The carbon atom contributes four outer-shell electrons to the bonding system, and each hydrogen atom contributes a single electron. Four covalent bonds result. In lithium fluoride (LiF, bottom right), the sole outer electron of the lithium atom fills the sole vacancy in the outer shell of a fluorine atom, leaving oppositely charged ions with complete outer electron shells.

atoms acquire noble-gas electron configurations. In the case of sodium, each sodium atom has a core of ten electrons in complete shells and a further electron that is alone in the outer shell. The eleventh electron is well shielded from the pull of the nucleus, so it requires little energy to detach from the atom, leaving a positive ion (Na^+). A chlorine atom has 17 electrons, and it can accept a further electron from sodium to form a negative ion with a complete noble-gas configuration (Cl^-).

Once the two types of ions have formed, they assemble into a regular structure called a lattice. Such lattices form the basis of crystals, which are cubic in the case of sodium chloride.

In a lattice, each positive ion has only negative ions as its neighbors, and vice versa. The strength of the electrostatic attractions between pairs of oppositely charged ions makes ionics lattices extremely stable substances. A great deal of thermal energy is required to break up a lattice, which is why salts typically have extremely high melting points. Salts are also inflexible, since a slight relative motion of the sheets of ions in a crystal lattice increases the separation between pairs of ions with opposite charges and brings like-charged pairs closer together, causing a resistance to flexing. When a crystal fractures, whole sheets of ions dislocate, so unlike-pair attractions are replaced by like-pair repulsions throughout the boundary between two sheets. This action causes the sheets to fly apart, leaving nearly perfect flat surfaces.

When physical chemists study the energy changes that happen when a salt forms from its component elements, they find that the energy released when the stable lattice forms more than compensates for the energy input required to split chlorine molecules (Cl_2) into separate atoms and to free sodium atoms from a block of the metal. The excess energy is released as heat.

Covalent bonding

Many elements are too far away from a noble-gas configuration to be able to form stable ions with such a configuration. Carbon, with six electrons, would have to form either C^{4+} ions (two electrons) or C^{4-} ions (ten electrons). The electrostatic forces in these ions would be so out of balance that they would rapidly acquire or shed electrons to reduce their charges. These elements usually complete their noble-gas configurations by forming bonds in which pairs of atoms share pairs of electrons. This is called covalent bonding.

In the case of hydrogen, a single atom would have just one electron in a shell that can hold two. In molecular hydrogen (H_2), two hydrogen atoms share their electrons in a single covalent bond. In effect, both hydrogen atoms complete their shells by forming such a bond. The two electrons move so fast that they behave as a cloud of negative charge that encompasses the two nuclei. There is a repulsion between the two like-charged nuclei, just as there is between the electrons, but a detailed calculation shows that this repulsion is compensated by the attractions between the electrons and the nuclei. Proof of the strength of the covalent bond can be found in diamond—the hardest known substance—in which carbon atoms are linked only by covalent bonds.

TRANSITION-METAL COMPOUNDS

The transition metals form many compunds in which they have more electrons than the related noble gas. This is because there is a fine balance between the energy required to remove their valence electrons and the energy recovered when the ions so formed enter into compounds. For the same reason, individual transition elements may exhibit a variety of apparent valencies.

The valency status of a transition metal is given as its oxidation state, which is equivalent to the number of electrons stripped from the metal atom on forming a given compound. In manganate (VII) salts, for example, the MnO_4^- ion can be thought of as being formed by Mn^{7+} combining with four O^{2-} ions. The oxidation number of manganese is +7 in this case. In fact, MnO_4^- ions are held together by covalent bonds, and the negative charge is spread over the four oxygen atoms.

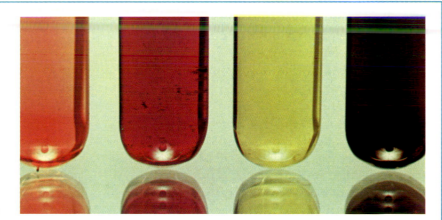

Characteristic of the chemistry of transition metals are complex ions, in which a number of negative ions or neutral molecules bond to a central metal atom. Attached groups of this type are called ligands. Many of the complex ions are colored as a result of electronic transitions that absorb visible light at visible wavelengths.

▲ From left to right, these salt solutions demonstrate the colors of manganese (II), manganese (VII), iron (II), and iron (III).

Polar bonds

The force of attraction that holds electrons in atoms is unique for each element. Differences between these attractive forces have an influence on the properties of covalent bonds that link atoms of different elements. A polar bond is a covalent bond that links atoms with different electronegativities (attractions for electrons).

Consider the electron pair that bonds the carbon and nitrogen atoms together in methylamine (CH_3NH_2). Both carbon and nitrogen have completed their noble-gas configurations by forming the appropriate number of bonds, but the nitrogen nucleus has one more proton than does the carbon nucleus. Hence, the nitrogen nucleus has a stronger pull on the electrons in the bond. The electrons spend more of their time near nitrogen than near carbon as they orbit the two nuclei, giving the nitrogen atom a slight negative charge and the carbon atom a slight positive charge.

Coordinate and hydrogen bonds

A coordinate bond is one in which the electron pair that forms the bond is contributed by only one of the bonded atoms. In nitrous acid (HONO), nitrogen is doubly bonded to one oxygen atom and singly bonded to a hydroxy group. The nitrogen atom also has an unbonded pair of electrons. In nitric acid (see the illustration above), an oxygen atom, which is two electrons short of a noble-gas configuration, accepts two electrons from nitrogen, and a coordinate bond forms.

A hydrogen bond is similar to a coordinate bond. When a hydrogen atom is bonded to an electronegative atom such as nitrogen or oxygen, it has a slight positive charge as a result of bond polarity. If a nearby atoms has a pair of electrons that is free to form a bond, that pair can form a partial coordinate bond with the hydrogen atom. This type of bonding is exclusive to hydrogen.

Resonance

Resonance occurs when the true structure of a molecule is a blend of two or more theoretical molecular structures. In the case of benzene (C_6H_6), a simplified structure can be drawn with the six carbon atoms linked by alternate single and double bonds. If this were the true structure, the pairs of doubly bonded carbon atoms would be closer together than the singly bonded pairs. In fact, all carbon–carbon bonds are equal and intermediate between single and double bonds.

Chemists originally called this effect resonance because they imagined molecules vibrating between alternate forms. In fact, no such vibration occurs: the "blended" structure is a weighted average of all the possible alternative structures.

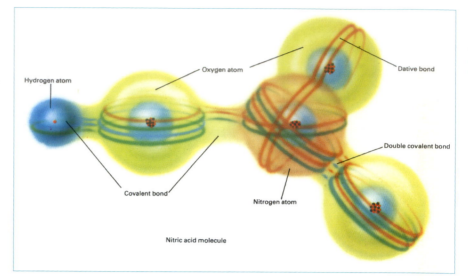

▲ This diagram represents the electron orbitals in a molecule of nitric acid (HNO_3). The hydrogen atom contributes one electron (blue), the nitrogen atom contributes five electrons (red), and two of the oxygen atoms contribute two electrons each. Each pair of electrons constitutes a covalent bond. The third oxygen contributes no electrons; instead, it accepts a pair of electrons from the nitrogen atom, forming a so-called coordinate bond.

Metallic bonding

After ionic and covalent bonds, a third type of bond is that which holds metal atoms together in large arrays. Atoms of metals all have one or more loosely bound electrons. In a block of metal, each atom has given up custody of its loose electrons, and they then become the property of the whole metallic crystal. It is the force of attraction between the positive ions left behind and the "sea" of electrons that bonds atoms in a lattice.

The nature of metallic bonding explains why metals are good conductors of electricity: their bonding electrons are relatively free to move under the influence of an applied electrical field. The free electrons can also carry thermal energy, which is why metals are good conductors of heat.

Forces between molecules

In a molecular substance, by far the strongest forces are those that hold atoms together in molecules. There are, however, milder forces of attraction that act between molecules, such as the electrostatic forces that form between regions of positive and negative charge as a result of polar bonding.

The strongest intermolecular force is the hydrogen bond, already described. Substances, such as water (H_2O), that form strong hydrogen bonding, have much higher melting and boiling points than similar substances that are less capable of hydrogen bonding, such as hydrogen sulfide (H_2S)—a gas at room temperature.

Finally, so-called London dispersion forces arise because the motions of electrons in adjacent molecules become coordinated. This coordinated motion reduces the strength of electrostatic repulsions between electrons.

SEE ALSO: ATOMIC STRUCTURE • CATALYST • CHEMISTRY, PHYSICAL • DIAMOND • METAL • PERIODIC TABLE • QUANTUM THEORY

Chemistry, Analytical

◄ This chemist is analyzing a chemical sample using a mass spectrometer. These instruments work by converting the molecules in the sample into ions. The ions are focused into a beam, which is then deflected by passing it through an electrical or magnetic field. Each element has a different charge-to-mass ratio and so will be deflected by a different amount. By analyzing the results on a graph, chemists can determine the composition and quantity of elements present and thus determine the likely chemical formula of the sample.

Analytical chemistry is the development and application of techniques that determine the chemical compositions of compounds and mixtures. Qualitative analysis reveals the identities of elements and compounds; quantitative analysis also reveals the proportions in which components are present in compounds and mixtures.

The applications of analytical chemistry are diverse. Chemical analysis is used by prospectors to determine the purity of ores in samples of rocks, by food scientists to assess the nutritional value of food products, and by drug manufacturers to ensure that harmful impurities are absent. Further uses of analytical chemistry are in the syntheses of new chemical compounds and in the industrial manufacture of established compounds. In either case, the analyst tests the product mixture to determine its composition.

An analyst might first seek to identify which elements are present in a sample. He or she might then perform tests to ascertain the percentage by mass of various elements in the sample. Further tests might establish the form in which elements are present. A sample might contain iron as a metal in a simple compound or in a complex compound such as hemoglobin, for example.

In many cases—particularly when information about the nature of a compound is required—it is necessary to start analysis by freeing a compound from impurities using a separation technique. Distillation, recrystallization, solvent extraction, and various forms of chromatography are among the most widely used separation techniques.

Distillation

Distillation separates the components of a liquid mixture according to their boiling points. The distillation temperatures of the components of a mixture can often be used to identify the components by referring to boiling-point tables. In vacuum distillation, a reduced pressure lowers the boiling points of the components, which helps in the separation of compounds that decompose near their normal boiling points.

Recrystallization

Recrystallization uses differences in solubility to separate mixtures. An impure solid is dissolved in the minimum amount of hot solvent that allows it to dissolve fully. As the solution cools, one of the components starts to separate as pure crystals, which can be isolated by filtration.

Pure solids have distinct melting points that can help identify them. A few crystals are placed in a capillary tube—an extremely fine glass tube—and viewed through a magnifying glass as they are heated. The temperature at which the crystals melt is then compared with tabulated values.

Solvent extraction

Solvent extraction, like recrystallization, uses differences in solubility to separate mixtures. An impure mixture is first dissolved in a solvent. The solution is shaken with a second solvent that is immiscible with the first. One of these solvents is usually water, the other is typically ethoxyethane (diethyl ether, $C_2H_5OC_2H_5$), hexane (C_6H_{14}), or trichloromethane (chloroform, $CHCl_3$).

The solvents are selected so that the main component of the mixture is more soluble in one solvent, while the impurities are more soluble in the other. After shaking, the solvents are left to form layers in a separating funnel—a flask in the shape of an inverted teardrop with a tap at the bottom. The lower solvent layer is run off first through the tap into a flask, and the upper layer is then run into a separate flask.

The layer that contains the main component is shaken with further portions of immiscible solvent to extract traces of impurities. After separation, the solution of the main component is evaporated to leave pure material.

Solvent extraction is particularly successful in isolating organic acids and bases, which can be converted into water-soluble salts by treatment with inorganic alkalis and acids, such as sodium hydroxide (NaOH) and hydrochloric acid (HCl). The salts are extracted into water and then extracted into water-immiscible solvent by converting them back into free acids or bases, which have little solubility in water.

Chromatography

In chromatography, the mixed sample—as a gas or in solution—is carried through an adsorbent material by a stream of inert gas or solvent. The adsorbent can be paper, silica gel in a column or on a glass plate, or kieselguhr—a type of clay.

In any given mixture, some components will have a greater affinity to the adsorbent, while other components will have less affinity. Substances that adsorb more strongly take longer to be washed through the adsorbent medium than do the less strongly held substances, so the different components move at different rates through the medium.

The amount of time each component spends in the medium is called its retention time. The retention time relative to that of a standard material can be used as a means of identification.

▼ These three biological experiments to test for signs of life were part of a miniature laboratory on board the Viking missions to Mars. The pyrolytic release looked for evidence of photosynthesis, the labeled release for signs of metabolic activity, and the gas exchanger for indications of respiratory activity. The laboratories had to be assembled under sterile conditions to ensure that samples were not contaminated with organisms from Earth.

Classical analysis

The determination of which elements are present (qualitative analysis) and the estimation of the percentage of each or of one important constituent (quantitative analysis) can be done by performing a series of chemical tests. Qualitative tests for metals are based largely on solubilities of salts following a standard procedure whereby groups of metals are precipitated (thrown out of solution) by the addition of specific reagents. Lead, mercury, and silver ions form precipitates of insoluble chlorides when hydrochloric acid is added to solutions of their soluble salts, for example. Further tests can then discriminate between these ions. Some metals produce characteristic flame colors when a tiny amount of their salt is heated on an inert wire in a gas flame. Sodium produces an yellow-orange flame, for example, while copper gives a blue-green flame.

Quantitative analysis for metals can be done by drying and accurately weighing the solid formed when an ion is completely precipitated by a particular reagent. This technique is called gravimetric analysis. The composition of carbon-containing compounds can be analyzed by determining the amounts of carbon dioxide, steam, and other gases formed when a known weight of the compound is completely burned.

Titration is a method of analysis in which a known quantity of a sample—almost always in solution—is treated with a reagent that reacts specifically with one component of the sample mixture. The reagent is added as a solution of known concentration. At the endpoint—the stage of titration when the material that is the subject of the test has all been consumed by the reagent—excess reagent starts to accumulate. The success of a titration method depends on there being a means to identify when this occurs. In the case of the titration of an acid-containing sample with a standard alkali such as sodium hydroxide, the pH of the solution increases from an acidic value (less than 7) to neutral (7) at the endpoint. The pH continues to rise if more alkali is added. The endpoint can be observed—and the acidity of the sample calculated—by using a pH meter or by adding a few drops of an indicator dye that changes color as pH changes. With practice, titration provides a convenient and accurate means of analysis for a wide variety of substances.

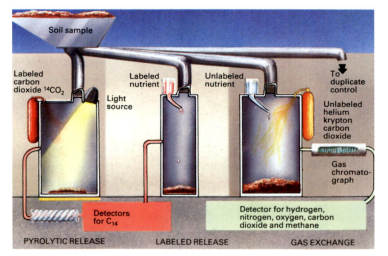

Soil sample

Labeled carbon dioxide $^{14}CO_2$

Light source

Labeled nutrient

Unlabeled nutrient

To duplicate control

Unlabeled helium krypton carbon dioxide

Gas chromatograph

Detectors for C_{14}

Detector for hydrogen, nitrogen, oxygen, carbon dioxide and methane

PYROLYTIC RELEASE

LABELED RELEASE

GAS EXCHANGE

Automatic titration

In manual titration, the sample solution is swirled in a flask while standard solution is dripped from a burette—a thin glass tube whose wall is marked to indicate volume. The flow of standard solution is controlled using a tap at the bottom of the burette, and the volume of standard solution added during the titration is obtained by subtracting the volume reading at the start of the titration from the reading at the endpoint.

In circumstances where large numbers of titrations have to be done on a routine basis, such as in industrial laboratories, the burette is replaced by a reservoir of standard solution and some form of dosing device that operates under instructions from an endpoint detector. One such device is an optical sensor that detects the color change of an indicator. Others use electrodes to monitor changes in conductivity, pH, or the concentration of some ion for which the electrode is sensitive.

Colorimetric analysis

Colored substances owe their color to an ability to absorb photons of light that have frequencies in the visible spectrum. The amount of light absorbed by a solution of such a substance depends on the concentration of that solution. Colorimetry uses the strength of absorption of visible light to measure concentration.

The simplest form of colorimetry uses a series of standard solutions prepared at a range of concentrations. These might be labeled A, B, C, and so on. The standard solutions and the test solution are placed in transparent tubes of identical dimensions and viewed under even lighting. The result is reported in terms of the closest standard solutions, so C–D would indicate a solution intermediate in color—and concentration—between solution C and solution D. This type of analysis is also used to monitor unspecified colored impurities in complex products such as resins. In some cases, the color of a test solution is developed by adding a reagent that forms a strongly colored compound by reacting with one component of the test sample.

More sophisticated colorimetry uses devices that measure the extinction, or amount of absorption, of a given wavelength of light. The test solution is placed in a transparent cell of standard dimensions. The colorimeter measures the change in light intensity of the test wavelength when the cell is placed in its light path.

Colorimetry depends on the ability of the electrons in a substance to absorb light. It is the simplest of a range of spectrometric methods that depends on the absorption or emission of different forms of electromagnetic radiation.

◄ Crystalline tartaric acid viewed through a microscope at ×30 magnification.

Spectrometry

Atoms, ions, and molecules absorb and emit electromagnetic radiation as they undergo changes in energy state. These energies are characteristic of these atoms or molecules and can often be used to identify them. The concentrations of substances can be calculated by measuring the intensity of absorption or emission of given wavelengths, as is done in colorimetry. In general, therefore, spectrometry can be used for both qualitative and quantitative analysis.

Atomic spectra

The lines in atomic spectra are produced by atoms absorbing and emitting photons of light as they move between permitted electron states of different energies. The lowest energy state is called the ground state; higher energy states are called excited states. Each line in a spectrum corresponds to a specific transition.

Atomic emission spectrometry is similar in principle to a flame test: hot, excited atoms in a flame emit light as their electrons fall to the ground state. If more than one type of atom is present, the relative intensities of the different spectra can be used to calculate the proportion of each element in the mixture.

In atomic absorption spectrometry, a beam of white light is shone through a vaporized sample. Atoms in the vapor absorb light at specific frequencies as their electrons move from lower energy states to higher ones. These frequencies match those in the emission spectra.

X-ray fluorescence is slightly different from other types of atomic spectrometry. High-energy X-ray photons knock electrons from deep in the cores of atoms. The excited ions so formed then emit characteristic frequencies of light as their electrons rearrange themselves into more stable configurations. The X-ray spectra that result can be used for qualitative and quantitative analysis, particularly of minerals and alloys.

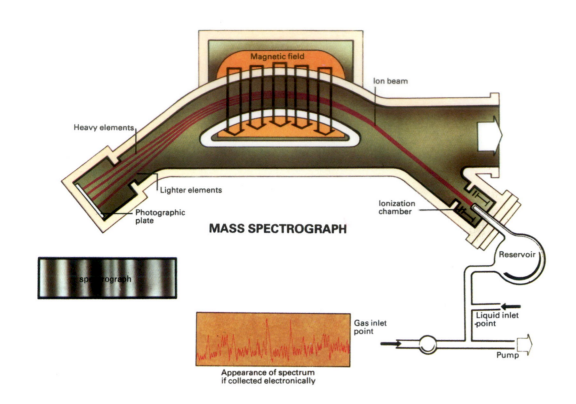

MASS SPECTROGRAPH

Heavy elements

Lighter elements

Photographic plate

Magnetic field

Ion beam

Ionization chamber

Reservoir

Gas inlet point

Liquid inlet point

Pump

Appearance of spectrum if collected electronically

◄ The study and analysis of spectra is called spectrometry. In mass spectrometry, molecules are broken up into charged fragments, which are accelerated through an electric field and then enter a magnetic field, in which they are deflected by an amount that depends on their charge-to-mass ratio. The amount by which each fragment is deflected depends on its mass. Knowing the mass and how molecules tend to fragment in general allows the spectroscopist to assign a chemical formula to each fragment, which can then be pieced together into a structure for the molecule as a whole.

Infrared spectrometry

Infrared absorption spectra probe transitions between the permitted vibrational states of a molecule. Since all but the simplest molecules have several possible modes of vibration, these spectra can contain many hundreds of lines. Certain groups of atoms absorb at frequencies that vary little from one compound to another. An example is the absorption of the C–OH group, which can be used to identify alcohol groups in a compound.

NMR spectrometry

The nuclei of certain elements—notably hydrogen and carbon-13—are magnetic; they can occupy different energy states when placed in a magnetic field. In nuclear magnetic resonance, or NMR, a sample is placed in an extremely strong magnetic field and subjected to pulses of radio-frequency radiation. Each pulse knocks nuclei into excited states, and the nuclei then emit radio-frequency radiation as they return to their ground states. The same effect is used in magnetic resonance imaging (MRI) of the human body as a diagnostic tool.

The exact energies of NMR transitions depend on the strengths of the local magnetic fields at each type of nucleus in a molecule, which are influenced by the neighboring atoms. Consequently, NMR spectra can be used to show how the atoms in a molecule connect together. Since the intensity of each peak in a spectrum is directly related to the numbers of nuclei of each type, NMR can also be used to calculate the relative proportions of components in mixtures.

Mass spectrometry

Mass spectrometry measures the charge-to-mass ratios of the positively charged molecular fragments that are formed when a vaporized sample is ionized by an electron beam. Fragments are separated according to charge-to-mass ratio by a combination of electric and magnetic fields.

The initial product of ionization is called a molecular ion. Since the molecular ion is missing an electron, its bonding system is weakened and it tends to break into fragments, some of which are charged. Certain fragments are more stable than others, and those will predominate in the mass spectrum that is observed.

High-resolution mass spectra can be used to identify the compositions of fragments from their relative masses, and a skilled operator can deduce a great deal about the composition and structure of a compound by studying its fragmentation.

Gas chromatography

In gas chromatography, a sample is vaporized and carried through an extremely thin, extremely long tube by a stream of inert gas such as nitrogen. In some cases, the tube is packed with an adsorbent such as silica or kieselguhr. In some cases, the relative retention times of the components are sufficient to identify them; in other cases, the gases that emerge from the tube are fed directly to a mass spectrometer for identification.

SEE ALSO: ACID AND ALKALI • CHEMISTRY, INORGANIC • CHEMISTRY, ORGANIC • CHEMISTRY, PHYSICAL • SPECTROSCOPY

Chemistry, Inorganic

Inorganic chemistry is the study of the chemical elements and all their compounds, excluding the organic compounds of carbon. Carbon oxides, carbonates, and metal carbides are among the compounds of carbon that are considered inorganic rather than organic.

Until the mid-19th century, inorganic chemistry dominated the field of chemical research. The organic chemicals known at that time were believed by many to be possessed of a life force, so their study was largely left to biologists.

Inorganic chemistry has its origins in the ancient art of alchemy—a pseudoscience whose followers sought to produce gold from so-called base metals, such as lead. Although their quest for gold would be in vain, alchemists succeeded in developing methods for extracting metals from their ores. They also discovered the usefulness of distillation for separating liquids from solids and for separating mixtures of liquids.

The manufacture of gunpowder—a mixture of saltpeter (potassium nitrate; KNO_3), sulfur, and charcoal—was an early inorganic chemical industry that became important when the gun was invented in the mid-14th century. By the mid-17th century, many common metals and alloys were known, as were some of the nonmetallic elements, such as phosphorus, and certain acids and alkalis, among them sulfuric, hydrochloric, and nitric acids; potassium carbonate (potash), sodium carbonate (soda ash), and sodium hydroxide.

Theories and discoveries of elements

Until the late 17th century, most chemists held the misguided belief that all matter consisted of different mixtures of four basic elements: air, earth, fire, and water. Then in 1661, the Irish chemist and physicist Robert Boyle published *Sceptical Chymist*, in which he disputed the theory of the four elements, proposing instead the existence of many more chemical elements of the type that is recognized by chemists today.

The 18th century was a period of great activity in the field of inorganic chemistry. The elements hydrogen, oxygen, nitrogen, and chlorine were discovered within a few years of each other in the 1760s and 1770s. Then in 1789—more than a century after Boyle's publication—the French chemist Antoine Lavoisier published his *Traité Elémentaire de Chimie* (Elementary Treatise on Chemistry), in which he listed several elements that he and others had discovered by experiment. Lavoisier also put forward the theory of conservation of matter, according to which the total amount of matter is unchanged by a chemical reaction. That is, the same elements are present in the same quantities before and after a chemical reaction—the elements merely change their combinations as a result of the reaction. Conservation of matter is the basis for writing chemical equations, in which the total numbers of atoms of each element are the same on both sides of the equation. Lavoisier, who died by guillotine in 1794, is widely regarded as the founder of modern inorganic chemistry.

Discoveries of elements continued into the 19th century. Nickel, chromium, and uranium were discovered in the late 18th century. In the early 19th century, the British chemist Sir Humphry Davy used the then-new technique of electrolysis to prepare samples of alkali metals of group 1 and alkaline-earth metals of group 2 from their fused salts. In 1817, silicon, a nonmetallic element, was detected within cast iron, and in 1825, aluminum, one of the last important metals to be discovered, was extracted from its chloride.

In 1869, the Russian chemist, Dimitry Mendeleyev published his periodic table, in which he classified all the elements then known into groups of ascending atomic weight. The original table had many gaps where Mendeleyev predicted the existence of elements that were unknown at the time. These gaps have since been filled and the periodic table extended by further discoveries and by the synthesis of unstable elements in nuclear reactors. The first elements to be synthesized in this way were neptunium and plutonium, which were both made in 1940 by bombarding uranium atoms with the appropriate subatomic particles.

▲ A technician supervises a pilot-plant production of anhydrous aluminum chloride. Pilot plants are an intermediate stage between small-scale laboratory preparation and full-scale production in purpose-built equipment. They help researchers to identify potential problems caused by increased scale. Such problems include the development of hotspots when a heat-releasing reaction mixture is not adequately stirred.

The Leblanc process

Much of the modern inorganic chemical industry can be traced back to the development of processes that converted common salt into alkalis. For this reason, the early inorganic industry was called the alkali industry. Since chlorine is an important by-product of these processes, the term *chlor-alkali industry* is sometimes used.

The first alkali-industry process was developed in the late 18th century in response to a prize offered by the French Academy of Sciences in 1775. The challenge was to develop an industrial process for manufacturing soda ash (sodium carbonate, Na_2CO_3), a product in great demand for the manufacture of soap and glass. In 1787, the French surgeon Nicolas Leblanc devised a method for producing soda ash from sodium chloride (NaCl). In the first step, sodium chloride reacts with sulfuric acid to form sodium sulfate:

$$2NaCl + H_2SO_4 \rightarrow Na_2SO_4 + 2HCl$$

The sodium sulfate produced by this reaction is then converted into sodium carbonate by heating it with limestone (calcium carbonate, $CaCO_3$) and coal, a source of carbon:

$$Na_2SO_4 + CaCO_3 + 2C \rightarrow Na_2CO_3 + CaS + 2CO_2$$

Washing the ashy black product mixture yielded a solution of soda ash that was then evaporated and crystallized and left a solid black mass of calcium sulfide mixed with unreacted coal.

While the original process succeeded in producing the desired sodium carbonate from cheap raw materials, it also produced large quantities of corrosive hydrogen chloride and foul-smelling calcium sulfide. In additional processes, hydrogen chloride—a cause of great environmental damage if released to the atmosphere—was converted into chlorine by oxidation. The chlorine so produced was then absorbed into slaked lime (calcium hydroxide, $Ca(OH)_2$) to make bleaching powder, a valuable by-product. The calcium sulfide was disposed of by roasting it in air to produce sulfur dioxide, a raw material for making the sulfuric acid used in the first step of the process. The development of Leblanc's process was halted by the French Revolution (1789–1799); the first Leblanc process plant started operation in 1823.

The Solvay process and electrolysis

In 1860, a Belgian chemist, Ernest Solvay, developed a process for making sodium carbonate that would replace the Leblanc process. In the Solvay process, brine, a solution of common salt in water, is treated with ammonia and then carbon dioxide. The initial product is sodium hydrogen carbonate (sodium bicarbonate, $NaHCO_3$):

$$NaCl + NH_3 + CO_2 + H_2O \rightarrow NaHCO_3 + NH_4Cl$$

The sodium salt crystallizes from the mixture and is collected by filtration. The crystals are then roasted, releasing carbon dioxide, which is reused, and water:

$$2NaHCO_3 \rightarrow Na_2CO_3 + CO_2 + H_2O$$

The Solvay process proved to be cheaper than the Leblanc process, mainly because the ammonia used in the first step could be recovered by treating the ammonium chloride with slaked lime.

Later in the 19th century, the availability of mains electricity made the electrolysis of brine a strong rival of the Solvay process. Electrolysis extracts hydrogen and chlorine from brine by the passage of an electrical current:

$$2NaCl + 2H_2O \rightarrow 2NaOH + Cl_2 + H_2$$

The cost of the electricity was offset by the value of the chlorine gas that formed as a by-product.

▶ Ammonium nitrate (NH_4NO_3) fertilizer—seen here being loaded into a rail truck—is produced by combining two key products of the inorganic chemical industry: ammonia (NH_3) and nitric acid (HNO_3). Ammonia is made by reacting hydrogen with nitrogen in the Haber process; nitric acid is made by oxidizing ammonia with air in the presence of a platinum–rhodium catalyst.

BUCKYBALLS AND BORANES

A growing field of research in inorganic chemistry concerns molecules in which several atoms of one or more elements form spheres, cages, rods, or clusters.

Buckminsterfullerene, formula C_{60}, is an almost perfectly spherical molecule that was first made in 1985 by using a laser to vaporize carbon from graphite rods in an inert atmosphere. It has since been identified as a component of soot.

The C_{60} molecule has twelve C_5 rings that form the points of an icosahedron—a twenty-sided regular polyhedron. The C_5 rings link together through bonds that form hexagons of carbon atoms. Larger fullerenes have sheets of carbon atoms arranged in hexagons between the twelve C_5 rings. The structures of the fullerenes, sometimes known as buckyballs, resemble the geodesic domes designed by Buckminster Fuller, the U.S. architect and inventor who inspired their name.

The fullerenes and their derivatives have potential uses as catalysts, solid lubricants, and superconductors, and the larger fullerenes might also be able to encapsulate toxic anticancer drugs.

Boron hydrides form another group of cluster compounds. The structures are based on deltahedra—solid forms with triangular faces—that have 6 to 12 vertices. The *closo* boron hydrides have the general formula $B_nH_n^{2-}$, *nido* boron hydrides have formula $B_{n-1}H_{n+3}$, and *arachno* hydrides have formula $B_{n-2}H_{n+4}$.

The *closo* forms are complete n-pointed deltahedra of B–H groups (with n values of 6, 10, or 12), while *nido* and *arachno* hydrides have more open structures that resemble nest- or bowl-shaped webs.

A related group of compounds, the carboranes, are mixed hydrides of boron and carbon. Since a carbon atom has one more electron than a boron atom, a C–H group has the same electron count as a B–H$^-$ group, so $C_2B_{10}H_{12}$ has the same electronic structure as $B_{12}H_{12}^-$.

Boron cluster hydrides and carboranes are remarkably stable when compared with simple hydrides, such as diborane (B_2H_2). Whereas the simple hydrides decompose rapidly in contact with air or water, for example, boron cluster hydrides are stable in the presence of these substances. When boron hydrides and carboranes react, they do so in ways that resemble the reactions of alkanes and aromatic hydrocarbons, so the hydrogen atoms attached to boron can be replaced by other functional groups.

In the reaction between carborane ($C_2B_{10}H_{12}$) and the methyl ester of trifluoroethanoic acid (CF_3COOCH_3), the product has the formula $C_2H_2B_{10}(CH_3)_{10}$. All the boron atoms are attached to methyl groups, leaving two hydrogens attached to carbons. Replacing them with functional groups is the starting point for building ring- and rod-shaped molecules that contain carborane icosahedra.

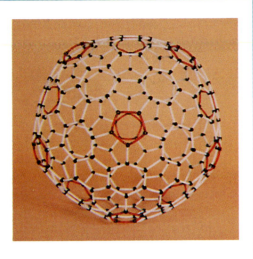

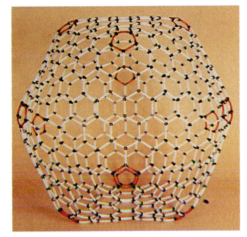

▲ These photographs show ball-and-stick models of two fullerenes. In each case, twelve C_5 rings, highlighted in red, form the vertices of an icosahedron. In the upper example, hexagonal C_6 rings complete the surfaces, making a total of 240 carbon atoms. The lower example has formula C_{560} and a more accurate icosahedral form.

Ammonia and nitric acid

In the late 19th century, the main source of ammonia was as a by-product of the carbonization of coal to produce gas and coke. Ammonia was much in demand, notably for use in making explosives and artificial nitrogen-containing fertilizers. By the end of the 19th century, it was clear that coal carbonization alone could not meet the demand for ammonia.

In 1913, the German chemist Fritz Haber developed a method for making ammonia by reacting nitrogen from air with hydrogen in the presence of an iron catalyst. Haber used hydrogen produced by passing steam over red-hot coke. The Haber process was modified for industrial production by the German chemist Karl Bosch, and it is this modification that is in use today.

One of the main uses of ammonia is in the manufacture of nitric acid—itself an important raw material for many industrial processes. Nitric acid is produced by heating ammonia with air in the presence of a platinum catalyst laced with a small amount of rhodium. The initial product—mainly nitrogen oxide (NO) mixed with nitrogen and oxygen—reacts further as the gases cool. The resulting nitrogen dioxide reacts with water and air to form nitric acid:

$$4NO_2 + 2H_2O + O_2 \rightarrow 4HNO_3$$

Much of the nitric acid produced by this process is combined with ammonia to produce ammonium nitrate fertilizer. Large quantities are also used to nitrate organic chemicals in the production of explosives and intermediates for drugs.

Sulfuric acid

Sulfuric acid is manufactured by oxidizing sulfur dioxide and reacting the resulting sulfur trioxide directly or indirectly with water:

$$2SO_2 + O_2 \rightarrow 2SO_3$$
$$SO_3 + H_2O \rightarrow H_2SO_4$$

The sulfur dioxide for the first step is produced by burning sulfur—one of the few elements that occur uncombined in nature—or by roasting metal-sulfide ores in a stream of air.

The oxidation of sulfur used to be effected by the use of nitrogen dioxide produced by ammonia oxidation. The reaction was performed in huge lead chambers where a water spray converted the trioxide into sulfuric acid that reached a maximum concentration of 68 percent in water. The chamber process was used to produce sulfuric acid to meet the demands of the Leblanc process.

In the more modern contact process, sulfur dioxide is oxidized by oxygen from air in the presence of a vanadium pentoxide (VO_5) catalyst. The sulfur trioxide so produced is passed into concentrated sulfuric acid, where it forms oleum ($H_2S_2O_7$). Adding water releases the acid. Sulfuric acid is used in the manufacture of detergents and other organic chemicals, as well as to make phosphoric acid and phosphate fertilizers from calcium phosphate ($Ca_3(PO_4)_2$).

FACT FILE

- *The annual production of sulfuric acid was for many decades used as an indicator of a country's economic activity. This relationship stemmed from the importance of the acid in many key industrial processes.*

- *Bioinorganic chemistry is the study of the action of trace metals and other elements in living systems. Many of the enzymes that catalyze reactions in living systems have metal atoms at their active sites, which is why small amounts of inorganic compounds play a vital role in the formation of these enzymes. Some inorganic compounds are toxic because they disrupt the normal course of bioreactions, while other compounds can be used to modify processes in living organisms in a therapeutic way. Lithium carbonate, for example, is an effective treatment for bipolar disorder, since it restores normal nerve activity by modifying the balance of other ions in the body.*

Inorganic research

Much of the current research in inorganic chemistry involves cooperation with other areas of scientific research. Combined efforts with theoretical chemists and X-ray crystallographers have led to an improved understanding of the structures and properties of materials. This understanding has paved the way for the synthesis of many exotic materials, including compounds that contain clusters of atoms and ceramics that become superconductors much closer to room temperature than any known combination of metals.

Inorganic chemists work with industrial chemists to develop catalysts that save millions of dollars by reducing the operating temperatures and pressures necessary for industrial reactions to occur. Some of these catalysts are synthetic minerals such as zeolites, where minute changes in composition or structure can have massive influences on catalytic activity. Other catalysts include compounds in which transition-metal ions are surrounded by ions and molecular fragments called ligands. Such compounds are called transition-metal catalysts, and their catalytic activity depends largely on how easily the metal can switch between oxidation states and how they connect with reacting molecules.

Other areas of interest include the development of new semiconductor materials for making electronic components and the use of materials that interact with light to split water into oxygen and hydrogen for environmentally clean fuel.

▲ This chemical plant in Louisiana produces chlorine by the electrolysis of common salt (sodium chloride, NaCl). Chlorine is used to sterilize water and in the manufacture of a vast range of inorganic and organic chemicals.

SEE ALSO: ACID AND ALKALI • ALKALI METALS • BIOCHEMISTRY • CATALYST • CERAMICS • CHEMISTRY, ORGANOMETALLIC • HALOGEN • NITROGEN • SEMICONDUCTOR • SULFUR • ZEOLITE

Chemistry, Organic

Organic chemistry is the study, synthesis, and manipulation of compounds that contain carbon and hydrogen, and of related compounds in which one or more hydrogen atoms are replaced by other groups of atoms. Organic compounds do not include metal carbides, carbon-containing alloys, and simple compounds of carbon with nonmetallic elements—carbon dioxide and carbon disulfide, for example. Such compounds are classified as inorganic carbon compounds.

The term *organic compound* stems from a belief held by 18th- and early 19th-century chemists that carbon-containing substances found in plants and animals possessed some form of life force. According to that belief—called vitalism—such substances could be formed only by living organisms: they could not be produced artificially from substances of mineral origin.

Vitalism was accidentally disproved by the German chemist Friedrich Wöhler. In 1828, Wöhler was attempting to produce ammonium cyanate (NH_4CNO) by mixing solutions of ammonium chloride (NH_4Cl) and silver cyanate ($AgCNO$). The mixture produced a solid precipitate of silver chloride ($AgCl$), which Wöhler removed by filtration. When he boiled the remaining solution to remove its water, Wöhler was surprised to find that the product was urea ($CO(NH_2)_2$), a component of urine and already a familiar organic compound at that time. As such, Wöhler had accidentally synthesized an organic compound from inorganic materials by the simple use of heat—an achievement that the vitalists had previously held to be impossible.

Early developments

By the mid-19th century, gasworks were producing large quantities of tar as they carbonized coal to produce gas for heating and lighting. At first, this tar had little use apart from that of surfacing roads and preserving and waterproofing wood. With time, however, experimenters discovered that the distillation of coal tar yielded numerous useful substances and mixtures. Given that these substances were largely compounds of carbon and hydrogen, chemists classified them with the organic chemicals found in plants and animals.

The first organic chemical to be synthesized on a large scale was a derivative of a component of coal tar: aniline (aminobenzene, $C_6H_5NH_2$). In 1856, the British chemist William Perkin was trying to synthesize quinine, an antimalarial compound extracted from the bark of cinchona trees. When he tried to convert aniline into quinine, the

result was a black sludge that formed a purple solution in ethanol. Finding that the solution was an excellent dye for silk, Perkin patented the process for making his dye, which he called mauveine. In 1857, he set up a mauveine factory and started selling his product to dye houses. Mauveine-dyed clothing reached the peak of fashion in the early 1860s, and the success of mauveine stimulated the development of new techniques for making useful products from components of coal tar.

Chemicals from petroleum

In the 20th century, petroleum distillation replaced coal tar as the principal source of raw materials for the organic-chemicals industry. Early in the 20th century, gasoline and diesel fuel were separated from crude petroleum by simple distillation. The greater part of each barrel could not be used as motor fuel, however, and it soon became apparent that uses would have to be found for the residues of petroleum distillation. Chemists developed a number of techniques for improving the yield of petroleum refining. One such technique, called reforming, converts chainlike alkane hydrocarbons into cyclic aromatic compounds. Aromatics improve the properties of motor fuels and are useful starting points for the manufacture of numerous useful chemicals.

Another significant development was the introduction of cracking, a process that splits large molecules into smaller ones. Cracking enables high-boiling distillation fractions to be converted into fuels and also produces small molecules with double carbon–carbon bonds. Such molecules can be made to link together in chains and are the raw materials for the production of plastics such as polyethene and polypropene.

▲ Chemists in research laboratories perform tests and experimental reactions on a small scale in glass flasks and test tubes. If a synthesis is successful in the laboratory, it might eventually become a large-scale industrial process.

Molecular structure

There are many more compounds of carbon than there are of any other element. In fact, of the ten million or so known and recorded compounds, more than four-fifths are organic compounds.

One of the reasons for the enormous diversity of carbon compounds is the ability of carbon to form stable chains and rings of atoms in molecules; another factor is each carbon atom's ability to form four covalent bonds. In many cases, multiple bonds connect atoms in carbon compounds. A third reason for the wide scope of carbon chemistry is carbon's ability to form covalent bonds with many other elements. Carbon can bond with nonmetals—notably halogens, hydrogen, nitrogen, oxygen, and sulfur—as well as with some main-group and transition metals.

Alkanes

Hydrocarbons are organic compounds of carbon and hydrogen only. The simplest hydrocarbon is methane (CH_4), which is the main component of natural gas. Methane is also the simplest of the alkanes—hydrocarbons in which the carbon atoms are linked by single bonds only. The next simplest alkanes are ethane (C_2H_6), propane (C_3H_8), butane (C_4H_{10}), and pentane (C_5H_{12}).

The alkanes form a homologous series, a group of compounds with similar structures whose members have formulas that differ by units of CH_2. The general formula for an alkane is C_nH_{n+2}, where n can be any whole number. The "-ane" suffix in the names of alkanes indicates membership of this series, and the roots of the names indicate the number of carbon atoms: methane has one carbon, ethane two, propane three, and butane four. Pentane, hexane, heptane, and higher hydrocarbons derive their names from Greek words for their numbers of carbon atoms.

In an alkane, each carbon atom is surrounded by four atoms that form the points of a tetrahedron. In so-called straight-chain alkanes, the carbon atoms form flexible zigzag chains. Higher alkanes are oily liquids and waxy solids because their molecules tangle together.

Alkanes with four or more carbon atoms can form branched chains. The simplest branched alkane is methylpropane ($CH_3CH(CH_3)CH_3$), which has four carbon atoms and ten hydrogen atoms, just as butane does. When two compounds have different structures but share a formula, they are called structural isomers, so methylpropane is a structural isomer of butane. Branched alkanes are named by adding the names of the branch alkyl groups—methyl ($-CH_3$), ethyl ($-C_2H_5$), propyl ($-C_3H_7$), and so on—to the alkane name of the longest chain of carbon atoms, so that $CH_3CH(CH_3)CH_2C(C_2H_5)_2CH_2CH_2CH_3$ is called 2-methyl-4,4-diethylheptane, for example. The numbers refer to the positions of the branching groups counting along the principal chain, so "4,4-diethyl" indicates that there are two ethyl groups attached to the fourth carbon atom along the heptane chain. Note that the numbering starts at the end of the chain that gives the lowest numbers in the final name, and methylpropane needs no numbering because there is only one possible position for the methyl group.

Alkenes and alkynes

Alkenes and alkynes are classes of hydrocarbons where at least one multiple bond joins adjacent carbon atoms. The alkenes have at least one double carbon–carbon bond per molecule, while the alkynes have at least one triple bond.

The simplest alkene is ethene (ethylene, $CH_2=CH_2$), followed by propene (propylene, $CH_3CH=CH_2$). In alkenes that have four carbons or more, the position of the double bond is indicated by the number of the first doubly bonded carbon atom along the chain: $CH_3CH_2CH=CH_2$ is but-1-ene and $CH_3CH=CHCH_3$ is but-2-ene.

When a carbon atom is attached to three atoms by a double bond and two single bonds, those atoms form the points of a triangle. Also, the structure of the double bond prevents the groups of atoms attached to the doubly bonded carbon atoms from rotating around the double bond. Thus, many alkenes can exist in two dis-

▼ Some of the simplest organic chemicals are chains of carbon and hydrogen known as hydrocarbons. Alkanes have single carbon bonds, alkenes have a double carbon bond, and alkynes have a triple-carbon bond. Many molecules can share the same chemical formula, but branching and isomerism can make the molecule look very dissimilar and react in a different manner.

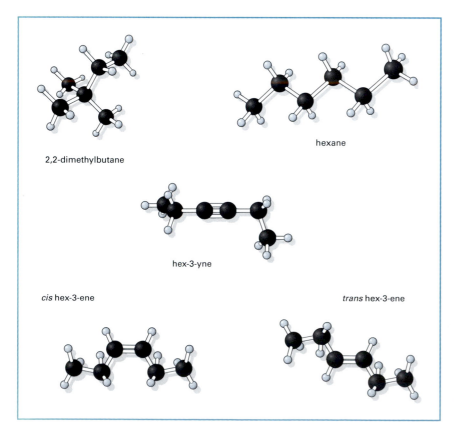

2,2-dimethylbutane

hexane

hex-3-yne

cis hex-3-ene

trans hex-3-ene

tinct forms, called geometric isomers. In the *cis* isomer of but-2-ene, for example, the two methyl groups lie on the same side of the double bond; in the *trans* isomer, they are on opposite sides.

Higher alkenes may have two or more double bonds, the number being limited only by the valency of carbon atoms. Each double bond represents a subtraction of two hydrogen atoms from the formula of the related alkane. The general formula for alkenes with one double bond is C_nH_{2n}, where *n* is greater than one.

The simplest alkyne is ethyne (acetylene, $CH{\equiv}CH$), followed by propyne ($CH_3C{\equiv}CH$). When carbon forms a triple bond and a single bond, the two atoms attached to the carbon atom lie on a line that passes through the carbon atom. Because of this arrangement, geometric isomerism does not occur among the alkynes. Higher alkynes may have two or more triple bonds, and each represents the subtraction of four hydrogen atoms from the related alkane. The general formula for alkynes with one triple bond is C_nH_{2n-2}, where *n* is greater than one.

Alicyclic compounds

Alicyclic hydrocarbons are alkanes, alkenes, and alkynes whose carbon atoms form one or more rings. The simplest cycloalkane is cyclopropane (C_3H_6), which is used as an anesthetic.

An unbranched cycloalkane can be thought of as a straight-chain alkane that has lost a hydrogen atom from each of the carbon atoms at the two ends of the chain as they bonded together to close the ring. Consequently, the general formula for cycloalkanes is C_nH_{2n}, and they are isomeric with open-chain alkenes that have one double bond. More complex cycloalkanes have alkyl groups or other groups attached to the central ring, and some molecules contain two or more rings.

The angle between the carbon–hydrogen bonds in methane is slightly greater than 109 degrees, which is the ideal angle for a singly bonded carbon atom. The geometries of small-ring compounds requires a tighter bond angle— 60 degrees in cyclopropane, for example. This angles strains the bonds that hold the ring together. The greater the strain in a ring compound, the greater its tendency to react with other molecules so as to cause the ring to open.

The angle between carbon–carbon bonds in cyclohexane (C_6H_{12}) would be 120 degrees if its molecules were simply flat hexagons. In fact, the six-carbon ring in cyclohexane is puckered, so the angle between bonds is reduced, as is the strain.

Some molecules have double or triple bonds between carbon atoms in a ring. These compounds are known, respectively, as cycloalkenes

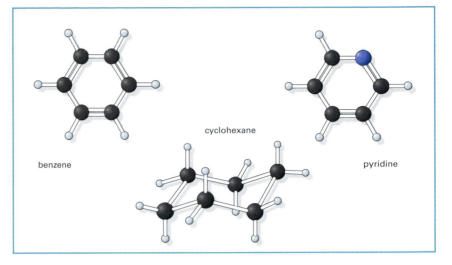

benzene   cyclohexane   pyridine

▲ A particular feature of organic chemistry is the ability of carbon to form ring structures. These structures can be flat molecules like benzene and pyridine, where the shared electrons resonate round the ring. Cyclohexane is a singly-bonded ring, but it is not a planar molecule because of strains between the bonds.

▼ Carbon not only forms chain and ring structures, it can also form ball-like structures called fullerenes. Fullerenes contain many carbon atoms linked in geometric patterns called polyhedra that are roughly spherical in shape. These samples contain C60 (left) and C70 (right).

and cycloalkynes. The simplest cycloalkene is cyclopropene (C_3H_4). Since the ideal bond angle for a carbon atom at the center of two single bonds and a double bond is 120 degrees, cyclopropene's geometry places even more strain on its bonds than does cyclopropane, and cyclopropene is correspondingly more reactive.

The constraints of bond angles are even more extreme with a triple bond, which would normally require four atoms to lie in a straight line. For this reason, the smallest cycloalkyne is cyclononyne (C_9H_{14})—smaller rings would be too strained to exist as stable molecules.

Aromatic compounds

Certain ring compounds have a particular stability owing to a property called aromaticity. The archetypal aromatic compound is benzene (C_6H_6). While the structure of benzene is sometimes represented by a ring of six carbon atoms linked by alternate single and double bonds, the reality is more complex. The three double bonds in benzene form a bonding system that spreads symmetrically around the ring, so the bond between each pair of carbon atoms in the ring is intermediate between a single and a double bond. This symmetrical bonding system provides the characteristic stability of aromatic hydrocarbons, called arenes, that are based on benzene rings.

Arenes are not the only compounds that exhibit aromaticity. In pyridine (C_5H_5N), for example, a nitrogen atom replaces one of the CH groups in benzene and contributes an electron to the aromatic system. In thiophene (C_4H_4S), a sulfur atom replaces two CH groups and contributes two electrons. Ring compounds in which carbon atoms are replaced by atoms of other nonmetals are known as heterocyclic compounds. Other aromatic compounds include polycyclic aromatics, such as naphthalene ($C_{10}H_8$), in which two or more benzene rings join at their edges.

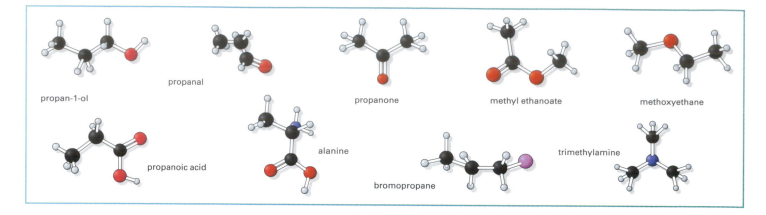

propan-1-ol

propanal

propanone

methyl ethanoate

methoxyethane

propanoic acid

alanine

bromopropane

trimethylamine

▲ Adding functional groups to carbon compounds changes their chemical properties and reactivity with other compounds and molecules. The addition of oxygen gives rise to substances such as alcohols, aldehydes, carboxylic acids, ethers, and acetates. It is this ability to form multiple bonds with other atoms that makes carbon such a unique element and the basis for a whole branch of chemistry.

Functional groups and reactivity

As the number of atoms in an organic molecule increases, so does the number of ways in which that compound can react with other substances. This increase in complexity is particularly striking for molecules that include atoms of elements other than carbon and hydrogen. As an aid to understanding the chemistries of complex substances, chemists consider molecules as consisting of groups of atoms that have characteristic sets of chemical properties. Molecular fragments such as these are called functional groups.

The multiple carbon–carbon bonds in alkenes and alkynes are functional groups. In their most typical reactions, they allow other molecules to add to the molecule that contains them by opening up and forming bonds with fragments of the attacking molecule. When an ethene molecule reacts with hydrogen, for example, the double bond in ethene opens and allows each of the carbon atoms to form a bond with a hydrogen atom.

Aromatic rings are also functional groups: the typical reaction of an aromatic system is called substitution. Attack by a positive ion, such as NO_2^+, causes a temporary disruption of the aromatic ring as a positively charged intermediate ion forms. This intermediate ion soon loses a hydrogen ion as it restores the stable aromatic system. The overall result is that at least one of the atoms or groups attached to the ring is replaced, but the aromatic ring persists.

Alkanes that contain chlorine, bromine, or iodine—collectively known as haloalkanes—have a tendency to lose negative halide ions, leaving a positive charge on the organic molecule that they leave. There is usually one of two end results: a substitution reaction, where a negatively charged species such as OH^- replaces the lost halide ion, or elimination, in which a hydrogen ion departs from a neighboring carbon atom and a double bond forms. Elimination is the opposite of an addition to a double bond. Fluorine forms extremely strong bonds with carbon that break only under extreme conditions.

The hydroxyl group (–OH) is characteristic of alcohols, such as ethanol (C_2H_5OH). Its oxygen atom can accept a hydrogen atom from an acid to form a positively charged species—$C_2H_5OH_2^+$, in the case of ethanol. This type of species can then lose a water molecule (H_2O), and the resulting positive ion reacts by substitution or elimination.

Strong bases and reactive metals, such as sodium, can remove a proton from the hydroxyl group to leave an alkoxide ion—$C_2H_5O^-$, in the case of ethanol. These ions attack compounds, such as bromoalkanes, that have functional groups that are prone to such an attack. The product of such a reaction between sodium ethoxide and bromoethane (C_2H_5Br) is ethoxyethane (diethyl ether, $(C_2H_5)_2O$), which contains the ether linkage (–COC–), also a functional group. Alkoxide ions are nucleophiles—species that react with centers of positive charge, such as those that form when halide ions split from haloalkanes.

The amino group ($-NH_2$) is characteristic of primary amines, such as ethylamine ($C_2H_5NH_2$). It is basic, and readily accepts a proton from acids to form an ammonium ion, such as $C_2H_5NH_3^+$. In its basic form, the amino group is a nucleophile that can attack species such as bromoethane (C_2H_5Br) to form secondary amine such as diethylamine ($(C_2H_5)_2NH$), tertiary amines, such as triethylamine ($(C_2H_5)_3N$), and sometimes even quaternary ammonium salts, such as tetraethyl-ammonium bromide ($(C_2H_5)_4N^+Br^-$).

The carbonyl group (CO) is characteristic of aldehydes and ketones. In aldehydes, such as propanal (C_2H_5CHO), the carbonyl group is attached to a hydrogen atom and usually an alkyl group. (Methanal, or formaldehyde (HCHO), is the exception.) In ketones, such as propanone (acetone, $(CH_3)_2CO$), the carbonyl group is attached to two alkyl groups. The chemistry of carbonyl compounds has a complexity beyond the scope of this article, but many of their reactions start with a nucleophile attacking the carbon atom of the group to leave a single carbon–oxygen bond and a negative charge on oxygen.

Compound functional groups

When two or more functional groups are attached to the same or neighboring carbon atoms, they cause profound modifications to one another's chemical properties.

When a molecule has a hydroxyl group attached to an aromatic ring, as does phenol (C_6H_5OH), an electron pair on the oxygen atom interacts with the bonding system of the aromatic ring, making it richer in negative charge. This makes phenol more attractive to positively charged attacking species—and hence more reactive—than, say, benzene or a similar compound. Also, when the hydroxyl group in phenol loses a proton, the resulting ion is stabilized by the aromatic ring absorbing some of the negative charge. This makes phenol much more acidic—more prone to losing a proton—than is an alcohol such as ethanol, where no such stabilization can occur.

The aromatic ring modifies an amino group in a similar way. Aminobenzene is much less basic than ethylamine because the electron pair that its nitrogen atom uses to attach a proton is drawn into the aromatic ring to some extent.

Carboxylic acids and derivatives

Perhaps the most striking interactions between functional groups occur in molecules that have a carbonyl group with a second functional group attached. The most familiar of these compounds are the carboxylic acids, such as ethanoic acid (acetic acid, CH_3COOH), which have a hydroxyl group attached to a carbonyl group. These molecules are acidic because, when they lose a proton, they form a highly stabilized carboxylate ion, such as ethanoate (acetate, CH_3COO^-). The negative charge of a carboxylate ion is split between its two oxygen atoms, and this dilution of charge provides its stability. In an amide, such as ethanamide (CH_3CONH_2), the carbonyl group makes the amino group lose all its basicity.

Amides form one class of carboxylic acid derivatives—substances in which the hydroxyl group of a carboxylic acid is replaced by another functional group. In acid chlorides, such as ethanoyl chloride (acetyl chloride, CH_3COCl) that group is a chloride ion; in esters, such as ethyl ethanoate (ethyl acetate, $CH_3COOC_2H_5$) it is an ether linkage to an alkyl group; and in acid anhydrides, such as ethanoyl ethanoate (acetic anhydride, $(CH_3CO)_2O$) it is an ether linkage connected to another carbonyl group.

Carboxylic acids and their derivatives react by a nucleophile attaching itself to the carbon atom of the carbonyl group and displacing the group that was originally attached there. Acid chlorides are the most reactive derivatives, and they are typically made by reacting a carboxylic acid with sulfonyl chloride (an inorganic acid chloride, $SOCl_2$). The next most reactive derivatives are anhydrides, followed by the acids themselves, esters, and finally amides. Each type is made by treating a more reactive derivative with the appropriate nucleophile: carboxylic acid for acid anhydrides, water for acids, alcohols for esters, and ammonia or an amine for amides. These reactions are fundamental to the manufacturing processes for polyamides, such as Nylon and Kevlar, and of polyesters, such as Dacron.

Fats and oils are esters of fatty acids (long-chain carboxylic acids) with 1,2,3-trihydroxy-propane (glycerol, $CH_2(OH)CH(OH)CH_2(OH)$), in which each molecule of glycerol has three fatty-acid groups attached. Soaps (salts of fatty acids) and glycerol are obtained by heating fats and oils with solutions of alkali in water. These break the ester linkages in faster than would water alone.

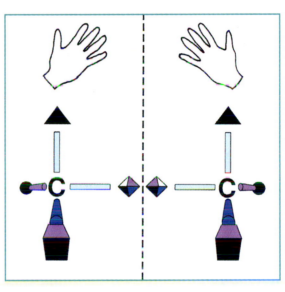

◀ The two forms of a chiral material can be compared to a pair of hands: they are mirror images, but cannot be superimposed. In the representation of a chiral carbon center, the bonds to the triangles and diamonds lie in the plane of the paper of this page. The spheres lie "below" the paper, and the cubes are "above" the paper.

Chirality

Natural organic compounds often include at least one carbon atom that is attached to four different groups. An example is lactic acid (2-hydroxy-propanoic acid, $CH_3CH(OH)COOH$): The second carbon atom in the chain is attached to four different groups: $-CH_3$, $-H$, $-OH$, and $-COOH$.

Ball-and-stick models of compounds such as lactic acid show that they can exist in two different forms, called enantiomers, that are mirror images of one another. This effect is called chirality, meaning "handedness," since the two forms, like a pair of hands, are reflections of one another and they cannot be superimposed.

A pure solution of one enantiomer or the other rotates the plane of polarization of light that passes through it, and the two enantiomers rotate light in opposite senses. This is why chirality is sometimes called optical activity.

Chiral synthesis

When a chiral substance reacts with a substance that is not chiral, both enantiomers react at exactly the same rate. However, if two chiral substances react together, certain combinations of enantiomers generally react more quickly than others. This has a profound effect on the action of synthetic drugs that have a chiral center.

Living organisms construct proteins from amino acids—simple molecules that have the general formula $CHR(NH_2)CO_2H$, where R is different in each amino acid. The carbon atom between the acid and amino groups is a chiral center, since it is attached to four different groups. Natural amino acids exist in only one of their two possible enantiomeric forms, which leads to the proteins they form having chiral activity. Since the enzymes that catalyze biochemical reactions are chiral proteins, their interactions with other chiral molecules are different for each chiral form of those molecules.

In the case of ibuprofen, a synthetic painkiller with a chiral center, one enantiomer is a more effective painkiller than the other. Both enantiomers are equally capable of causing stomach irritation, however, so the effectiveness of the drug would be increased and its side effects reduced if the enantiomer that is the more potent painkiller could be produced as a pure substance.

One approach that helps improve the yield of one enantiomer over the other is the use of chiral raw materials. This only works when the geometry of the chiral center is maintained (or completely reversed) in the synthesis.

Another approach uses one enantiomer of a chiral catalyst to promote the formation of the desired enantiomer. A special case of this approach uses natural or genetically modified enzymes—themselves extremely selective chiral catalysts—to yield a high proportion of one particular enantiomer in the product mixture.

Finally, if the product can be crystallized, one enantiomeric form can be separated from a product mixture by seeding its crystallization with a small crystal of the desired enantiomer. The other enantiomer remains in solution.

▲ Computer-generated molecular models such as this help chemists and molecular biologists to visualize the physical shapes of enzymes and understand how smaller molecules fit into the active sites where their reactions are catalyzed.

FACT FILE

■ *Crown ethers are ring compounds composed of repeated $-CH_2CH_2O-$ blocks. Crown ether molecules with four such blocks in a ring fit snugly around lithium ions, five-block crowns fit sodium ions, and six-block crowns fit potassium ions. These compounds are made in the presence of their target ions, and they help the salts of those ions to dissolve in nonpolar solvents, such as hexane, where their chemical reactivity is enhanced.*

■ *As fossil fuels become scarce, alternative sources of organic chemicals will gain importance. Potential sources include methanol, made by the fermentation of wood, and ethanol, made by fermenting cane sugar. These materials can be catalytically converted into hydrocarbon mixtures similar to petroleum. They have an advantage over petroleum in that the cultivation of their source plants is rapid and consumes carbon dioxide, a greenhouse gas.*

Retrosynthesis and synthons

When a research chemist first considers strategies for synthesizing a complex molecule, the number of possible raw materials and synthetic reactions can be bewildering. In the 1960s, Harvard professor Elias J. Corey addressed this problem with his methodology of retrosynthetic analysis.

Retrosynthesis works by picturing the target molecule as if it were a jigsaw puzzle. Each piece of the molecular jigsaw is called a synthon, and standard methods exist for introducing each synthon into a molecule. The chemist then uses his or her judgment to select the sequence of synthetic steps that is most likely to have success.

Using retrosynthesis, the modern chemist can create new chemicals with potential uses as diverse as biodegradable detergents, more intense dyes, and better drugs with fewer side effects.

SEE ALSO: AMINO ACID • ANILINE AND AZO DYES • CHEMISTRY, ORGANOMETALLIC • COAL TAR • DETERGENT MANUFACTURE • ENZYME • FAT • FIBER, SYNTHETIC • GAS INDUSTRY • GASOLINE, SYNTHETIC • HYDROCARBON • POLYMER AND POLYMERIZATION

Chemistry, Organometallic

Organometallic chemistry is the synthesis and study of molecules that contain at least one bond between a metal atom and a carbon atom.

This branch of chemistry embraces aspects of both organic and inorganic chemistry and has generated compounds that are useful for the research chemists and industrial chemists alike. Plastics such as polyethene and polypropene are manufactured using organometallic catalysts, and many pharmaceutical products are developed with the aid of organometallic reagents although these are often replaced by cheaper organic reagents when large-scale manufacture begins.

Until recent years, organometallic tetraethyl-lead ($Pb(C_2H_5)_4$) was added to gasoline to improve its performance in internal combustion engines. Such gasoline produces toxic lead compounds when it burns, however, so the use of lead additives is now strictly regulated.

Organometallic compounds are classified by the type of metal they contain—main group or transition—and by the type of bonding that holds them together. Compounds in which carbon is bonded to a metalloid such as silicon or boron are sometimes classified as organometallics.

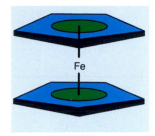

▲ Ferrocene, the pioneer organometallic compound, consists of an iron atom surrounded by flat aromatic molecule rings.

Compounds of main-group metals

The organometallic compounds of the metals in the s-block and p-block of the periodic table have the simplest type of bonding. The compounds of metals in the last column of the d-block—zinc, cadmium, and mercury—are usually classed with the compounds of main-block elements, since their properties are similar in many respects.

The metal–carbon bonds in organometallic compounds of main-group elements are simple covalent bonds, although their electrons are more strongly attracted to the carbon atom than to the metal atom. This effect, called bond polarization, leads to the carbon atom having a partial negative charge. The extent of polarization depends on the metal: the Li–C bond in methyllithium (CH_3Li) is much less polarized than the bond in methylpotassium (CH_3K), since potassium attracts electrons less strongly than does lithium.

Many of the organometallic compounds of s-block metals burst into flames or explode when they come into contact with oxygen or water. Therefore, such compounds have to be made and used in equipment that excludes air and moisture. The potent reactivity of main-block organometallics makes them useful in synthesis; they react as if they consisted of a metal cation and an anion whose negative charge is on carbon.

A number of methods for preparing main-block organometallics start with a reaction between a highly reactive metal, such as lithium or magnesium, and a haloalkane, such as chloromethane or bromoethane:

$$2Li + CH_3Cl \rightarrow CH_3Li + LiCl$$
$$Mg + C_2H_5Br \rightarrow C_2H_5MgBr$$

The latter equation shows the formation of ethylmagnesium bromide, which is an example of a Grignard reagent. Organometallic compounds of less reactive main-block metals are made by reacting their chlorides or fluorides with organolithium, magnesium, or aluminum compounds.

Alkyllithiums, Grignard reagents, and similar organometallic compounds react with organic compounds by displacing atoms and groups of atoms that form stable anions. Such species are called leaving groups since they have a tendency to detach from molecules of which they form a part. An example of such a reaction is the formation of hexane from butylmagnesium bromide (a Grignard reagent) and bromoethane, where the bromide ion is the leaving group:

$$C_4H_9MgBr + C_2H_5Br \rightarrow C_6H_{14} + MgBr_2$$

This reaction is typical of those used by research chemists to add groups of atoms to molecules in the synthesis of new compounds.

▶ Catalytic cracker units lie at the heart of all oil refineries. Many use metal compounds as catalysts to speed the conversion of oil into shorter hydrocarbons, alcohols, and aldehydes. Investigation of the organometallic complexes formed by the metals used in cracking can give chemists an insight into the reactions that take place between organic molecules at the metal surface of a catalyst.

Transition-metal complexes

The first known organometallic compound was first made by a Danish chemist, William Zeise, in 1827 and is known as Zeise's salt. It is a potassium salt that has a complex anion of platinum (II) with chloride ions and an ethene molecule: $PtCl_3(C_2H_4)^-$. While the electron pairs that form the bonds between the chlorine atoms and the platinum atom are from the chlorine atoms, the pair that forms the bond between ethene and platinum comes from the bond between the two carbon atoms in ethene. Consequently, a single pair of electrons forms a bond between three atoms: two carbons and one platinum. This is an example of multicentered bonding, a common feature of transition-metal complexes.

Carbonyl compounds

In 1890, Ludwig Mond, a British chemist, synthesized a volatile compound of carbon monoxide and nickel—tetracarbonylnickel ($Ni(CO)_4$)—that would form the basis of a method for obtaining pure nickel. This compound was the first of a new class of compounds: metal carbonyls.

Metal carbonyls are unusual in that the metal atom is in oxidation state zero, the same as that of the element, because each carbonyl group (–CO) contributes an electron pair to one bond while the metal atom contributes an electron pair to a second bond. Two bonds form between each carbonyl group and the metal atom with no net gain or loss of electrons at that atom.

Sandwich compounds

The chance discovery of ferrocene in 1951 opened up a field of research of immense variety. Ferrocene ($Fe(C_5H_5^-)_2$) was the first example of a metallocene—a compound in which a metal atom is sandwiched between two flat, aromatic rings. The metal atom in these complexes is typically iron or cobalt, and the aromatic rings tend to be cyclopentadienyl ions ($C_5H_5^-$), benzene molecules (C_6H_6), or closely related compounds.

The bonds in sandwich compounds form through complex interactions between the molecular orbitals of the rings and combinations of the atomic orbitals of the metal. Chemists simplify the description of such compounds by stating their hapticity, which is the number of carbon atoms that take part in bonding with the metal atom. In the full name of ferrocene—bis-(η^5-cyclopentadienyl)iron—"bis" indicates two rings and η^5 (pentahapto) indicates that each ring is attached to the metal through five carbon atoms. A number of half-sandwich compounds have now been synthesized in which the metal atom bonds to only one aromatic ring.

▲ The reactor cell of a Metal Organic Vapor Phase Epitaxy (MOVPE) system, where gaseous molecules pass over a heated substrate on which they are deposited. The technique is used in the synthesis of compounds such as gallium arsenide and indium phosphide, which are important in the semiconductor industry. The organometallic compound, for example, trimethyl gallium, decomposes at the high temperatures used, and the metal atoms produced combine to give very thin, pure, uniform layers of the semiconductor.

Uses of organometallic compounds

The uses of s-block organometallics in organic synthesis has already been discussed. Another important use of such compounds is in the formation of "living" polymers of materials such as butadiene ($CH_2=CH_2–CH_2=CH_2$). When butadiene is added to a solution of butyllithium, chains of polybutadiene form and grow until all the butadiene has been consumed. The reaction continues when more butadiene is added, which is why the polymer is described as "living." It is "killed" only when a substance is added to destroy the alkyllithium.

Ziegler–Natta polymerization catalysts are mixtures of titanium trichloride and trialkylaluminums that accelerate ethene and propene polymerizations and increase the structural order of the products. The species formed during these reactions are partially stable organotitanium compounds, and the study of related organometallics that are stable helps reveal the mechanisms of these reactions. Studies of other model organometallics help in understanding and optimizing a variety of catalytic systems, including those for the synthesis of hydrocarbons from mixtures of carbon monoxide and hydrogen made from coal. This process may become an important source of fuels as petroleum reserves become depleted.

SEE ALSO: CATALYST • CHEMISTRY, INORGANIC • CHEMISTRY, ORGANIC • GASOLINE, SYNTHETIC • POLYMER AND POLYMERIZATION

Chemistry, Physical

Physical chemistry is the study and description of the physical properties and behavior of atoms, molecules, ions, and their mixtures.

Physical chemists measure the properties of chemical systems using techniques that include calorimetry, which measures heat changes; spectrometry, which measures interactions between substances and electromagnetic radiation; and electrical measurements. They use the results of these measurements to confirm or disprove theories of structure, equilibrium, and change.

Early atomic theory

Atoms are the smallest particles that exhibit chemical properties, and an important branch of physical chemistry attempts to describe their structure. The British chemist John Dalton proposed that elements consist of atoms in 1803, and by the early 20th century, it was known that these atoms consisted of nuclei of protons and neutrons surrounded by electrons.

Scientists observed that atoms heated in a flame emit light and ultraviolet radiation and that each element emits characteristic frequencies of light that form an atomic spectrum. Astrophysicists used this knowledge to deduce the presence of helium, hydrogen, and other elements in the Sun and other stars. The Danish physicist Niels Bohr proposed that the lines in atomic spectra were a consequence of electrons moving between orbits of different energies.

Quantum mechanics

Since the 1920s, theoretical chemists have revolutionized theories of atomic structure with the introduction and development of quantum mechanics. Perhaps the greatest contribution came from the Austrian physicist Erwin Schrödinger, who devised an equation of motion for an electron in a hydrogen atom, which describes various permitted states of energy and angular momentum for an electron in motion around a proton. Each permitted electron state is known as an orbital, and the energy differences between these states are consistent with the energies of photons in the atomic spectrum of hydrogen.

The Schrödinger equation does not describe the path of an electron: rather, it describes a three-dimensional map of the probability of locating an electron in any a given instant. Atomic orbitals are often given a physical shape by defining envelopes that encompass high percentages of the probability of finding an electron.

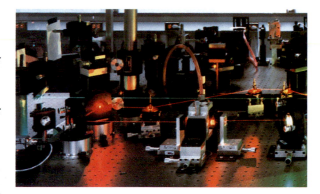

◀ Apparatus used at the California Institute of Technology to study the breaking of chemical bonds using 60-femtosecond pulses of laser light.

Complex atoms

Schrödinger's equation can be solved exactly only for atoms and ions in which a single electron moves around a nucleus because the motion of an electron is influenced by the electric field around the nucleus. In atoms and ions with two electrons or more, each electron experiences an electric field that is modified by all the other electrons in the same atom. It is this interdependence that makes it impossible to formulate exact equations of motion for electrons in complex atoms. Instead, a set of approximate orbitals is fed into a computer, and the computer then recalculates each orbital according to the electric field caused by the nucleus and the other electrons in the atom. Powerful computers allow several recalculations of this type to be performed in a reasonable time, with the exactness of the orbital set improving on each recalculation.

A further complication for polyelectronic atoms—those with more than one electron— arises with atomic spectra and transitions between electronic states. Every orbital must be calculated before and after the transition since the electron that changes orbital alters the electric field felt by all the other electrons as it does so.

Physical chemists use spectroscopy to confirm the energy differences between the electronic states of atoms and ions. Movements of electrons between high-energy orbitals are accompanied by the emission of visible or ultraviolet photons.

The energies of orbitals close to the nuclei of atoms can be explored by bombarding atoms with fast-moving electrons. The collisions knock electrons from deep within atoms, leaving vacancies in low-energy orbitals. When electrons drop into these vacancies from higher-energy orbitals, they give out X-ray photons. These photons have more energy than ultraviolet and visible photons,

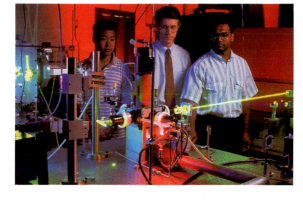

▲ Researchers at the University of Wisconsin-Madison have been using lasers to control the rate of chemical reactions by stretching bonds.

since the energy gaps between low-energy orbitals near the nucleus are considerably larger than the gaps between higher-energy orbitals.

Molecular structure

According to basic theories of chemical bonding, molecules are held together by electron pairs that form between pairs of bonded atoms. Although these models help to explain the shapes and reactions of molecules, they are oversimplifications of reality. In fact, the electrons in molecules occupy electronic orbitals that span several atoms of a molecule, or even the whole extent of a molecule.

In theory, a Schrödinger-type equation could be written to describe the motions of electrons in molecular orbitals; in practice, it would be an extremely complex task to calculate even approximate solutions for such an equation partly because an infinite number of possible molecular geometries would have to be assessed.

X-ray diffraction is widely used by chemists who are trying to establish the structure of molecules. Where possible, a single crystal of the substance under investigation is placed in an X-ray diffraction apparatus. A beam of X-ray photons is aimed at the crystal, and detectors measure the intensity of X rays scattered at different angles from the crystal. This forms an interference pattern from which the shape of the molecule can be calculated. The use of a single crystal simplifies the calculation by ensuring that all molecules in the sample have the same orientation.

Once an X-ray crystallographer has elucidated the geometry of a molecule, a theoretical chemist can calculate electronic orbitals that are consistent with that geometry. The simplest technique for this calculation is linear combination of atomic orbitals, or LCAO.

In the LCAO technique, orbitals of the atoms in a molecule are combined mathematically to form molecular orbitals. Orbitals can combine only if they have similar symmetries: dumbbell-shaped p orbitals can combine only if their two lobes lie along parallel axes, for example. The symmetry requirement simplifies the choice of basis sets of atomic orbitals for calculating the individual molecular orbitals.

▼ Physical chemists are studying the properties of microtubes made of fullerene carbon molecules, as shown in this computer-generated structure.

Molecular spectroscopy

Some of the atomic-orbital combinations form orbitals that hold the atoms in a molecule together; these are called bonding orbitals. Other combinations correspond to a repulsion between atoms and are called antibonding orbitals. Those that have no effect on the strength of the bond between atoms are called nonbonding orbitals. In a stable molecule, electrons occupy bonding or nonbonding orbitals. Such electrons can move to higher-energy antibonding orbitals as they absorb energy in the form of ultraviolet radiation. The frequencies at which these ultraviolet absorptions occur correspond to energy differences between molecular orbitals, so they help to complete the bonding models calculated by LCAOs.

Electronic motions are not the only molecular motions for which permitted energy states exist: molecules also rotate and vibrate. A molecule such as carbon monoxide (CO), for example, can rotate head over tail around either of the two axes at right angles to that axis. The energy gaps between permitted rotational energy levels depend on the size of the moment of inertia about an axis. Since a molecule's mass is almost entirely in the nuclei of its atoms, the moment of inertia can be used to calculate the distance between nuclei: the C–O bond length in the case of carbon monoxide. The photons that correspond to changes between rotational energy levels lie in the microwave region of the electromagnetic spectrum.

Vibrations in molecules occur when groups of bonds lengthen and contract in a coordinated manner. In the case of carbon monoxide, the only vibration is the stretching of the carbon–oxygen bond. The energy gap between vibrational energy levels is an indication of the strength of the bond. This information is valuable for chemists who are trying to determine how easily a bond can be broken in a chemical reaction. The photons that correspond to vibrational transitions lie in the infrared region of the electromagnetic spectrum.

A molecular vibration will appear in the infrared spectrum of a molecule only if it causes its electric dipole to oscillate. An example of a vibration that does not appear in infrared spectra is the "breathing" mode of tetrachloromethane (CCl_4). All the C–Cl bonds stretch at the same time, so the molecule remains tetrahedral and has a zero electric dipole throughout the vibration.

Calorimetry

Calorimetry is the measurement of heat changes in systems as they undergo physical and chemical changes. A simple form of calorimetry measures the heat input required to increase the tempera-

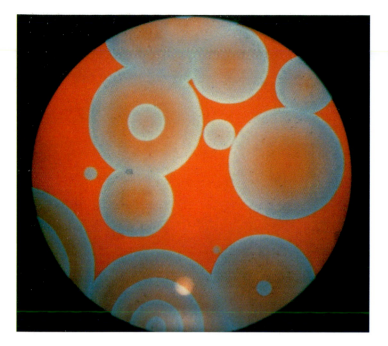

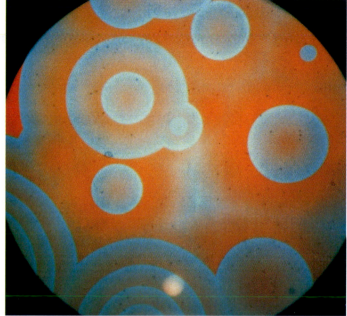

ture of a substance without that substance undergoing physical or chemical change.

In the case of a solid being warmed by an electrical heater of a known power rating, the rate at which that solid's temperature increases indicates the amount of energy required to increase the temperature of the solid by one degree. This is the heat capacity of the solid.

In general, the molecules or atoms in a solid vibrate around fixed positions in the solid lattice. There are permitted energy levels for this type of vibration, just as there are for molecular vibrations and rotations in the gas phase. As the temperature of the solid increases, the vibrational energy increases, and the atoms vibrate over larger distances. Molecular motions in a liquid are intermediate between those in solids and gases, with the molecules vibrating at all times, but only occasionally rotating or moving over a greater distance.

A branch of physical chemistry called statistical mechanics uses a mathematical function called a Boltzmann distribution to calculate the proportion of molecules that will occupy each of the translational energy levels at a given temperature. It is the change in this distribution with temperature that governs the heat capacity of a substance in a given physical state—solid, liquid, or gas.

Heat changes also occur when a substance changes state. As a solid melts, for example, the strong forces of attraction between molecules in the solid form are replaced by weaker attractions in the liquid form. The substance absorbs an amount of energy, called the latent energy of fusion, to enable this change. The same amount of heat is evolved by the substance as it changes from liquid to solid. A similar heat change occurs

▲ Waves of chemical change occurring in a mixture of reagents undergoing the Belusov-Zhabotinski reaction. In an apparently uniform mixture points of instability appear, which begin radiating waves that spread through the solution at several millimeters per minute.

when a substance boils or condenses, in which case it is called the latent heat of vaporization.

Chemical changes generally involve the release or absorption of heat energy as bonds break and form. When a solid rocket fuel burns, for example, the energy released on the formation of new bonds appears as the translational energy of the gaseous products, which are much hotter than the reactants. The heat change involved in a chemical reaction is measured in a device called a calorimeter.

In one form of calorimeter—the bomb calorimeter—a combustible substance is placed in a cylinder that is filled with oxygen, sealed, and placed in water. The substance is ignited, and the heat released by its combustion is calculated from the increase in temperature of the water bath, the cylinder, and its contents. This method is used to measure the calorific values of foods and fuels.

Thermodynamics

Thermodynamics is the study of the rules that govern physical and chemical changes in terms of changes in the energy and disorder of a system. The concept of entropy is used to quantify the disorder of a system, and one of the fundaments of thermodynamics is that a chemical or physical change must be accompanied by an increase in entropy for it to be able to occur spontaneously.

Different forms of energy and matter have different values of entropy. The energy in a chemical bond is highly ordered, low-entropy energy, while heat energy can spread through a system and is a disordered, high-entropy form of energy. An ordered, crystalline solid has little entropy, while a gas has a large amount of entropy by virtue of its randomly distributed particles.

Most spontaneous chemical changes are exothermic (heat releasing), and at least part of their entropy increase comes from the conversion of low-entropy chemical energy to high-entropy heat energy. Some spontaneous reactions are endothermic (heat absorbing), however, and their entropy must be provided by the formation of high-entropy gaseous products from low-entropy solid or liquid reagents, for example. An example is the formation of carbon disulfide (CS_2) from carbon and sulfur. The bonds in carbon disulfide are weaker than the carbon–carbon and sulfur–sulfur bonds that have to be broken to make carbon disulfide, so a heat input is required. The product is a gas under the conditions of the reaction, and it is the entropy of carbon disulfide gas that is the driving force of the reaction that forms it. Carbon disulfide readily forms carbon dioxide and sulfur dioxide with oxygen (CO_2 and SO_2). The bonds so formed are much stronger than those in carbon disulfide, and large amounts of chemical energy are released as heat.

Kinetics

While thermodynamics determines whether a reaction can happen at all, kinetics determines how quickly a reaction will happen under a given set of circumstances. Thermodynamics favors the combustion of gasoline in air, for example, but unfavorable kinetics prevent this from happening until a spark or flame is applied.

For a chemical reaction to occur, two or more molecules must collide and possess the energy required to rearrange the bonds between atoms to form products. A reaction may consist of a series of chemical changes, and the slowest of all those stages is the one that governs the speed of the whole reaction. The rate of that step increases in proportion to the concentrations of the chemical species that take part in that step. Therefore, a concentrated acid will react with a metal more vigorously than a dilute acid does.

If the temperature of a reaction mixture increases, the molecules in that mixture will move more rapidly, so they will collide more violently. This means that a greater proportion of collisions will have sufficient energy to transform reagents into products, and the rate at which the reaction proceeds increases with increasing temperature.

Catalysts increase the rate of a reaction by reducing the energy threshold for a reaction to occur. In many cases, the catalyst changes the route of the reaction. The reactions of solids can also be made to proceed more rapidly by using fine powder rather than lumps, because the reaction occurs at the surface, and powder has a greater surface area.

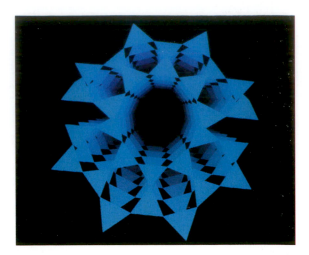

► Computer-graphics representation of the structure of unidirectional channels through the synthetic zeolite Theta-1. This can be prepared with a variable silicon content, thus enhancing its properties as a catalyst and molecular sieve.

Photochemistry

Certain reactions are initiated by the action of light on molecules. This happens when the absorption of a photon causes electronic transitions that split a molecule into reactive fragments called free radicals, or leave the molecule in an "excited" state that is more prone to reaction than the unexcited "ground" state of that molecule.

An example of a photochemical reaction is the fading of dyes on prolonged exposure to sunlight. The color of a dye stems from its ability to absorb photons of visible light and convert their energy into heat or another form of energy. Occasionally, an excited dye molecule will undergo a photochemical reaction that converts it into another substance that is unable to absorb light.

Gas laws

The gas laws were one of the earliest developments in physical chemistry. They describe how the pressure, temperature, and volume of a gas are related to the number and mass of molecules in a sample. The pressure on the surfaces that contain a gas depends on the frequency and momentum with which gas particles hit those surfaces. These factors depend on the number and mass of gas particles per unit volume and the speed of those particles, which is determined by the temperature of the gas sample.

Electrochemistry

Electrochemistry studies oxidation and reduction reactions that produce or consume electrons at electrodes. This field of study is important for the study of electrochemical cells and other power-generating systems and for developing methods for extracting and purifying substances by passing a current through liquids. These processes are called electrolysis and electrorefining.

 SEE ALSO: ATOMIC STRUCTURE • CATALYST • GAS LAWS • ION AND IONIZATION • SPECTROSCOPY • THERMODYNAMICS

China and Porcelain

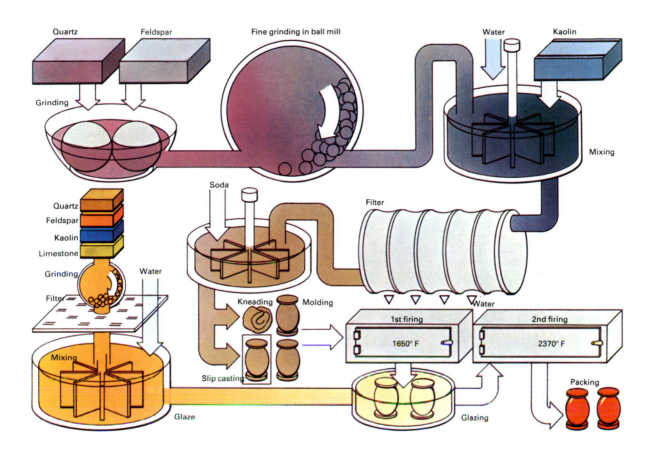

China clay (kaolin), the basic material for the ceramic industry, was known to the Chinese at least as early as 1000 B.C.E. and probably much earlier than that. Its use for the making of porcelain was known by that time, as examples of this ware from the Western Chou period (1000–700 B.C.E.) have been found in graves at Anhui and Honan, near Hangchow. In Britain, china clay was known to the Cornish in the Middle Ages as "pot growan" or "growan clay," but they did not realize its true value. The first person to recognize its potential was William Cookworthy, a Quaker apothecary from Plymouth, in 1746. Cookworthy was the first person in Europe to produce true hard porcelain identical to the Chinese ware. Johann Böttger at Meissen had produced a type of hard porcelain in 1710, but it contained no china stone, a silicate related to the feldspars, which is essential for the production of true porcelain as invented by the Chinese.

Today the term *china* is used to describe general articles of tableware such as cups, saucers, and plates, pottery teapots, various jugs, basins, and articles of ornamental ware. There are several kinds of chinaware, all of it white. Translucent vitreous china is used for feldspathic china, porcelain, and bone china, while opaque vitreous china

is used for hotel ware and some domestic china. Earthenware is made from opaque porous china.

Although the ingredients of china, which when compounded together are known as the body, vary somewhat from country to country, the major one is clay. The exception to this is bone china, which consists of about 50 percent bone ash (calcium phosphate produced from burnt animal bones).

The body

Whatever the specific formula of the body, the way it is prepared is fairly standard, and the methods described here refer principally to the manufacture of vitreous domestic ware.

The nonplastic ingredients, such as quartz and feldspar, have to be reduced to particles sufficiently fine to be mixed with the clay by grinding them in rotating mills lined with ceramic brick to avoid metal contamination of the ingredients. Small balls of very hard porcelain are put into the mill to assist the grinding process, and these are separated from the ingredients after milling.

Each of the ingredients has an important role to play. The quartz, for example, reduces shrinkage during drying and firing; the feldspar acts as a flux. The fineness of the particles is important,

▲ The main stages in making porcelain and glaze. Quartz, feldspar, kaolin, and water are mixed together and then filtered to remove excess water. Soda is added to make the mixture more fluid, then the ware is shaped and fired.

CHINA CLAY

China clay, or kaolin, is a soft white earth consisting principally of the mineral kaolinite, which is a hydrated aluminum silicate, $Al_2O_3 2SiO_2 \cdot 2H_2O$. In its natural state, however, it invariably occurs with some of the alumina replaced by iron together with titanium and alkalis. China clay is the product of the natural decomposition of granite and other igneous rocks (formed by the cooling of molten rock masses) when the rocks were still unconsolidated. The conversion of these rocks into clay may have been achieved by a number of different processes, but all of them involve the breaking down of alkaline constituents in

◀ A monitor hose in action, blasting clay out of the rock face.

feldspathic minerals by acidic solutions, usually from weathering or hydrothermal activity underground.

To extract the clay, first of all the topsoil, or overburden, is removed by mechanical diggers and scrapers together with any discolored clay, and then the clay face is washed by high-pressure water hoses, known as monitors, operating at pressures of up to 350 psi (24 bar). The hoses produce a raw wash containing clay, quartz, and mica, and this wash is pumped to a sand-separation plant, where the coarse quartz sand is separated out. The clay is then dewatered, thickened, and screened before going to the filter presses, where more water is squeezed out of it. The press-cakes of clay are then broken up and dried in rotary driers to the required moisture content and milled if powdered clay is wanted.

and often these ingredients are purchased ready-milled. The china clays are supplied as dry lumps or powder, and other white-firing clays, such as ball clay, which is similar to china clay but more plastic, may be used in addition to the china clay.

Mixing

To ensure complete mixing of the ingredients, it is usual to disperse each one in water, the resulting suspensions being known as slips. Each slip has its own tank, or blunger, and is continuously agitated to prevent wasteful sedimentation from forming.

These slips are pumped into a mixing vat called an ark in the desired proportions. Typical proportions are, for example, 40 to 50 percent clay, 20 to 35 percent quartz, and 20 to 35 percent feldspar, the proportions varying according to the type of ware being made. Sometimes the nonplastic ingredients are added to the ark in powder form.

The next stage is to turn the body slip into a plastic form that can be shaped or molded using large filter presses that force out some of the water through filter cloths. The resulting filter cakes are sheets of plastic body, usually about two feet square and two inches thick.

These cakes are not yet ready for use, however, as they are wetter on the inside than they are at the edges. To prepare them for use, they are fed into pug mills, which are really giant mincing machines. These mills cut up the cakes in a vacuum to remove air and then extrude the clay as consolidated cylinders.

Molding

The oldest known method of shaping clay is by hand alone: a later invention of profound importance was the potter's wheel. Both these techniques, however, are slow and unsuitable for producing articles of uniform size and thickness. In a modern china works, most of the shaping is done automatically.

To make flatware—a plate for example—a slice of plastic clay is cut from the extruded cylinder of clay from the pug mill. This slice is then fed onto a plaster of Paris mold, which is rotated and squeezed against a rotating heated roller, the latter being profiled to the shape of the plate.

The next stage is the drying. It is here that the mold plays another essential part, as plaster of Paris can absorb water. The molds are slowly conveyed through a drying oven and emerge with the ware sufficiently dry to be removed and strong enough to withstand rough edges being tidied up, or fettled, prior to firing.

Cups are produced by forcing a lump of clay against the sides of cup-shaped molds with a rotating tapered roller. Hollow wares that are not symmetrical cannot be made in this manner and are formed by another process called slip casting.

Slip casting

To make a complex shape such as a teapot, a plaster mold is prepared and cut in half lengthwise. The halves are temporarily joined together and slip is poured into the mold. As the plaster of the mold begins to absorb the water, the slip at the sides begins to thicken, and a thin wall of clay is built up. After a suitable time, the excess slip is poured out and the mold put into the drier. When dried, the mold is opened up, and the pot in its unfired, or green, condition is removed. The handle is cast separately and fixed in position with a little slip as the adhesive. When completely dry, the pot is ready for firing. Other items of domestic ware, such as basins, sinks, and toilets, are made by the slip-casting method, although on a much larger scale.

Firing

Early pottery was simply left to bake in the sun, a practice that produced vessels that were quite rigid enough to store dry solids but that were porous and easily reverted to their plastic state when wet. Baking the wares over a wood fire or, later, in a wood-fired kiln was a great advance, as these wares remained permanently hard. The porosity remained, and thus the vessel would always be damp, but the pot would not become plastic and liquids could be stored in it. An example of such pottery is terracotta, of which some garden wares and baking containers are still made. The Chinese, however, discovered that given a high enough temperature over a sufficient period of time clay would vitrify, that is, its physical nature would alter so as to render it nonporous.

The modern kiln is usually a tunnel up to 100 yds. (90 m) long with a carefully controlled temperature gradient: the temperature increases gradually along the tunnel, reaching its maximum in the middle and decreasing steadily toward the

◀ The dry ingredients are mixed separately with water to produce the slips—finely divided solid materials held in suspension in water.

▶ A hand gilder decorates a jar in an old Imari design at the Royal Crown Derby factory, England.

exit. This means that the ware reaches its maximum temperature in the middle of the tunnel and is cooling off as it emerges.

Each item has to be carefully placed on a kiln car that is then slowly pushed through the tunnel. The setting of the pieces on the car calls for skill and experience because they shrink by about 12 percent as they are fired. A cup, for example, is set on a cone-shaped piece of refractory material so that it can ride up freely as it becomes smaller. Bad setting will cause distortion and cracking.

Vitrification requires a temperature of about 2190°F (1200°C) and takes between 10 and 30 hours. What emerges from the first, or biscuit, firing is ware with a relatively rough texture that is nonporous, white, and mechanically strong and ready for decorating and glazing.

Glazing

A glaze is a thin layer of glass completely and evenly covering the biscuit ware. It is applied as a suspension spraying or hand dipping, the suspended solids melting sufficiently in a second, or glost, firing to form a skin of glass. The glaze adds a shine and smoothness to ware and, in the case of a body that is porous, renders it impermeable.

The composition of a glaze has to be carefully matched to suit the body. Both glaze and body must, when cooling, shrink to the same final extent so that the layer of glaze fits the body properly. A bad fit can cause the crazing that appears on older pieces of pottery. The glaze may be either clear or colored; a common use of colored glazes is in the manufacture of bathroom fittings.

Decoration

Decoration is ideally applied before glazing so that the pattern is protected by a hard layer of glaze. Many of the color materials used in decorating will not, however, stand up to the high temperature of the glost firing, which is a little over 1830°F (1000°C). Thus, the decorating may have to be done after the glazing, necessitating a third, or enamel, firing at about 1380°F (750°C) in order to fuse the pattern into the glaze. The two basic methods of decoration are called underglaze and onglaze.

The oldest method of applying color is by hand and requires considerable skill, as the raw materials used often change color during firing and this possibility must be allowed for when the colors are chosen. The hand method is expensive.

The usual way of decorating tableware is by means of paper transfers, or lithos, printed from lithographic plates using varnish instead of ink. The powdered colors, usually metal oxides, are dusted on and stick to the varnish. Normally a manufacturer will buy lithos made to his designs by a specialist. The lithos are wetted and carefully pressed onto the ware by hand. The silk-screen printing technique can be applied to pottery too, either directly or by transfers.

A recent development in silk-screen offset decoration is the total color transfer process developed by British Ceramic Research in the United Kingdom. Four different colors can be applied as half tones, heavy decorations, and even thick bands of color. The process not only gives variety and quality but is inexpensive.

Some of the most expensive tableware has patterns enriched by hand painting, and gold and platinum are often used in the decoration. The powdered metal is mixed with resin and applied by the normal onglaze methods or with just a brush. The resin burns out, leaving the metal on the glazed surface. In really elaborate pieces, several enamel firings may be needed to bring up the various colors.

Porcelain

Porcelain may be defined in modern terms as a vitreous (glassy) ceramic body, white in color, and translucent. This definition can be enlarged to include certain early Chinese wares and any Chinese ware sufficiently highly fired and giving a high ringing note when sounded (struck lightly). The manufacture of modern porcelain is essentially the same as that for other chinaware.

True porcelain was first made in the Tang dynasty by mixing china clay (kaolin, or pai tun) with petuntse (the less fully decayed feldspar and quartz). The typical body composition was 50 percent kaolin and 50 percent petuntse (25 percent quartz and 25 percent feldspar). Hard-paste porcelain is made by firing the body at between 1650 and 1830°F (900–1000°C) then applying the glaze and firing a second time at about 2500°F (1375°C).

The hard-paste tradition came to Europe in the late 17th century by the sea trade route from China. The first European to succeed in imitating porcelain was a German chemist, Johann Böttger, who produced hard-paste porcelain between 1710 and 1714 in the castle at Meissen, which was the beginning of the Meissen porcelain industry.

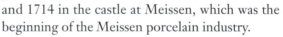

▲ Sheets of the body mixture being removed from the filter press, where most of the water is forced out of the slip.

Soft paste

Soft-paste porcelain manufacturing spread along the overland trade routes from China through the Islamic empire until it reached Italy. The first successful European experiments in soft-paste porcelain took place in Florence using a white burning clay with the addition of frit (ground glass), which gives a vitreous body when fired at 2010 to 2190°F (1100–1200°C). This biscuit ware was then dipped in a lower-firing lead glaze, which matures in the second firing at 1920°F (1050°C). Variations on this soft-paste theme were tried throughout Europe for 350 years with varying degrees of success.

In England, William Duesbury and Andrew Planché used soft paste at their Derby factory in 1750. The next development was the addition of bone ash to the traditional hard-paste body by Josiah Spode in 1794, using 50 percent bone ash, 25 percent kaolin, and 25 percent Cornish stone (a mixture of quartz and feldspar). This formula was soon adopted by Derby, Minton, and Coalport and became the typical English bone china body, an exclusive blend of hard- and soft-paste porcelain. The porcelain industry in the United States began at the end of the 18th century, making mainly soft-paste and bone china.

SEE ALSO: Ceramics • Kiln • Mass production • Mining techniques • Paper manufacture • Toilet

Chromatography

Chromatographic techniques separate mixtures by exploiting differences between the physico-chemical properties of their components.

Techniques such as gas chromatography can provide detailed quantitative and qualitative analyses using samples that are only a few microliters in volume. These tests can detect traces of pesticide residues in food and drugs in blood and urine samples. In industry, chromatography is used to check the purity of products and to control pollution by testing the contents of effluents before they are released to the environment.

Scientists in laboratories use columns packed with silica to separate the substances in product mixtures from experimental syntheses; a thin layer of silica on a glass plate can be used to the same effect for minute quantities of products.

Chromatographic methods were developed as a means of purifying complex natural products that were difficult or impossible to extract by other methods. As early as the 19th century, dye chemists tested the contents of dye vats by dipping the edges of rags into the liquid and watching the individual dyes form separate bands as the liquid seeped through the rag. In 1903, the Russian botanist Mikhail Tsvet used a column packed with calcium carbonate powder to split mixtures of plant pigments into colored bands. Tsvet called his technique *chromatography*, from the Greek words meaning "color writing."

Principles of chromatography

In any form of chromatographic technique, the components of a mixture are split between a mobile carrier phase, which can be a gas or a liquid, and a stationary phase, which can be liquid or solid. The mobile phase flows through or along the stationary phase, but the two do not mix.

The various chemical compounds in the mixture pass back and forth between the mobile phase and the stationary phase as the one flows past the other. Components of the mixture that have a stronger affinity for the stationary phase than for the mobile phase spend more of their time trapped by the stationary phase, so they pass through more slowly than components that have a greater affinity for the mobile phase.

The time taken for a component to pass though the stationary phase is called its retention time; it depends on the nature of the mobile and stationary phases, the length of the path through the stationary phase, and the flow rate of the mobile phase. Often, the retention time is stated relative to that of a calibrating substance.

◄ The recorder of this thin-layer chromatography apparatus plots a peak for each substance that emerges from the separation column. The relative retention times of the individual substances help in their identification, while the area under each peak is proportional to the amount of that substance in the sample mixture. Other detectors provide a photographic image that indicates concentration.

Column chromatography

Two British chemists, Archer Martin and Richard Synge, developed column chromatography in the 1940s. Their goal was to separate the components of mixtures of amino acids derived from wool. At first, they tried to effect this separation by making two immiscible solvents flow in opposite directions while in contact with each other. The amino acids separated according to differences in their relative affinities for the two solvents.

Martin and Synge had limited success with their efforts until they hit on the idea of binding one of the solvents—water—to finely powdered silica (SiO_2) packed in a vertical glass column. While their equipment resembled that used by Tsvet some 40 years before, the technique differed in that the stationary phase was a liquid. The mobile phase was trichloromethane (chloroform, $CHCl_3$), which does not mix with water.

A chromatography column is prepared by pouring a suspension of hydrated silica in solvent into a cylindrical glass column that has a tap at the bottom and a sintered-glass disk just above. The disk allows solvent to pass through while preventing silica from escaping through the tap. When the silica has settled as a layer, solvent is drained from the column until the upper surface of the silica is just wet with solvent. The sample solution is then added, and solvent is drained until the sample soaks into the top of the silica bed. The operator then adds more solvent at the top of the column and partially opens the tap to control its rate of flow through the column. Those substances that have a high affinity for the solvent of the mobile phase move down the column more rapidly than other components. The liquid that emerges from the column is collected in small portions that yield the individual components of the mixture when the solvent is removed by evaporation.

Paper and thin-layer chromatography

Chemists now have grades of chromatography-quality silica at their disposal. These contribute to highly consistent chromatography results by virtue of their uniform particle-sized distributions. The grades of silica available when Martin and Synge were developing chromatography were much less uniform, however, and consequently their results were variable. Frustrated by this, Martin and Synge sought a more reliable medium for their separations. They found that filter paper, which consists of water bound to cellulose fibers, was an acceptable medium for their tests.

In paper chromatography, drops of sample solutions are spotted along a line near the bottom of a sheet of filter paper and allowed to dry. The sheet is then put in a glass tank that contains a layer of solvent and positioned so that the sample spots are just above the surface of the solvent. The solvent slowly seeps up the paper, carrying the sample components at different rates as it goes. The process is complete when the solvent front—the line that separates wet and dry filter paper—reaches the top of the sheet. The sheet is then removed from the tank and allowed to dry.

In thin-layer chromatography—developed in the 1940s and 1950s—a glass sheet coated in a uniformly thin layer of silica gel replaces filter paper as the stationary phase. The plate is run in a solvent tank just as in paper chromatography.

In both paper and thin-layer techniques, the positions of spots of colored substances are visible throughout the separation. Colorless substances can be revealed by viewing their fluorescence under ultraviolet light and marking their positions or by spraying the spots with reagents that convert them into colored compounds.

Compounds can be identified by spotting known substances alongside the test spots and comparing the distances traveled by components of the mixture with the known spots. If the spots are applied using micropipettes—capillary tubes that dispense known volumes of solutions—the concentrations of components can be estimated by comparing the areas of their spots with those of the spots left by standard solutions.

Gas chromatography

Although Martin and Synge suggested in the early 1940s that gases could act as the mobile phase in chromatography, it took until the late 1950s for research chemists and chemical corporations to start developing gas chromatography (GC) as a practical technique. The first automatic GC equipment went on sale in the 1960s.

Since the 1960s, gas chromatography has developed as an extremely versatile method for performing rapid, accurate analyses of mixtures as diverse as urine, hydrocarbon blends from oil-refining units, amino acids, and perfumes.

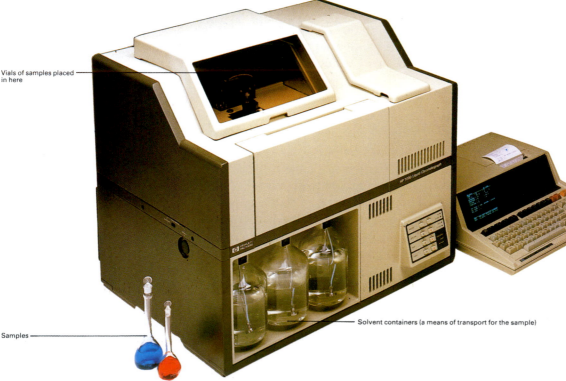

Vials of samples placed in here

Samples

Solvent containers (a means of transport for the sample)

◀ The development of liquid chromatographs, such as the Hewlett Packard 1090, has speeded up chemical analysis. Readouts from this machine indicate the presence of particular chemicals by the height and placing of peaks that occur at specific times, depending on how quickly each chemical moves through the stationary phase.

In a GC apparatus, the column is in fact a long, thin tube—typically 300 to 600 ft. (90–180 m) in length with an internal diameter of ⅟₁₀₀₀ in. (0.25 mm). The column is coiled inside an oven that operates over a typical temperature range of around 100 to 750°F (around 40–400°C).

The stationary phase is a thin layer of non-volatile liquid coated on the inside of the column; this is why GC is sometimes called gas-liquid chromatography, or GLC. The mobile phase is a pressurized inert gas, such as nitrogen, that does not react with the sample components at the temperature used for the separation.

The duration of a GC analysis can be a few seconds or several minutes, depending on the substances in the sample mixture. The separation starts when a sample is injected by hypodermic syringe either directly into one end of the column or into a heated block where the sample vaporizes before being adsorbed as a plug of vapor at the start of the column. Carrier gas then sweeps the components of the mixture through the column.

The end of the column leads to a detector that uses flame ionization, thermal conductivity, or some other physical property to record a peak as each component emerges from the column. A pen recorder plots the peaks versus time. The retention times, heights, widths, and areas of the peaks provide both qualitative and quantitative data about the components of the mixture.

The heart of a GC apparatus is its column, and column conditions such as length, gas flow, temperature, and stationary phase can be modified to suit the mixture under analysis. In some cases, the oven temperature is programmed to increase with time so as to accelerate the passage of low-volatility components in the sample.

In an analytical technique called GCMS—gas chromatography and mass spectrometry—a large-bore column separates the components of a mixture and feeds them directly into a mass spectrometer. The mass spectrometer identifies each component by providing high-accuracy mass determinations for each compound and the fragments that it forms in the mass spectrometer.

High-pressure liquid chromatography

High-pressure liquid chromatography—also called high-performance liquid chromatography, or HPLC—is a refinement of the method used by Tsvet. The stationary phase is a finely powdered adsorbent solid; the mobile phase is a liquid pumped under pressures that can be as high as 2,000 lbs. per sq. in. (140 kg/cm²). The rapid flow and the uniformity of the column packings ensure chromatographic separations almost as effective as those produced by gas chromatography.

As the components of a sample mixture emerge from a column, some are detected by their absorption of ultraviolet light; others are better observed by measuring changes in the refractive index of the column output as each component leaves the column.

As with GC, a peak is plotted on paper for each component that emerges from the column. The peak shapes and retention times of the components help in their identification by reference to standard results.

The critical advantage of HPLC over GC is that it is suitable for the analysis of chemical substances that are so sensitive to heat that they would not survive the high temperatures often used for GC. A second advantage over GC is that a large-scale HPLC apparatus can separate large enough samples to make it useful for preparing high-purity samples for chemical testing.

Other techniques

While the techniques mentioned above separate compounds according to differences in their volatilities or relative affinities for solvents, certain techniques use other physical properties as a basis for separation. Gel-permeation chromatography, or GPC, is one such technique. GPC uses a semisolid porous gel as the stationary phase and a liquid solvent as the mobile phase. The speed at which the components of a sample mixture pass through a GPC column is related to their size: smaller molecules pass through the pores in the gel faster than do larger particles. GPC can reveal the molecular weight distributions in product mixtures from polymerization reactions.

Ion-exchange chromatography separates ions according to their strengths of attraction to oppositely charged sites in a porous solid matrix. The first examples used zeolites—porous natural clays—to separate mixtures that contained cations of rare-earth and transuranic elements.

▲ Analysis of the chemical constituents of a pesticide by means of paper chromatography. This process is relatively slow.

SEE ALSO: AMINO ACID • CHEMISTRY, ANALYTICAL • CHEMISTRY, PHYSICAL • DRUG AND ALCOHOL TESTING • ION AND IONIZATION • OSMOSIS • PEN RECORDER • POLYMER AND POLYMERIZATION • ZEOLITE

Chromium

Chromium is a white, hard, lustrous metal, which can be highly polished. It tends to be brittle at low temperatures, but it is extremely resistant to oxidation and corrosion and so is widely used to provide a protective coating. Many of its compounds are brightly colored—hence its name, which comes from the Greek *chroma*, meaning color. The colorations in some gemstones, green in emeralds and red in rubies, come from traces of chromium compounds.

Chromium, chemical symbol Cr, is a member of the first transition series in the periodic table classification. There are nine other members, including manganese, iron, cobalt, and nickel. These metals all have high melting points and form a range of compounds where the various metals show different valencies (that is, combinations with different numbers of atoms).

Chromium melts at 3465°F (1907°C). The chromium atoms are arranged in a body-centered cubic lattice in the metal, that is, with one atom in the center of a cube surrounded by eight others—one being positioned at each corner.

Occurrence and extraction

The main source of chromium, which does not occur uncombined, is a mixed oxide of iron and chromium called chromite. This mineral, $FeCr_2O_4$, has a cubic crystal structure known as a spinel with the chromium atoms in octahedral sites and the iron in tetrahedral ones. Nearly 90 percent of the world's supply comes from six countries: Zimbabwe, Russia, Turkey, South Africa, the Philippines, and Albania.

To extract chromium the chromite ore has to be reduced (oxygen removed) to convert the chromic oxide, Cr_2O_3, to the pure metal. If the chromium is going to be used to make a steel alloy, then the iron content in the ore does not have to be removed. So the ore is reduced to give a mixture of chromium and iron (an alloy called ferrochrome). The addition of coke to the ore followed by heating in an electric arc furnace will produce a ferrochrome with a high carbon content. This result can be undesirable in some steels, so silica, SiO_2, is added to oxidize the carbon. By controlling the reducing conditions, the carbon level can range from 5 to 0.01 percent.

Chromium has to be separated from the iron for most other uses. The first stage is to separate the chromic oxide, Cr_2O_3. Medium-grade ores with about 45 percent chromic oxide are roasted with sodium carbonate to make sodium chromate, which is next dissolved out in water, separating it

▲ Chrome plating is a popular decorative process in the automobile- and motorcycle-customizing world. A high-quality finish requires meticulous preparation, the most important part of which is the polishing.

▲ Chromite—a mixed oxide of iron and chromium—has a cubic crystal structure known as spinel and is the main source of chromium.

from the rest of the ore. The chromate is then treated with sulfuric acid to make sodium dichromate, which is reduced back to chromic oxide by various processes, including the chemical action of sulfur or carbon.

Chromium of commercial purity is made by a thermal process. Powdered chromic oxide is reduced using powdered aluminum. The reaction is highly exothermic (that is, it produces heat) once the aluminum is ignited and produces chromium metal of between 97 and 99 percent purity. If a highly pure form of the metal is required (99.9 percent), a solution of chromic acid is decomposed by electrolysis using ammonium sulfate and sulfuric acid.

Alloys

Additions of relatively small amounts of chromium are made to steel to improve the heat-treatment properties, enabling thicker sections to be quench-hardened and tempered.

If vanadium, nickel, or manganese is added as well, the steel produced can be used for springs, ball and roller bearings, and other uses where a stronger steel is required. Steel used for making vessels and pipes that are resistant to oxidation includes about 5 percent chromium. Stainless steels, which have particularly high resistance to atmospheric corrosion and oxidation, contain between 10 and 20 percent chromium. Their ability to be heat treated depends on the carbon content. If the chromium content is high and there is low carbon content (0.1 percent), the steel cannot be heat treated. Such steels are used to handle nitric acid. Stainless steel used for cutlery contains about 13 percent chromium and 0.3 percent carbon, and it can be heat treated. High-carbon (1 to 2 percent) chromium steels are used where hardness and abrasion resistance is needed. If the chromium content is raised to 30 percent, the resistance to oxidation is good enough to use the alloy for burner jets and heat exchangers in domestic and industrial boilers.

Nickel is often added to chromium steels to increase the ease of working the alloy. For example, stainless steel sinks can be pressed out from a flat sheet of 18:8 stainless steel (18 percent chromium and 8 percent nickel).

The addition of nickel to chromium greatly improves its high-temperature corrosion resistance; electric fire heating elements operating around 1380°F (750°C) are made of 20 percent chromium, 80 percent nickel alloy. The nimonic series of alloys that have been developed to withstand the very high temperatures encountered in gas turbine blades are based on the same alloy with small but important additions of aluminum, titanium, and molybdenum.

Uses of chromium

Chromium compounds are extensively used in the leather industry, for chromium plating, for use in the production of timber treatment salts, and in the manufacture of pigments. Chromium is used as a coating on metals to prevent corrosion, while low-grade chromite ores are used for refractories.

When leather is tanned, complex inorganic chromium compounds are frequently used to remove water from between the protein fibers in the hide. Other chromium compounds are used to provide a range of pigments, although there is increasing competition from synthetic organic compounds. The main pigment colors are green from chromic oxide, yellow from lead chromate, and orange from a mixture of molybdenum salts and lead chromate.

The shiny trim on automobiles is today generally stainless steel rather than electroplated chromium. A few manufacturers also use chrome-plated plastic for bright trim inside their vehicles.

Although chromium is highly resistant to corrosion, it is difficult to deposit a layer that does not crack. So the main resistance to corrosion is obtained by a nickel layer, often one hundred times thicker, which can be deposited to form a crack-free surface. The chromium layer is then put on top of the nickel to give a scratch-and-tarnish-resistant surface. The ability of a layer of electroplated chromium to form minute cracks is useful in piston rings and cylinder liners. The cracks can hold sufficient oil to lubricate these parts for short periods when the main lubricant is not circulating, such as when an engine is started. The purest form of chrome covering (known as chromizing) is obtained by heating the object in an atmosphere of a chromium halide. The article is heated to around 1800°F (1000°C), and the volatile chloride or iodide of chromium diffuses to the surface of the article and deposits chromium. Layers deposited in this way do not have the same cracking tendencies as the electroplated coverings. Since they are cheaper than stainless steel, deposited layers of chromium on steel are used in gas stove burners, furnace parts, and some hand and machine tools. Low-grade chromite ores containing about 35 percent chromite and a low silica content are used to make refractory bricks.

◀ Chromium compounds are used extensively in the leather industry for tanning and pigmentation. Tanning removes water from the hide, making it tougher and suitable for fashioning into shoes, belts, and purses.

 SEE ALSO: Alloy • Carbon • Corrosion prevention • Electrolysis • Iron and steel • Leather • Nickel • Paint

Civil Engineering

Civil engineers design and build roads and railroads and the structures associated with them, such as bridges and tunnels. They also have a wide role in the overall planning of transportation systems and are responsible for water supply, including the planning and construction of dams.

Today, more than ever before, civil engineers will be expected to demonstrate an awareness of environmental issues when planning such large projects. They will have to work closely with scientists to prepare environmental impact assessments of the effects the new structure will have as well as the demands on resources needed for construction.

Bridges

Of all the projects in which civil engineers become involved, bridges are probably the most dramatic and prestigious. During the 1990s, a number of significant bridges were completed around the world. The record for the world's longest-span bridge, set in 1981 by Britain's Humber Bridge with its 4,625 ft. (1,410 m) main span, was surpassed by a number of other structures. Denmark's Great Belt (Store Baelt) East Bridge, which is part of an 11 mile (18 km) bridge and tunnel link between the islands of Zealand and Funen, has a huge main span of 5,330 ft. (1,624 m) and was opened to traffic in late 1999.

This is not the longest structure, however; it is surpassed by the 6,500 ft. (1,990 m) Akashi Kaikyo Bridge in Japan, completed in 1998, which spans the Akashi Straits between the islands of Honshu and Shikoku. This bridge has been designed to withstand an earthquake measuring 8 on the Richter scale, but the ten-year construction period was complicated by the fact that this is an area of frequent typhoons.

Also in a typhoon area is Hong Kong's Tsing Ma Bridge, part of the Lantau crossing serving the new Chek Lap Kok Airport. Its length is slightly less than that of the Humber Bridge. Unusually, road and rail traffic is protected from typhoons inside the bridge's specially designed, ventilated box-section deck. Six lanes of road traffic are carried on top. Construction was comparatively swift—it began in 1992, and the airport and bridge opened to the public in 1998.

Rise of the cable-stayed bridge

All the examples mentioned so far have been suspension bridges, which have held a monopoly on the world's longest spans since the Brooklyn Bridge was built in 1883. They consist of a high-strength steel cable hung between two towers and anchored to a heavy concrete block or to solid rock at each end. The bridge deck is hung from the main cables by suspender cables.

However, cable-stayed bridges have been increasing in popularity over the last two decades. In this type of bridge, the deck is supported by cables, usually in a fanlike arrangement, running diagonally from the deck to the towers. Cable-stayed bridges have come into their own only since computers became available to assist with the complex design calculations involved. The method of construction of this type of bridge leaves the deck more vulnerable to high winds in its partly complete state; this vulnerability has also restricted the length of span achieved.

One of the most striking modern cable-stay bridges, the Alamillo Bridge in Spain, designed by Santiago Calatrava, is a road bridge at the north end of La Cartuja island, with a 460 ft. (142 m) high pylon visible from Seville's old town. The Alamillo Bridge's striking feature is its forcefully

▼ Building Hong Kong's new airport at Chek Lap Kok was an enormous feat of civil engineering. First, engineers had to flatten a 300 ft. (100 m) rocky island to just 23 ft. (7 m) above sea level. The island was then extended to four times its size by a land-reclamation project that involved 70 percent of the world's dredging fleet. Contracts for the materials used were some of the biggest in history, and at the peak of construction, a force of 21,000 workers was needed on site. Two bridges and a railroad terminal were also built to service the airport.

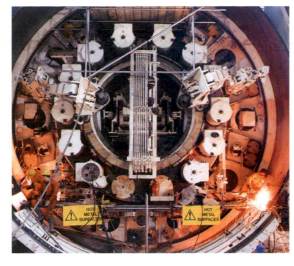

▶ One of the 16 ft. (4.8 m) diameter tunneling machines used during construction of the 30-mile (49 km) Channel Tunnel, connecting France and the United Kingdom.

asymmetric design. Its single pylon inclines away from the river, and supports the 650 ft. (200 m) span with 13 pairs of cables. The weight of the concrete and steel pylon provides a counterbalance for the bridge deck. The single plane of cables support a beam down the middle of the road, maintaining the bridge's image of a harp. The roadway itself is cantilevered out from the beam.

The record span for a cable-stayed bridge remained between 1,300 ft. and 1,600 ft. (400 m and 500 m) from the mid 1970s for more than two decades. The record holder was Canada's 1,525 ft. (465 m) Alex Fraser, or Annacis, Bridge in Vancouver until the construction of the Pont de Normandie, with a main span of 2,808 ft. (856 m), over the Seine River between Le Havre and Honfleur in France. This bridge, completed in 1995, represented a significant leap forward for the genre.

Tunnels

Tunnels present civil engineers with perhaps the greatest challenges of their career. Even with the most detailed site investigation, the danger of the tunnel face collapsing or of a sudden inflow of water resulting from an unsuspected fissure is always present to some extent.

In 1993, a long-standing goal of the tunneling industry was achieved with the construction of the 30 mile (49 km) Channel Tunnel between France and England. The project had been discussed for over a century, and started and abandoned on two occasions, before it became reality. Political rather than technical problems dogged the project: geological surveys had suggested at an early stage that the material under the Channel was chalk, a good tunneling material. Apart from some early problems on the French side, when unexpected fissures were met, this information proved largely correct. The Channel

Tunnel is actually three parallel tunnels; two running tunnels, one in each direction, that carry the high-speed rail tracks, with a service tunnel in between.

A 1980s development for tunneling in difficult ground conditions with noncohesive soils or high groundwater pressures was the earth pressure balance tunneling machine. Historically, when driving tunnels through waterlogged ground, contractors worked in a compressed-air atmosphere to prevent water inundating the face. However, workers under such conditions must observe strict decompression procedures to avoid injury, and as more has been discovered about long-term adverse health effects, acceptable working pressures have been reduced.

The earth pressure balance machine eliminates the need for compressed air. Material excavated by the cutting head is fed by screw conveyor through a sealed bulkhead behind the face, from where it is taken to the surface by belt conveyor. The solid plug of material in the screw conveyor supports the face and allows operators behind it to work in normal atmospheric pressure. Earth pressure balance machines were used on the eastern tunnel of the Danish Store Baelt crossing, Europe's biggest construction project to date.

The New Austrian Tunneling Method

As a tunnel is excavated, a permanent lining, usually made of cast-iron or precast concrete segments, is generally fixed in place to support the ground. However, increasing use is being made of the New Austrian Tunneling Method, especially for large-diameter caverns. Sprayed concrete is used to line the tunnel immediately after excavation, followed by a secondary concrete lining applied later. Engineers monitor the sprayed concrete lining for movement, and if necessary, they can increase its thickness.

Because the initial lining can be formed very quickly, there is less risk to workers from a collapse of the face or from settlement at ground level, which would also lead to the danger of damage to existing buildings. However, intensive monitoring is required and the technique has been reexamined since a major collapse during construction of the Heathrow Express railroad tunnel in London in 1995.

Transportation

Tunnels and bridges are usually constructed as part of road or rail links, and civil engineers are heavily involved in the wider picture of transportation planning. Rail travel has been enjoying something of a revival in recent years after being eclipsed by the automobile for most of the cen-

tury. France, Germany, and Spain have all built new high-speed rail links and the United Kingdom is currently building the high-speed Channel Tunnel Rail Link through Kent.

The French TGV (Train à Grand Vitesse) is typical: it carries passengers at 188 mph (300 km/h) and has proved able to compete with domestic air flights. The special track that allows the TGV to operate at full speed currently runs from Paris to Lyon, Le Mans, and Tours. Another line, TGV Nord, connects with the Channel Tunnel and Brussels; TGV Interconnexion is a ring service running round Paris; TGV Provencale runs south from Lyon.

Less glamorously, there has been a huge revival of interest in rail-based and light-rail solutions to urban traffic congestion, particularly in older crowded city areas. More and more experts are convinced that building roads to accommodate predicted levels of traffic merely causes the predictions to fulfill themselves, so the emphasis is increasingly turning toward encouraging people to use public transportation whenever possible.

Water supply

Improvements in the public health of the developed world last century owed as much to civil engineers providing sanitation and clean drinking water as to advances in medical science. Providing adequate water of a similarly high standard in developing countries remains a major concern.

Water supply is causing concern in the developed world, too, for a variety of reasons. Increasing levels of pollutants, particularly nitrates from agricultural fertilizers and fecal contamination from inadequate sewerage provision, coupled with increasingly stringent health standards mean that water-supply companies need to invest in more sophisticated treatment plants before they deliver water to customers.

Even well-established treatment techniques have begun to be called into question for a variety of health reasons. Water engineers have long seen chlorine as offering the ideal way of killing waterborne bacteria because it remains effective after the water leaves the treatment plant. However, studies have shown that surface water sources contain organic substances that react with chlorine to form compounds called trihalomethanes. Research in the United States has linked these substances with forms of cancer. Accordingly, alternative disinfectants, such as ozone, which is already widely used in France, and granular activated carbon, which traps the organic compounds within its chemical structure, are increasingly gaining favor. Because ozone has no residual effect, however, some chlorine still has to be added to the water to provide a satisfactory level of protection in the distribution system.

FACT FILE

■ Bridge spans have increased in length by a factor of 3.5 every 100 years since 1770. Longer bridges have been made possible by the development of new materials, such as wrought iron in the 1800s, steel later in the same century, and high-strength steel in the 1930s. These materials gave progressively greater strength with less weight.

■ What is thought to be the world's first plastic bridge, a cable-stayed footbridge with a modest 200 ft. (61 m) main span, was built at Aberfeldy, Scotland, in 1992. Apart from its foundations, it is completely made of composite plastics: cellular glass-fiber-reinforced polyester for the deck and "Aramid" cables. This project should stimulate considerable interest in the use of such new materials.

■ The world's widest bridge is Boston's new ten lane Charles River Bridge, with a main-span bridge deck 56.4 m wide. Two of the lanes are minor traffic feeders, cantilevered outside the pair of inverted-Y concrete towers that form the main support for the bridge. Both feeder lanes are on the same side, and this makes the cable-stay bridge into a complex asymmetrical design.

SEE ALSO: BRIDGE • BUILDING TECHNIQUES • DAM • GEODESIC STRUCTURES • RAILROAD SYSTEM • ROAD CONSTRUCTION • TUNNELING • WASTEWATER TREATMENT • WATER SUPPLY

Climatology

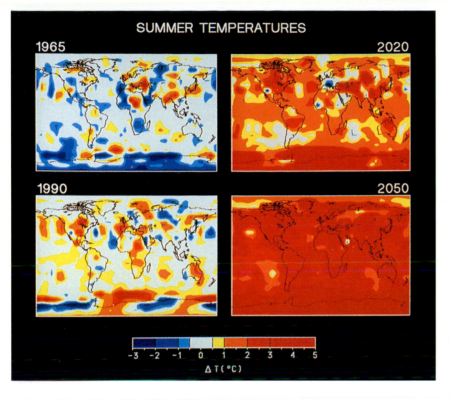

SUMMER TEMPERATURES

1965   2020
1990   2050

-3 -2 -1 0 1 2 3 4 5
ΔT (°C)

Climatology is the study of past, present, and future climates. The effects of climate are fundamental to everybody, influencing where they live and how they live their lives. Climate also plays an important role in almost every human economic endeavor, from agriculture to aviation to construction. Less obviously, it influences medicine, insurance, and sports. Predicting patterns and trends in how the climate changes over seasons, years, and centuries is an enormous challenge to climatologists.

The work of climatologists has become even more important with the discovery of potentially disastrous environmental effects, such as global warming, the attendant rise in sea levels, and ozone thinning. There is also a wide range of more localized effects, some natural and some caused by human activities, that could have profound consequences for agriculture. The ability to predict such changes would give policy makers the chance to avert them or, where they could not do this, give plant breeders time to develop new varieties and farmers time to adapt their methods.

Weather records

Accurate measurements of rainfall, temperature, and air pressure began in the mid-18th century. While they are useful to climatologists, 250 years is a comparatively short length of time to determine fluctuations that may occur over hundreds and thousands of years. Some information can be

▲ Computer predictions showing past and projected global surface air temperatures. Red and orange indicate increased temperatures. The data come from NASA's Global Climate Model and show that if levels of greenhouse gases, such as carbon dioxide, continue to rise, most of the planet will experience a significant increase in average temperature by the year 2050.

determined, however, from agricultural records, such as the size of harvests, when they were gathered, and the prices fetched at market. Other information can be gleaned from individual diaries and records kept by officials. China has summer rainfall records dating back 1,000 years that have been used to grade droughts and floods for the last five centuries. Though such records cannot be viewed as reliable, they can provide background detail in assessments of the social impact of climate variations.

Determining past climates

It is essential to discover whether the apparent climatic changes that we see around the world are really permanent or are simply temporary fluctuations from some overall long-term average. For example, we must expect occasional long runs of years that are particularly hot and dry, like those that occurred over much of the Northern Hemisphere in the 1990s.

Such anomalies give added urgency to the study of climates over long stretches of time, both in historical times and at earlier geological periods (where the discipline becomes known as paleoclimatology). If scientists can determine the range and duration of long-term climatic fluctuations, it should help them to predict what will happen in the future, provided—and this is a very important proviso—that they truly understand the underlying mechanisms at work.

Many different types of material provide information about past climate. Historical records are an obvious source, but there are many other types of evidence. Ancient bodies can be preserved in peat bogs, as Tollund Man was in Denmark and Lindow Man was in Britain. Rarely, one may be found in a glacier, as the "iceman" named Ötzi was in the Alps in 1991. Study of clothing and other items or sometimes even the remnants of the person's final meal gives valuable clues about the plants (and thus the climate) in the area at the time. The stomach contents of frozen mammoths discovered in Siberia have been used for the same purpose. The oldest known roadway, the Sweet Track, found in an English peat bog, gives evidence about the climate prevailing around 4000 B.C.E., the time it was constructed. The fossilized remnants of a particular form of beetle were found alongside the wooden walkway. Such beetles exist only where summers are about 3 to 5°F (2–3°C) warmer and winters 3 to 7°F (2–4°C) colder than those found in southern England today.

◀ The world's oldest roadway, the Sweet Track in Somerset, England, has timbers preserved from 3806 B.C.E. Beside it were remains of beetles that can exist only in a warmer climate than found in Britain today, giving clues to climate change.

Other major techniques include dendrochronology, the study of tree rings. The thickness of a ring indicates the temperature and rainfall in a particular year. Pollen analysis shows the prevalence of particular species in the past, which gives an idea of the prevailing climate.

Ice ages

Studies of past climate have revealed that, although many climatic changes take decades or centuries to become established, sudden alterations can occur when the whole climate switches from one stable state to another. Evidence from ocean sediment cores taken from the Atlantic and Carribean has shown that there have been seven ice ages in the last 700,000 years interspersed with shorter, warm interglacial periods. Overall, ice ages have two main contributory factors: Milankovitch cycles, which are regular changes in the direction of Earth's axis of rotation and in its orbit around the Sun and geological changes, particularly continental drift. When (as at present) land masses surround or cover the poles, warm ocean waters fail to reach them, thus giving rise to ice caps. This phenomenon occurs rarely, so that, over the whole of geological time, ice ages are infrequent events.

Analysis of ice cores and sediments has shown that the last ice age began about 117,000 years ago and lasted 100,000 years. Large ice sheets built up in northern latitudes, reaching a maximum thickness of about 2 miles (3 km) roughly 18,000 years ago. Locking up water as ice had the effect of reducing the global sea level by up to 400 ft. (120 m), and the average global temperature dropped by 14°F (8°C). However, the climate at this time was not constantly cold—ice ages are characterized by sudden dramatic warmings, the last of which began 15,000 years ago and is responsible for the current climate.

El Niño

A key aim of climatologists is to find regular patterns in the weather to help them predict what may happen in future years, an aim they achieve by analyzing huge quantities of weather statistics. Once they have established a pattern, they then have to determine the causes behind it, which may be natural variability or an external factor, such as sunspots, lunar cycles, or ionized particles in the upper atmosphere. One such pattern that has been determined is the El Niño-Southern Oscillation (ENSO), and climatologists have made great progress in modeling it.

Off the west coast of South America, the winds normally blow westward, and cause water to move away from the coast, producing an upwelling of cold, nutrient-rich waters that support large fish stocks. However, every four to seven years, there is a failure of the fisheries accompanying a reversal of the wind direc-

▼ The iceman found in 1991 in the Alps between Austria and Italy had been preserved in the ice for 4,000 years. His body yielded clues to the climate during the Bronze Age when he lived.

tion and increased rainfall in the area. This phenomenon is El Niño, and it normally lasts about a year.

Climatologists now know that this is only one feature of an ENSO event, which disrupts oceanic and atmospheric circulation over a large portion of the globe. High pressure builds up over the western tropical Pacific, and eastward-blowing winds spread a broad tongue of warm surface water toward the east. There is a decrease in rainfall over the western Pacific, Indonesia, and Australia. The circulation over the Indian Ocean and the rest of the Southern Hemisphere is also disrupted. An ENSO event in 1997–1998 contributed to forest fires in Indonesia and droughts in Papua New Guinea and Guyana. Devasting floods also occurred in China, Ecuador, Peru, and Kenya, as El Niño suddenly switched to its opposite effect, termed La Niña. The switch also delayed the start of the 1998 Atlantic hurricane season, which produced 14 named storms, one of which killed 9,000 and displaced 2.5 million people in Central America.

There are several computer models of the ENSO, and they show some success in predicting its severity and duration but not yet its timing or that of the cold event (La Niña) that follows it. Climatologists now think that these changes in circulation are linked to slow-moving undulations in the thickness of the surface waters of the Pacific Ocean that affect the depth of the thermocline between the warm surface and the deeper cold water currents. Models have shown that this process corresponds to the switch from El Niño to La Niña atmospheric circulation patterns every three to five years.

Global warming

Global-change research is one of the most important fields in contemporary climatology, and in 1988, the World Meteorological Organization (WMO) and the United Nations Environment Program (UNEP) set up the Intergovernmental Panel on Climate Change (IPCC). In addition, the WMO and other international scientific unions were establishing the Global Climate Observing System (GCOS) to collect data on climate variations all round the world.

Of chief concern is the impact of global warming on Earth's environment. Since the Industrial Revolution, levels of carbon dioxide in the atmos-

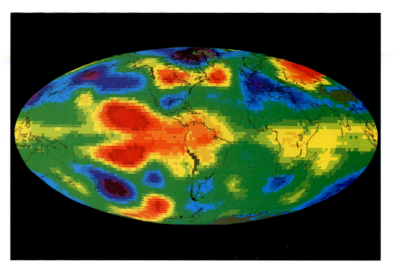

▲ Temperature anomaly map of the globe, using data from the TIROS-N weather satellite, shows an El Niño event in progress, marked by the large orange and red areas in the middle of the Pacific Ocean.

phere have risen by roughly 25 percent, and global surface temperatures appear to have increased by 1°F (0.4–0.6°C), with a significant jump of 0.5°F (0.2–0.3°C) occurring over the last 40 years. However, this warming has not been uniform—some parts of the southeast United States have actually cooled.

Carbon dioxide is a natural constituent of Earth's atmosphere and is radiatively active, that is, it absorbs heat from Earth's surface and reflects it back. Water vapor and ozone have the same effect and act as a blanket to stop too much heat escaping into space. If the balance of these gases changes, more heat will be trapped and the climate will become progressively warmer.

Scientists trying to model the effects of global warming have been surprised by some of the results from observations of the 20th century. They have not been able to find a direct correlation between the amount of warming that has taken place and the increase of greenhouse gases in the atmosphere. Also, during two periods in the 1940s and 1970s, the warming effect abated.

One explanation could be the influence of another product of fossil fuel combustion—sulfate aerosols. Unlike carbon dioxide, these particles reflect sunlight back out into space, producing a cooling effect. At the U.K. Meteorological Office, scientists have attempted to predict the likely effect of carbon dioxide levels doubling using a sophisticated model that takes into account the interaction between the atmosphere and the oceans. They performed three experiments over a timescale from 1860 to 2050. The first kept carbon dioxide levels constant, as a control. The second increased carbon dioxide gradually. For the third, they introduced sulfate aerosols that increased in line with the concentration of carbon dioxide.

What they discovered with this last experiment was that if carbon dioxide were to double by 2050, the sulfate aerosols would counterbalance the rate of warming and, in certain parts of the world, would actually slow it down. These findings correlate with what has been observed over the last 100 years and give rise to a prediction that global temperatures will rise by 4.5°F (2.5°C) by 2050, or by 3°F (1.7°C) if sulfates are taken into account. It is widely thought that global warming should not exceed a rise of 3.5°F (2°C).

THE OZONE LAYER

The ozone layer that surrounds Earth plays a key role in protecting the planet's inhabitants from harmful ultraviolet rays. It is formed in the stratosphere when ultraviolet radiation stimulates some oxygen molecules into splitting into energized atoms that quickly recombine with other oxygen molecules to form ozone (O_3). Most ozone is produced in the tropics, where sunlight is strongest, and transported round the globe by stratospheric winds.

The ozone layer is particularly vulnerable to attack by other chemicals present in the atmosphere such as nitrogen oxides and chlorine compounds. During the 1980s, scientists discovered a hole in the ozone layer over Antarctica. Measurements taken every month since then showed that the hole appeared between September and November every year and was growing. In September 1998, it reached a size of 10.5 million square miles (27.3 million km²), bigger than the entire Antarctic continent, and lasted for more than 100 days.

The reason for a hole developing in the ozone layer is unclear, but a group of man-made chemicals containing halogens called chlorofluorocarbons

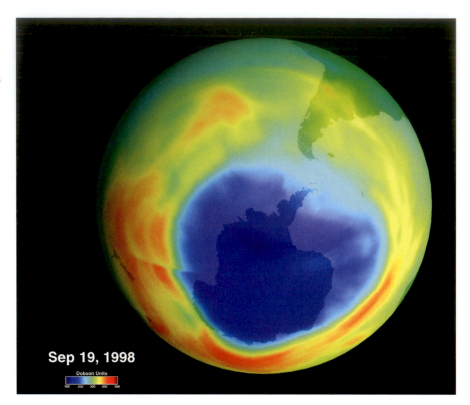

Sep 19, 1998

Dobson Units
100   200   300   400   500

(CFCs) are suspected of having played a key role. These highly reactive compounds were used as aerosol propellants and, when released, were transported to the upper layers of the atmosphere. Here, they broke down into highly reactive chlorine compounds that interfered with the process of ozone formation. Once the connection was made between these compounds and destruction of the ozone layer, CFCs were banned by international agreement. It is expected that the ozone hole will eventually shrink as CFCs are depleted, though it is also thought that thinning of the ozone layer could be a natural process owing to the presence of hydrochloric acid at high altitudes.

Consequences of warming

The impact on the weather at a local level if the planet gets hotter is much harder to predict. If, as expected, polar regions become warmer, there would be less of a temperature gradient between the equator and the pole, which would force storms to move to a higher latitude. Although there is a perception that storms and hurricanes have increased over the last century, it is not supported by weather statistics. What has increased is the cost of repairing the damage, particularly in built-up industrialized areas. Similarly, though an increase in flooding has been attributed to global warming, the damage that flooding causes has been augmented by land-use changes such as deforestation of upland areas, urbanization, embankments, and building on floodplains.

Inundation of great areas of land by rising sea levels is widely thought to be a likely impact of global warming. Measuring these changes is difficult, as the thermal expansion and contraction of the oceans is influenced by fluctuations in the amount of water stored in rivers, aquifers, and glaciers. How fast levels might rise also depends on whether melting of the glaciers and ice sheets is balanced by increased precipitation at high latitudes. The WMO has indicated that if carbon dioxide doubles by 2030, the sea level could rise by 2½ in. (6 cm) per decade, which is five times faster than has been seen in the last 100 years. Coastal cities and small island states would be at particular risk, though the release of the weight of the ice may cause some continental land masses to rise. However, until temperatures rise by at least 14°F (8°C), snowfall is expected to accumulate further on the ice sheets and glaciers, actually reducing sea levels rather than making them increase.

SEE ALSO: Barometer • Environmental science • Flood control • Glaciology • Hurricane and tornado • Meteorology • Rain and rainfall • Thunderstorm • Water

Clock

Clocks are essential to modern life. Apart from acting as timekeepers for everyday matters, their uses extend to the automatic programming of factories, timing in industrial and sporting activities, time switches in street lighting and domestic controls, and for all navigation and space travel.

History

People in the early settlements along the shores of the Nile and Mediterranean first indicated the passage of time by noting the length or position of the shadow of an upright stick in the ground. By 1500 B.C.E., these sticks had been replaced by elaborate obelisks in community centers. Cleopatra's needle (now in London) was one of them. Many elaborate and portable sundials followed over the next millennia, but none was of any value at night or out of the Sun. For use at any time, the clepsydra (water clock) was invented about 1500 B.C.E. It was followed by the sand timer, working on the same principle of filling or emptying a vessel at a controlled rate.

The hour was one of the first artificial divisions of time, probably invented by the Egyptians about 4000 B.C.E. Previously humans

▶ Sundials were an early way to tell the time. As the Sun travels across the sky, the shadow of the sundial's gnomon moves around the face of the dial to indicate the time with great precision. Unfortunately, they were of little use in cloudy weather or at night.

◀ A table clock signed "Nicholas Lemaindre, Blois, France, 1619." The clock has a mainspring movement with a fusee on which is wound a chain that keeps mainspring tension constant as it unwinds.

depended only on natural divisions of day, determined by the Sun, and of month, determined by the Moon. The 12 daylight hours started at dawn and the 12 night hours at dusk, so the hours were of different lengths and varied during the year. Early astronomers, however, used hours that were of equal length all the year round. As civilization advanced, more and more human activity was controlled by the horologium, as early timekeeping devices were called (horology is the science of time measurement). A monastery, the center of learning, would have a horologium, operated by water, upon which the sexton would depend for sounding the monastery bell to call the monks to rise, work, prayer, and bed.

The first mechanical clock

At an unknown point in history, but believed to be in Burgundy, France, around 1275 C.E., an unknown man, probably a monk, devised a new kind of horologium, a mechanical one that struck a single note on a bell at the hour instead of indicating the time visually. It was worked by a falling weight instead of water and became known as a clock, after the Latin *clocca*, bell. The first clocks also had alarms that could be set to ring continuously at a selected hour to warn the sexton, or the watchman of a civil community, when to toll his big bell. Such alarm clocks were quite small to judge by those shown in early paintings of this era.

The frame was a vertical double strip of iron or brass that stood on a base or was hung on a wall. The wall version had a hoop or stirrup at the top for hanging from a hook and two spurs at the bottom to prop it away from the wall. It was powered by a stone weight on a rope that was wound around a wooden barrel. Small pegs in the barrel allowed it to be turned to wind up the weight by hand. A click (ratchet) prevented the weight from falling down again without rotating the barrel in the opposite direction to drive the clock. To the barrel was attached a large toothed wheel, called the great wheel, that drove a very small toothed wheel or a wheel with rods for teeth, called a pinion. On the same shaft as the pinion was another large wheel, but of a different kind, called a crown wheel, with teeth on one side. (The name arose because of its likeness to a king's crown.) Across the crown wheel was another shaft with two small "flags" (pallets) attached to it placed to intercept a tooth on each side of the wheel. This vertical shaft was called the verge, after the staff with two small flags carried by a verger. As the weight fell, it turned the crown wheel, which was checked by a tooth striking a pallet at one side. Movement of the pallet turned the verge and caused the opposite pallet to intercept another tooth. The action was then repeated, so that the verge was oscillated to and fro as the weight descended. At the top of the verge was a horizontal crossbar with a weight at each end, the foliot, which had its own period of oscillation, or timekeeping, which it tried to impose upon the clock. Moving the foliot weights inward increased the rate, and outward decreased it.

Development

Very soon after the invention of the mechanical clock, it became divided into three separate mechanisms. The main one controlled the other two. It incorporated the crown wheel and verge (the escapement) and indicated time of day by a moving hand or moving dial. It was known at the time as the "watch" and is now called the going train. The second was the striking train, originally called the "clock," which had its own weight drive. It was released by a lever moved by a pin on a wheel in the going train. The third part was the alarm, which was also released by the going train and had a separate weight to drive it. It was first set by placing a removable pin in one of a radial series of holes representing the hours. Later a friction-held disk with a pin in it was rotated to set the alarm. On smaller clocks, a balance wheel with one spoke was used instead of a foliot. It was not adjustable, but weight could be added or subtracted from the driving weight to change the rate of drive.

The first improvement to striking clocks was to make them sound the correct number of blows

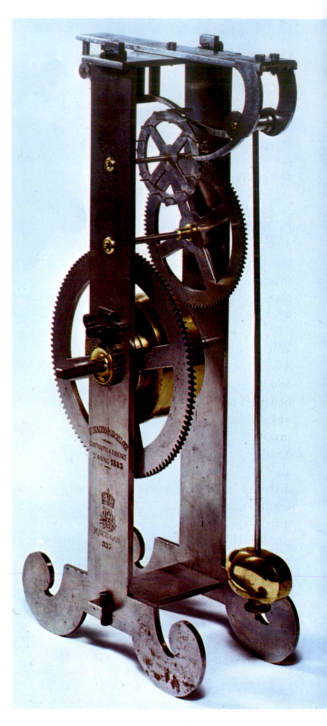

▶ A model of a pendulum escapement mechanism designed by the Italian astronomer Galileo Galilei. Clocks of this design were inaccurate until Christian Huygens hung the pendulum separately and connected it to a horizontal verge by means of an arm called a crutch.

on a bell to represent the hour, sometime around 1330. A form of cam wheel was developed to control the number of blows struck. It had 12 slots of increasing width around its periphery into which an arm dropped at every blow. When the arm could not drop into a slot, the striking stopped. Count-wheel striking of this type is commonly found on English longcase clocks and French ormolu clocks. An improved control called rack striking (or rack-and-snail), invented in 1676 by an English parson clockmaker, the Rev. Edward Barlow, not only prevented the striking from becoming out of phase with the time shown by the hands, as does the count-wheel system, but also made repeating clocks possible.

The early form of winding was soon replaced by a single rope fitting snugly in a grooved pulley. One end held the large driving weight and the other a small weight to keep the rope in the groove. The clock could be wound by pulling down the smaller weight by hand.

One hand indicating hours on a dial marked in hours with divisions for quarters was sufficiently accurate for some centuries on domestic clocks, although astronomers had used minute hands, even second hands, from the 16th century. One problem was in setting the clock to the time as shown by the sundial. At first, it was necessary to disengage the verge from the crown wheel to allow the hand to turn. Soon an unknown inventor thought of providing the hand with a slipping clutch so that it could be turned without affecting the clock.

Winding mechanisms

All clocks until about 1475 were weight driven and were therefore not portable. If moved, they had to be carefully set up again. Someone unknown, possibly a locksmith or swordsmith, invented a coiled spring to replace the weight, giving birth not only to the portable clock but also to the personal watch. The first spring-driven clocks were modified-weight clocks. Instead of a weight pulling on a line around the driving barrel, another barrel immediately below the driving barrel had a coiled spring inside it and wound the line around itself. The earliest known version of such a clock is dated 1480 and is in the Victoria and Albert Museum in London, England.

The mainspring alone was not an accurate enough power source for the clock, because it was strong when wound up and became progressively weaker as the spring ran down, unlike a weight, which could provide an absolutely constant source of power. So clockmakers introduced a device known as a fusee to provide a relatively constant source of power from the spring. This was a trumpet-shaped pulley, first illustrated for clockwork by Leonardo da Vinci in 1407 and originally used in his time to make the winding of war catapults easier. It effectively increased the leverage as the spring ran down gradually.

Precision devices

The biggest advance in precision, until very recent times, came with the invention of the practical pendulum clock by the Dutch scientist Christiaan Huygens, also famous for his contributions to dynamics and optics, in 1657–1658. His most effective design was a wall clock with a short pendulum about 1 ft. (0.3 m)

long connected with a horizontal verge acting on a horizontal crown wheel. Huygens hung the pendulum separately and connected it with the clock movement through an arm called the crutch. For weight-driven clocks, he employed an ingenious endless rope or chain that still provided drive while the clock was being wound. It was subsequently used in thousands of English grandfather clocks wound daily and for modern electrically wound turret clocks. His spring-driven clocks incorporated a going barrel instead of a fusee. The going barrel was wound in the same direction that it drove the clock, instead of being wound back, and therefore provided power during winding, whereas the fusee, although more accurate, had to have a complicated addition in order to provide this maintaining power. Most clocks by this time were wound with a key.

About 1675, William Clement, an English clockmaker, introduced an escapement designed for the pendulum known as the anchor, or recoil, escapement. It employed an ordinary flat escape wheel with teeth on the edge instead of the crown wheel, which had teeth on the side. The arrangement substantially reduced the arc of the pendulum so that a long one could be used, which determined the rate of the clock much more effectively. The most satisfactory length was just over 3 ft. (1 m), allowing the pendulum to swing from one side to the other in one second. This seconds pendulum, also called the Royal

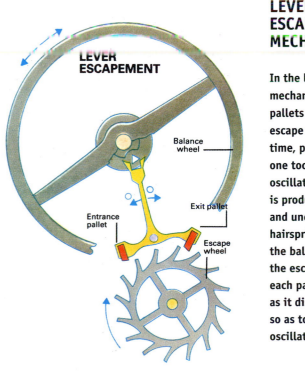

LEVER ESCAPEMENT

Balance wheel

Exit pallet

Entrance pallet

Escape wheel

LEVER ESCAPEMENT MECHANISM

In the lever escapement mechanism, the two pallets engage with the escape wheel, one at a time, permitting it to turn one tooth at a time. The oscillation of the pallets is produced by the coiling and uncoiling of a hairspring mounted within the balance wheel, and the escape wheel gives each pallet a small push as it disengages from it so as to keep the oscillations going.

▲ The early history of science is profoundly linked to astronomy—this miniature clockwork orrery (mechanical model of the solar system) dates from the first half of the 18th century. It was by measuring the movements of the stars and planets that early man was able to calculate years, seasons, and increasingly smaller units of time.

George Graham, invented the deadbeat escapement and in 1721 the mercury pendulum, which compensated for temperature changes with a column of mercury on the pendulum that expanded upward to keep it the same effective length. The deadbeat escapement, by changing the shape of the teeth on the escape wheel, avoided recoil in the mechanism and provided a shorter pendulum swing. These inventions increased the availability of precision clocks. The most remarkable feat of the time was the development of a marine timepiece with a balance wheel and compensated spring by a carpenter, John Harrison. It was tested in 1761 on a sailing ship voyaging to Jamaica and was only 5.1 seconds out during the 81 days' passage. That year initiated accurate navigation and the charting and control of the seas by the British Royal Navy.

The deadbeat escapement was improved upon, especially for tower clocks, which tend to slow down because of weather conditions. The new idea was to raise weights (by means of the movement of the escape wheel) that when released give an impetus to the pendulum. The most successful device of this type was invented by E. B. Denison (later Lord Grimthorpe), who used it in the Westminster tower clock called Big Ben, which was installed in 1859.

A German clockmaker, S. Riefler, built a precision pendulum clock in 1889 that was adopted by many observatories. In 1921, an English engineer, W. H. Shortt, devised the free-pendulum clock, the ultimate form of pendulum clock. The one in Edinburgh Observatory kept time to within 0.1 second a year. It is partly electric and has two pendulums, one to swing freely and the other to do the work. It was so accurate that it detected a regular wobble in the Earth's rotation, subsequently confirmed and analyzed by quartz clocks, used later by observatories, that kept time to the equivalent of a second in 30 years. Today the timekeeper from which all time standards are derived is the atomic clock, developed by the British scientist L. Essen, which has an accuracy equivalent to one second in 3,000 years. The atomic clock has detected a slowing down in Earth's rotation.

Manufacture of clocks followed trends set by the inventors. At first, all clocks were made by individual clockmakers, and the casings were held together originally by mortise and tenon, as in early wooden furniture, and after about 1500, increasingly by nuts on threads. Each part was made separately, and a wedge would fit only a particular slot and a nut only one particular thread. Some removable pieces were marked to

pendulum, reduced the error of a clock from about a quarter of an hour a day to only about 20 seconds a day. The minute hand, which had been used on a few astronomical clocks from the 16th century, became almost universal on clocks with all lengths of pendulum, and the second hand became orthodox on longcase clocks.

Better timekeeping by artificial clocks, as mechanical clocks were called, made two uncomfortable facts apparent. One was that the days varied in length throughout the year. The other was that sunrise time varied across the country, occuring gradually earlier eastward and later westward. The first was solved by accepting the "equal hours" shown by the clock (except in Japan, where complicated arrangements made the clock show hours of different length). The second was not solved until over two centuries later in 1884, when Greenwich mean time was adopted in most of the world, adapted by means of local time zones.

It was now apparent that clocks were better timekeepers than the rotating Earth, and increasing precision became the driving force of leading clockmakers from the early 18th century. Thomas Tompion, most famous of all English clockmakers, provided the first Astronomer Royal, appointed in 1676, with two high-precision clocks for the newly built Greenwich Observatory. In 1715, his friend and successor,

ATOMIC CLOCK

The very accurate measurement of time is important in many areas of modern technology, such as space exploration, satellite tracking, navigation, and scientific research; since the mid-1950s it has been provided by scientific instruments known as atomic clocks.

There is very little resemblance between an atomic clock and a normal one. It has no clock face or digital or audible readout normally associated with recording the time. It does not, therefore, tell the time but provides a reference standard frequency, which is used to calibrate other clocks.

All atoms in their natural state emit and absorb pulses, or quanta, of energy, owing to the switching back and forth of electrons from one orbit, or energy level, around the central nucleus to another. These energy levels of an atom are more constant than any other known natural phenomenon and are therefore ideally suited to determining standard frequencies. Certain elements, such as the alkali metals cesium and rubidium, are especially useful for this work. They have only one electron in their outer orbit to emit and absorb energy, and their respective frequencies are relatively uncomplicated and easier to use than those from atoms with more electrons in this orbit.

A cesium atom can be at one of two energy states, depending on whether the outer electron is spinning in the same or opposite direction to that of the nucleus. These different states influence the path of a free cesium atom as it travels through a magnetic field.

If a beam of cesium atoms is passed through such a field, then the maximum number of state transitions will occur when the field frequency is tuned precisely to the natural frequency of the cesium. The cesium clock measures the number of transitions and constantly tries to achieve the greatest possible number by means of a feedback circuit to the field frequency controller. Once locked on to the cesium frequency the controller can be used to control the accuracy of a quartz clock.

In practice, the method by which this is done is to heat cesium in a small electric oven set inside a straight tube from which all the air has been removed by vacuum pumps. Atoms stream out of a slit in the front of the oven and down the tube—there is no air to slow their progress. On the way, they pass a magnet that deflects atoms in one state to one side and atoms in the other state to the other side. This has the effect of deflecting some atoms off axis but focusing the rest into a converging beam.

The beam converges on a cavity resonator, a hollow antennalike device that passes an electromagnetic field across it. This field is kept at a frequency of 9,192 MHz by electronically multiplying the 5 MHz signal from a quartz clock. Provided that the quartz clock is running at exactly the right frequency, the field will change the spin direction of nearly all the atoms passing through it but without affecting the focusing of the beam in which they travel.

The beam comes to a focus at a narrow slit in the middle of the resonator, which stops any off-course atoms. The beam spreads out on the other side of the slit, but the focusing has made it cross over, and an atom that was on the left side of the beam before the slit is on the right side after it.

At the same time, the resonator has changed the spin direction of nearly all the atoms. Since atoms in one state are on one side of the beam (and vice versa), the net result is that the two changes cancel each other out. The beam then passes through a second magnet, which focuses it on a detecting device at the end of the tube. The few atoms that have not changed their state are on the wrong side of the beam to be focused and are thrown out to one side. The atoms striking the detector cause it to emit a signal that is fed back to the quartz clock.

If the frequency of the quartz clock slips, none of the atoms will strike the detector. The absence of any signal causes the quartz clock to change its frequency until it receives the signal again.

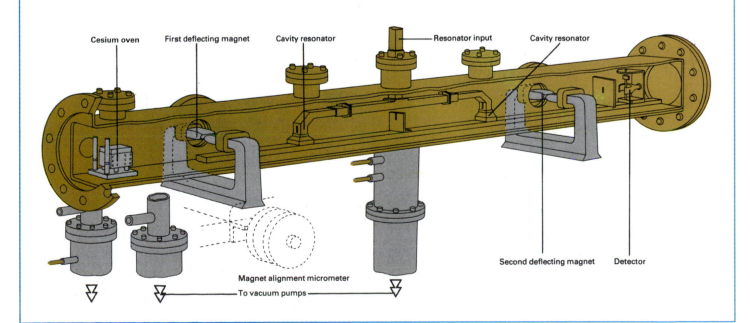

Cesium oven   First deflecting magnet   Cavity resonator   Resonator input   Cavity resonator

Magnet alignment micrometer

To vacuum pumps

Second deflecting magnet   Detector

show mating parts. From about 1700, some clockmakers began to make interchangeable parts so that clocks could be produced in batches by workers specializing in one part or another—a process pioneered by Tompion.

In the 19th century, after failed attempts in France, mass production was finally achieved in North America. In a water-powered mill, Eli Terry mass-produced wooden grandfather clock movements in thousands. Cheap mass-produced clocks of rolled brass also first appeared in the United States and then flooded Europe's markets, bankrupting many factories and forcing the reorganization of national industries.

Electric clocks

The first electric clock was invented in 1840 by a Scotsman, Alexander Bain, and an English clockmaker, Barwise, and worked off earth batteries: coke and zinc buried in the ground. The French manufactured an electric pendulum clock, worked by a Leclanché cell, that was small enough to stand on a mantelpiece. An American, H. E. Warren, invented the first synchronous electric clock in 1916; it is not a true clock, as it contains no time standard, merely counting the frequency of the alternating current and translating this into time of day. The biggest breakthrough was the dry-battery clock developed since World War II, particularly in Germany, which is an accurate timekeeper and will run for a year on a battery (some versions will run for five years).

The first battery clocks, remontoires, overcame variations in driving power by winding up a small weight (Huygens, 1659) or a small spring (Harrison, 1739) to drive the clock, a task originally done mechanically. The battery wound a light spring every quarter of an hour or so to drive a normal clock controlled by a balance and

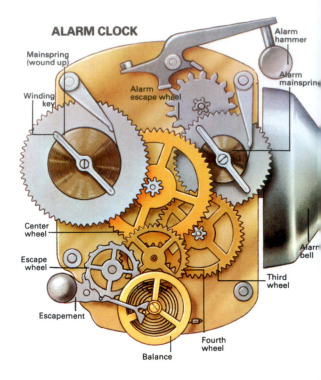

▶ The mechanism of an alarm clock features an additional spring for driving the alarm hammer, which strikes the alarm bell via the directly driven alarm escape wheel. It is always the smaller spring.

ALARM CLOCK

Mainspring (wound up)
Alarm hammer
Winding key
Alarm escape wheel
Alarm mainspring
Center wheel
Escape wheel
Alarm bell
Escapement
Third wheel
Fourth wheel
Balance

spring, a system invented for watches by Christiaan Huygens in 1675 but used also for almost all small clocks in the 20th century.

Most accurate of all is the battery-driven quartz clock, in which the time standard is a wafer, or "tuning fork," of rock crystal controlling a solid-state oscillator that drives the hands. Some are driven by storage batteries charged automatically by natural or artificial light.

Alarm clock

The alarm clock, now the basic household clock, has always been made in one form or another since the end of the 19th century. Because of a desire to keep prices low, it has followed a rather different direction of development. The mechanical alarm has not changed much horologically, but production has been refined to a considerable extent so that some factories can turn out every minute of the working day a complete and going alarm regulated automatically to an accuracy of 99.6 percent. Electric alarms avoid the task of daily winding.

Quartz clock

A mechanical clock consists of a regular oscillator and a mechanism for counting and recording the number of completed oscillations. In the case of the quartz clock, the oscillating part is a piece of quartz cut in a suitable direction from a quartz crystal, and the number of oscillations, which may be as high as one million per second, is counted by electronic dividing circuits that operate the clock dial.

▼ Three quartz clocks. The diagonal bands move around the cylinder and enable a more precise measurement to be made of the time than can be made from the rather small face.

Quartz crystal

Quartz crystal is piezoelectric and possesses very stable mechanical and electric properties that make it suitable for maintaining continuous oscillation in an electronic circuit. When an electric voltage is applied across the piece of quartz, it suffers a small extension or compression; conversely, mechanical strains produce electric charges on its surfaces. The charges are transferred to metal electrodes connected in an electronic circuit, including a transistor for amplification. As it oscillates, the quartz induces alternating voltages into the circuit, and continuous electric oscillations are produced, the power for these being obtained from the electric supply to the circuit.

Frequency division

The simplest circuit for dividing the frequency consists of two transistors connected through capacitors and resistors in such a way that only one of them can conduct current at a time. Such a device is known as a bistable circuit because it has two stable states. An electric impulse applied to the bistable circuit switches the current from one transistor to the other—that is, changes it from state one to state two. Another pulse changes it back again. Thus, for every two pulses entering the device, one pulse comes out; the circuit acts as a scale of two (or binary) divider. A number, n, of dividers connected in series divides by 2^n (that is, two to the power n).

A more complicated circuit divides by ten and is usually used in quartz clocks. It consists of a number of bistable circuits with other logic circuits. Quartz clocks were developed initially for the measurement of radio frequencies. It is convenient, therefore, for the oscillator frequency to be a power of ten so that frequency division and multiplication provide a decade scale of standard frequencies throughout the radio-frequency spectrum.

Design features

The crystalline form of quartz is complex, and its mechanical and electric properties are different in different directions. This fact complicates the design of oscillators but makes it possible to obtain a wide range of characteristics. For a high-performance clock, the oscillation is chosen with the greatest possible stability, low damping losses, and a zero-temperature coefficient of frequency.

One of the most difficult practical problems is that of supporting the quartz without damping the oscillations. One solution is to mount it at the nodal points of an overtone mode of vibration (that is, a harmonic of the fundamental oscillating frequency). These principles are illustrated in the Essen ring developed at the National Physical

▼ An Essen ring, showing electric axes and points of no displacement (nodes). The ring is supported at three of the six nodes. By using frequency dividers, the frequency of the quartz can be scaled down to operate a clock display.

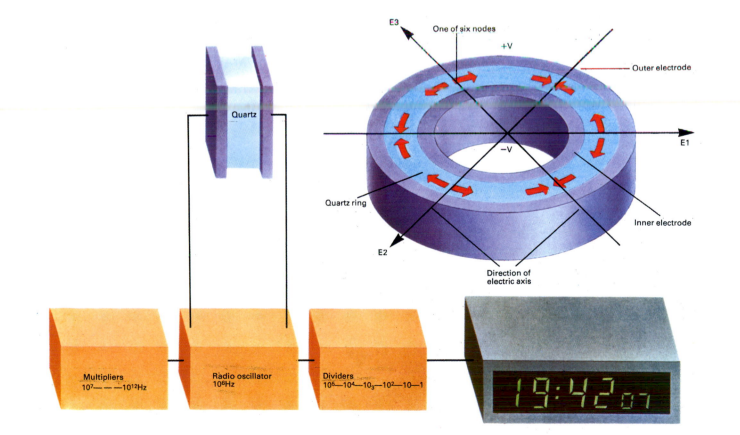

487

Laboratory in Britain and used as the standard at many observatories. The quartz is in the form of a ring about 2.2 in. (55 mm) in diameter and oscillates at a frequency of 10^5 cycles per second (10^5 Hz). The overtone mode is excited by electrodes consisting of metal rings coaxial with the quartz and surrounding its inner and outer surfaces. There are three electric axes in the radial direction, 120 degrees apart. A voltage between the electrodes causes one 60 degree segment to extend along the circumference and the neighboring 60 degree segment to contract. The quartz thus vibrates in its third overtone mode (third harmonic) with six nodes around the circumference, at three of which it is supported. The temperature coefficient depends in part on the radial width and can be made zero at a convenient working temperature.

Applications

Although made for frequency measurements, the best quartz clocks proved to be much better timekeepers than pendulum clocks, and the ring type kept time to 10^{-5} seconds (the 100,000th part of a second) per day. Astronomical observations

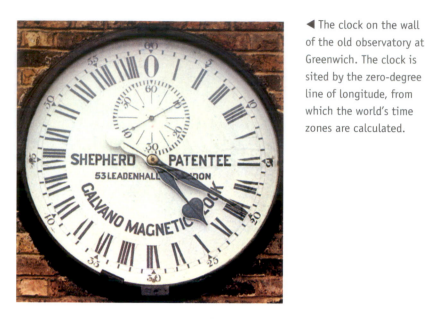

◄ The clock on the wall of the old observatory at Greenwich. The clock is sited by the zero-degree line of longitude, from which the world's time zones are calculated.

▶ A clepsydra, or water clock, from the Egyptian temple at Karnak, which was built between 1495 and 1380 B.C.E. On the inside of the original are 12 series of dots at different water levels; there was a different scale of time for each month. The water ran out of a spout at the bottom.

are themselves accurate to only 10^{-2} seconds (the 100th part of a second) per day, and the quartz clocks are used to smooth out the errors of observation and provide a uniform time scale. They must of course be adjusted so that on the average they keep time with atomic clocks and the rotation of Earth.

In the 1930s, when quartz clocks were developed, they could not be considered seriously for home use because of their size and cost. The situation has been completely changed by the introduction of the microprocessor and various digital styles of display. The most common today is the LCD (liquid crystal display).

Another advance is the radio-controlled clock. These clocks can automatically set themselves to the correct time after they have been plugged in to the electricity supply. They tune in to a radio frequency that transmits the exact time and automatically check their own accuracy once a day.

FACT FILE

- *In 1696, a mathematician called Burdeau created a clock for Louis XIV in which the figure of the king sat on a throne, and at the quarter hour the electors of the German states and the princes and dukes of Italy advanced, bowed, and retreated at the hours similiar obeisances were made by the monarchs of Europe.*

- *The hours represented by water clocks, or clepsydrae, from the time of the ancient Egyptians onward, varied in length from 50 to 70 minutes to suit the different lengths of day and night. Some Egyptian clepsydrae measured the movements of the stars and other heavenly bodies.*

- *New levels of accuracy were achieved by the caesium atomic clock devised at the National Physical Laboratory in Britain. An oscillating electrical circuit is tuned to synchronize with the vibration of a caesium atom in a vacuum. Subsequent models of the caesium atomic clock have an accuracy equivalent to an error of only one second every 3,000 years.*

SEE ALSO: BATTERY • CRYSTALS AND CRYSTALLOGRAPHY • PENDULUM • RADIO CONTROL • SUNDIAL • TIMING DEVICE • WATCH, ELECTRONIC • WATCH, MECHANICAL

Clothing Manufacture

The clothing industry is one of the few remaining trades that rely on the basic skills of the operative on the factory floor for the major contribution to the article produced. However, faced with the problem of skilled personnel leaving the industry and the need for high production rates, clothing manufacturers have increasingly turned to the use of automatic and semiautomatic machinery for designing, cutting, and making up garments.

Computer-aided design (CAD) has helped reduce the time between the designer's original drawing of a garment and the making up of samples. CAD allows the designer to experiment with different fabrics, styles, and patterns without cutting a piece of fabric until a version of the garment is agreed upon by the designer and the retailer.

Once production costs for the garment have been calculated, a series of basic patterns called slopers are cut and made into wearable samples. These samples are then tested on models to ensure that the fit is good and to finalize sizing of the pattern. Manufacturers use tables of body measurements to scale patterns to larger or smaller sizes. These measurements are fed into the CAD system, which calculates where the pattern needs to be enlarged or cut down to fit a particular size. When all the pattern pieces have been determined, a marker is produced, that is, an optimum layout for how the pieces are arranged for cutting, depending on the width of the material, any pattern or pile on the fabric, and how the garment is to hang on the body.

Cutting

The next stage in the manufacture of all types of clothing is the laying out and cutting of the material. This stage must be carefully planned so that there is a minimum of wasted cloth; in the past, it required a number of fairly skilled personnel and was done by hand. Laying out of material prior to cutting must be done very accurately, and modern machines are so precise that even checked and striped fabrics can be aligned.

When the material has been layed out on the cutting table, the patterns are marked out on the top layer as a guide for the cutting-machine operator. Couture garments are still cut by hand, but mass production cutters are manual- or computer-controlled operations, using straight-knife cutters. In manually controlled cutting, the cutter has to take care that the knife remains perfectly straight as it passes through the layers of fabric to ensure that each piece remains the same size. With computerized cutting, a vacuum is used to

► This multispool open-ended spinning machine transforms raw fiber into thread ready for weaving. The finished cloth will have to undergo a number of cutting, sewing, and fitting operations before it is turned into a wearable garment.

▼ The clothing industry still harbors a reputation for sweatshop labor throughout the world. Here, Chinese textile workers in Beijing shape knitted cotton socks on heated molds.

compress the layers and prevent them from moving while cutting is taking place. Up to 10 in. (25 cm) of fabric can be compressed down to 3 in. (7.5 cm) with a vacuum, the maximum thickness of material that can be cut. Laser cutting machines cut fabrics with a laser beam rather than a knife, and machines have now been developed that use high-pressure water or plasma jets, especially for use on plastic or leather.

The machine room

Many clothing factories use an assembly line method to sew the cut pieces of cloth into garments. The bundling system has the machinists working on single operations, such as sewing the front of the garment to the back, setting in sleeves, or joining tops and bottoms of collars. The unit production system is similar but uses an overhead hanger to move the garment on to the next stage in the operation. Modular systems need fewer workers, and each is responsible for completing an entire garment. The machinists move around the factory with the clothes

◀ An automatic fabric cutting machine. Thousands of pieces can be cut in one day using preprogrammed design instructions fed into a computer.

they are sewing, making it more interesting for them, as they get to work on a number of different operations, and reducing the manufacturer's costs, as there is less unfinished work in progress at any one time.

Sewing garments

At one time, the only machine used in making clothes was the ordinary industrial sewing machine (the flat machine). These are still in use, but modern versions incorporate several refinements. Some machines have under-bed trimming devices to cut away the threads left at the end of a stitched seam. Previously the operators had to trim the seams by hand, but with these machines, they need simply to touch a button and the thread is cut cleanly and the cut ends carried away by a stream of compressed air.

One of the more skilled operations in the making of dresses, skirts, and trousers is the insertion of the zipper. The need for this skill has been reduced by the automatic zipper machines that work from a continuous roll of zipper. The operator simply feeds the two pieces of fabric and the zipper into the machine, which both inserts and makes the zipper at the same time. This machine makes a perfect channel zipper, without the need for a skilled operator, at the rate of 60 zippers per hour.

Other operations that were considered highly skilled jobs have been turned into simple tasks by the use of machinery. For example, the shaping of collars, cuffs, and pockets has been greatly simpli-

fied. A simple conversion can be made to any modern flat machine so that by using a shaped plastic tracker to guide the fabric around the needle the operator can produce a perfect shape every time and at a high speed. Collars for men's shirts can be produced in large numbers by the use of templates that punch out the same collar shape every time. This method is only practical away from the fashion side of the clothing industry, where shapes do not change quickly and long runs of one style can be anticipated with significant economic safety.

Seam stitching

The stitching together of two edges of uneven contour, such as the waisted side seam on a dress, is another process that required a high degree of skill from the machinist. Today this same process can be done by an unskilled operator using, for example, the Durhopp Long Seamer, which does the whole operation automatically. Overlock machines, often used in a preliminary operation to seaming, bind the edges of the fabric and prevent them fraying.

Perhaps the most difficult operation of all in the making of clothing is stitching on the sleeves, which requires much skill in positioning and sewing the material. The entire operation can be completed using a machine such as the Pfaff 3801-1/01 sewing unit, which can be programmed to insert the sleeve and stitch seam tape around the armhole completely automatically.

Pressing

The final operation in clothing manufacture is the pressing of the finished garment, either by hand iron or mechanical press. In the past, the presser spent much time removing unwanted creases, but today all creases can be removed before pressing by passing the garment through a steam tunnel. The presser puts in only the creases required.

Materials

Until the 20th century, all clothing was made from natural materials like wool, cotton, silk, or animal skins and furs. Today, synthetic fibers, such as rayon, nylon, polyester, and acrylic, are used widely in the clothing industry, either alone or in combination with wool or cotton, and account for over 40 percent of the world's textile consumption.

SEE ALSO: COTTON • FABRIC PRINTING • FASTENER, CLOTHES • FIBER, NATURAL • FIBER, SYNTHETIC • HOSIERY AND KNITWARE MANUFACTURE • LOOM • MASS PRODUCTION • SEWING MACHINE • SPINNING • TEXTILE

Clutch

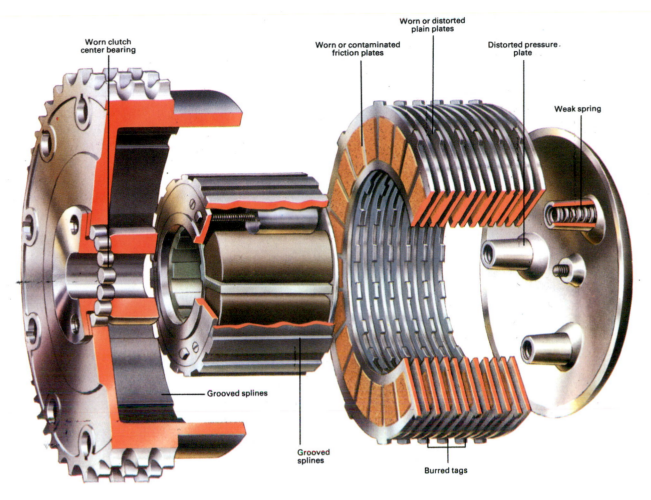

Worn clutch center bearing

Grooved splines

Worn or contaminated friction plates

Worn or distorted plain plates

Distorted pressure plate

Weak spring

Grooved splines

Burred tags

A clutch is a device that allows two components, usually drive shafts, to be engaged or disengaged by its operation. Although a clutch is commonly used on motor vehicles, various types are available for industrial applications. Electromagnetic, single dry plate, multi dry plate, multi oil-immersed plate, centrifugal, and vane are just some of the various types of clutch available.

The job of the clutch on a motor vehicle is to disconnect the engine from the road wheels while changing gear and then to allow the engine to pick up speed smoothly, which is especially important on starting. There are several designs used: the single dry plate type for vehicles with a manual transmission, and the vane type fluid coupling or torque converter, or centrifugal clutch, for automatic transmissions.

Single-plate clutch

In a single-plate clutch system, a flywheel made of cast iron is bolted to the rear end of the crankshaft. The face of the flywheel, which touches the clutch plate, is very smooth so as not to promote wear. The clutch plate is a two-piece disk about 8 in. (20 cm) in diameter. In the center of the plate

is a hole with splines (similar to gear teeth) in it that correspond to the splines on the input shaft of the transmission. The inner splined portion of the plate is connected to the outer friction part via buffer springs that absorb the initial take-up shock. Both sides of the plate are covered with friction material on the outer 1½ in. (4 cm) of the diameter. This is a high-friction, low-wearing, heat resistant material that is attached to the plate by rivets and bonding. The clutch cover consists of a pressed-steel casing that houses a pressure plate backed up by several coil springs or a diaphragm spring, which provides the force to press the plate hard up against the flywheel.

When the clutch pedal is pressed down, a release bearing under hydraulic pressure, or operated by a cable, presses down on the center of the clutch cover and forces the pressure plate away from the clutch plate. This action allows the clutch plate to remain stationary between the revolving flywheel and clutch cover. Gears may now be selected, and the slow release of the clutch pedal gradually clamps the clutch plate to the flywheel, allowing a direct drive from the crankshaft to the transmission.

▲ Potential trouble spots—leading to either clutch slip or clutch drag—on a multiplate clutch, found on the vast majority of motorcycles. Slippage and drag can make it hard for power to be transmitted from the engine to the gearbox efficiently.

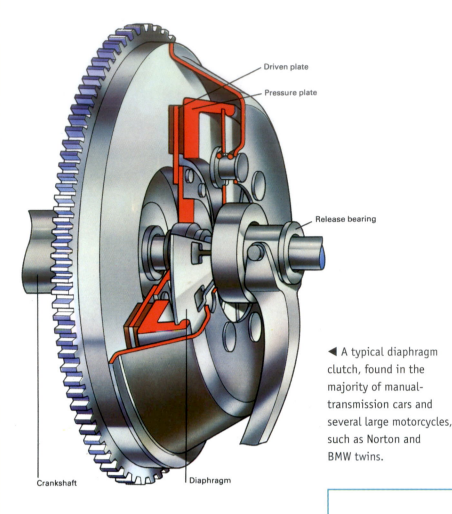

Driven plate

Pressure plate

Release bearing

Crankshaft   Diaphragm

◀ A typical diaphragm clutch, found in the majority of manual-transmission cars and several large motorcycles, such as Norton and BMW twins.

the drive shaft. Such clutches are found on the simpler or semiautomatic systems.

Other applications

Clutches are also used in industrial applications such as machine tools that have to stop and start without the motor being switched off. For this, any of the methods described for a car, in a modified form, or an electromagnetic clutch can be used.

The latter is a device which contains two electromagnets facing each other inside an outer casing. If the power is switched off, both halves of the clutch are independent. When current is passed through the magnets, they come together with a self-engaging coupling or friction plates in between, thus providing a straight-through drive. This type of clutch provides no graduation of the power engagement, which is unnecessary in production machinery, for example.

Since this sort of power engagement is direct and instantaneous, for safety reasons, shear pins may be included in the clutch or somewhere else in the machine. They are designed to break, causing loss of power, if the torque on the shaft increases sharply, for example, if the machine becomes jammed.

Vane and centrifugal clutch

On automatic transmissions, a fluid type clutch is used. As with the dry clutch assembly, a large casing bolts onto the flywheel and contains all the parts. The casing is a casting that has impeller vanes attached to the inside of it. Another large wheel, which is attached to the transmission input shaft, has the output vanes around its edge. It is fitted inside the outer casing to allow both parts to turn independently. The inside of the device is filled with oil and sealed. As the flywheel rotates faster around the inner (output) vanes, the oil sets up a turbulence that makes the inner wheel rotate. This action now provides drive from the flywheel to the transmission through the oil. The design allows the car to remain stationary when the engine is idling, but when the engine revs up, the oil is distributed, thus giving a smooth takeoff. Apart from the convenience of the automatic feature, this system eliminates a lot of moving parts. The only maintenance needed normally is the periodic replacement of the special transmission oil.

Centrifugal clutches contain a system of "bob" weights, which are attached by pivots to the flywheel. When the flywheel increases in speed, the weights are thrown out from the center until they provide contact between the power source and

DIAPHRAGM-CLUTCH OPERATION

The clutch is used to connect and disconnect the engine from the gearbox. For a vehicle to move, the clutch has to gradually raise the speed of the gearbox input shaft to the speed of the engine shaft. To do this, the clutch transmits a torque while the slip, owing to the difference in speed between the engine shaft and the gearbox input shaft, steadily increases. When the clutch pedal is depressed, the release bearing is thrust against the diaphragm, moving the friction pads away from the flywheel.

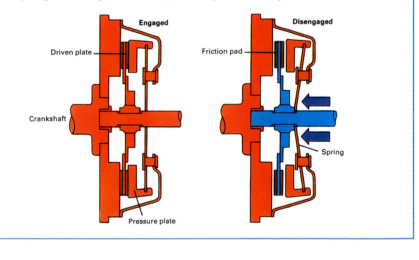

Engaged   Disengaged

Driven plate   Friction pad

Crankshaft

Spring

Pressure plate

SEE ALSO: AUTOMOBILE • CENTRIFUGE • ELECTROMAGNETISM • FLYWHEEL • FRICTION • INTERNAL COMBUSTION ENGINE • TRANSMISSION, AUTOMOBILE

Coal Mining

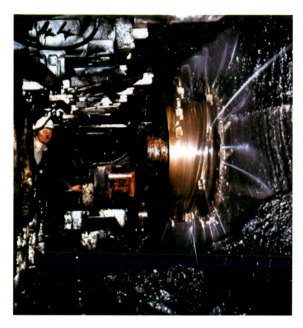

Coal deposits were formed from the remains of vast forests of trees, shrubs, and plants that flourished in the hot and humid climates of 250 to 400 million years ago. These flora died and rotted and were buried and consolidated under sediments deposited by encroaching seas. The coal seams so formed lay undisturbed except for geological upheavals until the coming of humans.

The Chinese are said to have used coal three thousand years ago, but there is no evidence that other ancient civilizations used it. The Venetian explorer Marco Polo, in the account of his 13th century travels through Cathay, records that the natives burned a black stone dug out of the mountains as fuel for cooking and heating.

Many hundreds of years ago, Europe and the British Isles were extensively covered with forests, but in modern times wood as a source of fuel has become comparatively scarce and therefore expensive. The discovery and exploitation of coal has had an important economic motivation. About 1200 C.E., a monk near Liège (in Belgium) made reference in a chronicle to a black earth similar to charcoal used as a fuel. From the 13th to the 16th centuries, the area around Liège made the most extensive use of coal in the world. The town of Liège dug its mine shafts in hills overlooking the town and drained them in such a way as to obtain its main water supply from them, thus deriving more than one advantage from the mining operation.

Coal outcrops had been exploited in Britain since the Middle Ages. In the Middle Ages, London began to import coal from mines in the northern part of Britain; from then until the late

◄ The cutting drum of the Anderton Shearer loader is raised and lowered by electrohydraulic controls; dust is suppressed by water jets.

▼ Control of the uniform advance of the coal face is increasingly relying on electronic monitoring and surveying rather than human skill.

Victorian period, Britain had no near rival in its production of coal. London's factories and homes produced so much coal smoke that it quickly became the dirtiest city in the world. The poisonous, acrid fumes combined with climatic conditions finally became a health hazard, leading to the introduction of the Clean Air Act in 1956, which prohibited the burning of coal.

The rise of coal as a fuel

The switch from wood to coal that occurred in the 17th century provided the foundation for the Industrial Revolution that followed. A coal fire is so dirty compared with a wood fire that a whole new technology had to be developed in many industries in order to deal with it. For example, in the breweries, when coal fires were first used to dry the ingredients, the resulting beer was undrinkable. The use of coal also encouraged the beginnings of modern mass production: in the glass industry, coal fires made possible greater production of plate glass than ever before, meanwhile the creation of beautiful objects one at a time by glass blowers became much more difficult in the smoky, poisonous atmosphere.

Parallel with the development of the economic and technological aspects of coal has been the problem of safety in the mines. The earliest workings were undoubtedly sporadic surface diggings in places where coal was easily accessible; as these surface deposits began to be depleted, the technical difficulties of ventilation, drainage, and roof support in the early mine shafts were insuperable. The first underground workings consisted of little more than vertical shafts some 6 ft. (1.8 m) in diameter, sunk to a depth of 30 ft. (9.1 m) or so. The coal around the bottom of the shaft was then hewn out to a radius of several feet and pulled or carried manually in baskets up the

and pressures, which caused it to undergo chemical and physical changes. With age, these processes created various types of coal that increased in hardness and carbon content. The three main types of coal are lignite, bituminous, and anthracite.

Lignite is brownish to black in color, crumbles after exposure to air, and is subject to spontaneous combustion. These characteristics give it very poor storage quality. Bituminous coal, including several lower grades called subbituminous, is the most common type of coal, it has very good storage qualities. Anthracite, also called hard coal, has a shiny black color and is sometimes made into costume jewelry. It burns slowly and is highly valued as a domestic heating fuel.

Coke is a substance made from certain types of bituminous coal, sometimes mixed with anthracite. It is almost pure carbon and is used in smelting iron ore. Coke is made by heating coal in an airless chamber almost to its burning point, which causes the volatile components (gas, tar, and others) to distill off. These products themselves can be valuable by-products. A great number of organic compounds, for example, can be derived successfully and economically from coal tar and crude benzol.

Mining statistics

By the middle of the 16th century, British coal production had reached about 250,000 tons (227,000 tonnes) a year. By 1700, this figure climbed to 3 million tons (2.7 million tonnes) a year; the Industrial Revolution that followed led to a staggering increase in the demand for coal. Britain entered the 20th century with an annual output of about 225 million tons (205 million tonnes), almost one quarter of total world production. After World War I, British

shaft. Such diggings are called bell pits and postwar strip mining operations in Britain have uncovered several of them.

As mines went deeper and became more complicated, technological progress was made only at the cost of human life. Each advance in the daring of the miners led to disasters against which safeguards were then developed. One early solution to the problem of ventilation was to sink a parallel shaft deeper than the one being worked. Birds were taken into mines because they use oxygen faster than humans, and if the air supply became inadequate the birds would die soon enough to give an early warning. Another problem was the flammable methane gas that is given off by coal seams when they are exposed by digging. In the early days of mining, a man would wrap himself in wet rags and crawl along the floor of a shaft holding a burning torch on a pole above and ahead of him to ignite the gas, whereupon the mine would be considered safe. Today safety methods are considerably advanced compared with these, but even so, disasters taking many lives occurred throughout the 20th century.

Types of coal

Coal is classed according to its characteristics when burned, its weathering qualities in storage, and its content of volatile materials. As plant material became buried in the swamps and peat bogs, it was subjected to increasing temperatures

▲ A pit head at Ebbw Vale, a valley in Wales famous for its coal mining traditions. The winding mechanism is used to haul the cage that takes the miners up and down the mine shaft.

▶ Once underground, high-speed trolley locomotives are used to transport men to and from the working seams. Vehicles are fitted with rubberized wheels to prevent sparks from forming. Coal mines harbor explosive gases as well as the potential that fires will break out along the coal seam.

coal output decreased, and the downward trend has continued.

In the United States, coal was not mined on a commercial scale until the mid-18th century, and it was not until 1840 that production reached an annual 1 million tons (0.9 million tonnes). As in Britain, industrial activity in the 19th century ran parallel to coal mining expansion; by the end of the century, annual production stood at about 370 million tons (335 million tonnes). By the 1990s, average output in the United States had reached over 1 billion tons (0.9 billion tonnes) per year. Recoverable global coal reserves have been estimated at 1.1 trillion (1.1×10^{12}) tons (1 trillion tonnes), nearly half of which is hard coal. At the rates of production current at the beginning of the 21st century, these reserves should last for another 200 years, significantly longer than the 45 years and 65 years predicted for oil and gas, respectively. Unlike oil and gas, coal reserves are found in more than 100 countries around the world and therefore make nations less vulnerable to shortages because of economic or political turbulence in regions that supply them.

Modern coal mining methods

Coal is mined by two distinct methods: surface mining and underground operations. The choice of method is dictated by many factors, such as the seam thickness, the depth and inclination of the seam, the location of the deposit, surface topography and land value, environmental considerations, economics, and a host of technical factors.

Surface mining—usually known as opencast, or strip, mining—is carried out by stripping away the strata overlying the coal seams and then removing the exposed coal. Until comparatively recently, it was feasible to remove only a maximum of about 100 ft. (30 m) of surface strata (overburden), but the postwar years have seen the development of huge excavating machines capable of stripping several hundred feet of overburden. The loading buckets on such machines are capable of scooping up several hundred tons with each operation. Not only has the size of the machine increased but there has been a general increase in the scale of strip mining operations, and some surface mines are now producing up to 50,000 tons (45,000 tonnes) of coal a day.

For use under certain favorable conditions, a special surface mining technique known as auger mining has been developed in the United States. This method involves boring a series of parallel holes into coal seams that have outcropped or been exposed by removing overburden. These augers are simply large rotary drills 2 to 5 ft. (0.6–1.5 m) in diameter that bore into the coal

seam for some 300 ft. (91 m). The coal that is cut away by the auger travels back along the scroll of the drill rod and is collected at the mouth of the hole. Augering machines are usually used where the thickness of the overburden becomes too great for further removal, but they can sometimes be used underground as well. In circumstances where it can be used, the auger machinery provides the cheapest coal mining method of all.

Producing a ton of coal may require stripping as much as 30 tons (27 tonnes) of overburden, a task whose extent provides some concept of the size of a modern open pit. In such pits, the removed material may be loaded onto trucks capable of hauling 100 to 200 tons (90–180 tonnes) or else onto conveyors that can move 10,000 tons (9,000 tonnes) an hour. The productivity of miners in open pits is very high compared with underground workers', and outputs of 50 tons (45 tonnes) each shift are commonly recorded.

Total mining costs are low by underground standards and may be only one quarter of those in deep mining operations. For these reasons strip mining is favored where possible. In Britain less than 10 percent of national output is strip mined, but in the United States nearly half the output is extracted this way.

▲ A mechanical scraper used to remove overburden in the Brunswick strip mine, Helmstedt, Germany.

◀ A cactus grab sinking an airway for a mine at Broken Hill, New South Wales, Australia. Grabs like this are often used to gouge out vertical shafts.

Strip mining has become an emotional issue among conservationists, particularly in the United States. In some places whole tops of mountains are being cut off. This affects not only the natural beauty but also the drainage of the land, the wildlife habitation, and so on. One solution would be to put some of the overburden back and replant it when the surface mine is exhausted, possibly using rubbish collections brought from cities as additional, cosmetic landfill.

Underground mining

Most of the world's coal is won from underground mines, some of which are 3,000 to 4,000 ft. (900 to 1,200 m) deep. Productivity in underground mines varies widely, depending on mining conditions, geological factors, and the degree of automation. In such depths, access to the seams is by vertical shafts equipped with hoisting machinery, but in shallower depths down to 1,000 ft. (300 m) the workings may be connected to the surface by inclined tunnels. Conveyors are usually installed in these surface slopes.

There are two principal methods of underground working: room and pillar, and longwall working. With the former system, once access to the seam has been gained, tunnels (rooms) are driven into the seam in two directions at right angles, dividing the seam into a number of rectangular blocks of coal (pillars), which may or may not be subsequently extracted. Depending on certain practical considerations, such as the degree of roof support needed from the pillars and the type of machinery being used, the rooms are 9 to 24 ft. (3–7 m) in width and the intervening pillars from 30 ft. (9 m) square to 150 x 300 ft. (45 x 90 m). Machines have been developed for driving these tunnels that eliminate the need for manual breaking or shovelling of coal. Such machines can cut tunnels in the seam at speeds of up to several inches a minute to produce coal at a rate of up to 10 tons (9 tonnes) a minute. This coal is mechanically taken to the rear of the machine and loaded onto conveyors or wagons for transport to the surface.

Room and pillar working is favored when mining beneath surface buildings or under lakes and seas. Under such circumstances, the pillars are left in position to minimize movement of the ground at the surface. However, this method can leave between 50 and 60 percent of the coal underground. Sometimes the pillars are removed at a later date, in a controlled collapse.

Longwall working is a total extraction system: all the coal within a specified area is extracted in

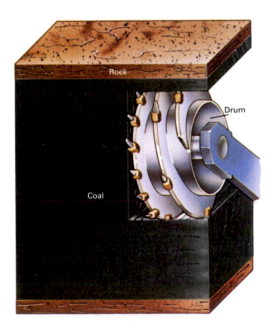

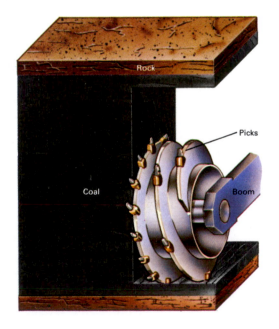

◀ A coal face is a tunnel that moves sideways. The cutting machine, or shearer, has a rotating cutting drum fitted with short picks and moves back and forth along the face conveyor by hauling itself along a heavy chain. As the face advances, the conveyor is snaked forward by rams in the chocks, which then advance in line. On many faces, the cutting edge makes two passes and the angle of the boom is altered accordingly.

FACT FILE

- Up until the late 17th century in Britain, coal was regarded as a poor person's fuel; most people preferring to use charcoal or wood for heating and cooking. In London, coal was known as "seacoal," because it was transported by sea from the coastal collieries of the northeast and to distinguish it from charcoal.

- Sometimes coal miners come across a substance known as fusain, also called mineral charcoal or mother-of-coal. It is formed by forest fires at the peat stage of coal formation. This process leaves a charcoal residue—a dull, black, brittle substance—which becomes incorporated into the coal bed.

- Modern coal mining is no longer viewed as the dangerous occupation it once was, thanks to improved methods of working and safety standards. U.S. Bureau of Labor statistics show that more injuries occur in the construction, timber, farming, and furniture-making industries. In Canada, strip mining is even regarded as less dangerous than working in the retail trade.

one operation. Two parallel tunnels are driven into the seam some 150 to 600 ft. (45–180 m) apart. These tunnels (gate roads) are then joined by a road at right angles, this third road forming the longwall face. Successive strips are then taken off the side of the face road, and the coal is deposited on a face conveyor that delivers it to the gate road conveyor and the shaft. As the longwall face moves forward, the roof behind the face is allowed to collapse, the gate roads being correspondingly advanced and supported. Such faces can advance several yards a shift and produce a daily output of 7,000 tons (6,350 tonnes). The most advanced systems in Britain include automatic steering of the coal-cutting machine. A microprocessor using data from a natural gamma radiation sensor, together with other transducers, automatically controls the machine's steering system to keep it cutting within the coal seam.

Once the coal is above ground, it undergoes a process called beneficiation to remove rock and dirt and is then crushed and graded. Techniques include flotation tanks, where rock and impurities sink to the bottom; centifugation; and froth flotation, where coal particles are blown into a chemical bath that makes them stick to bubbles that are then skimmed off and dewatered to recover the coal fines.

▲ A coal liquefaction plant at Baytown, Texas, where the Exxon Corporation is investigating an oil synthesis process that would generate petroleum derivatives for use in the chemical industry.

SEE ALSO: CARBON • COAL TAR • ENERGY RESOURCES • HYDRAULICS • MINING TECHNIQUES • POWER PLANT • TUNNELING

Coal Tar

The first commercial distillation of coal tar was carried out by Dr. Longstaff and Dr. Dalton near Leith, Scotland, in 1822. They sold the light distillate obtained to Charles Macintosh as a solvent for his rubber-proofing process patented in 1823. Throughout the 19th century, interest in the discovery of new organic compounds grew, especially aromatic compounds. In 1843, the German chemist August Wilhelm von Hofmann reported the presence of aniline in coal tar, followed by benzene in 1845. By 1900, more than 50 compounds had been isolated from coal tar. As well as dyes, compounds such as aspirin and saccharin were discovered.

Coal carbonization

When bituminous coal is carbonized, that is, heated at a temperature ranging from 1650 to 2370°F (900–1300°C) in refractory (able to withstand high temperatures) brick ovens in the absence of air, the coal becomes converted to coke. At the lower temperatures, this process is used for producing coal gas, which between the 19th and 20th centuries was required for domestic supplies, while the higher temperature is used to make metallurgical coke. In both cases, the byproducts are fuel gas, ammonia, tar, and water vapor, which distills off and is collected.

Coal tar distillation

One ton of coal yields about 9.5 gallons (36 l) of tar, which condenses on cooling to a thick black oil containing a mixture of various chemical compounds. These are separated by fractional distillation, followed by washing in alkali to extract weakly acidic aromatic compounds, such as phenol and washing in dilute sulfuric acid to remove the basic aromatic compounds. A final distillation of each extraction process affords further separations. The coal tar also contains about 5 percent dissolved crude benzol (light oil), the bulk of which remains in the gas stream because it contains lower-boiling-point components and is stripped from the gas stream by a separate process. For many years, the distillation of coal tar was the principal source of benzene. Today, however, it is obtained by stripping coal gas or from petroleum processing.

Four fractions based on a range of boiling points are collected: crude benzol is distilled from 175 to 340°F (80–170°C), middle or carbolic oil from 340 to 445°F (170–230°C), heavy or creosote oil from 445 to 520°F (230–270°C), and anthracene or green oil from 520 to 750°F (270–

▶ The British chemist William Perkin, who founded the dyeing industry based on coal tar chemicals. Synthetic dyes are widely used today because of their colorfastness and the range of colors that can be produced.

400°C). The residue that remains is pitch, a useful product used to make road tar and as a binder for smokeless fuel briquettes and the large carbon electrodes required for aluminum smelting.

The benzol fraction contains benzene, toluene, and xylene; the middle oil fraction includes phenol and naphthalene; the heavy oil cut contains cresols; and the anthracene distillate includes anthracene and related compounds. Altogether coal tar contains well over 200 chemical compounds, though commercially only the main ones are of interest.

Gas stripping

Every ton of coal yields about 3.5 gallons (14 l) of benzol, which is recovered from the coal gas by oil washing or absorption on activated carbon (a porous type of charcoal). The high-boiling-point oils used for washing may be a petroleum product such as spindle oil, creosote (a tar oil), or tetralin, an organic solvent. The crude benzole dissolves in the oil and is distilled off when the mixture is heated with steam. This distillate includes benzene, toluene, xylene, and solvent naphtha. Steam is also used to recover the benzole absorbed by the activated carbon.

SEE ALSO: ANILINE AND AZO DYES • CHEMISTRY, ORGANIC • GASOLINE, SYNTHETIC • HYDROCARBON • OIL REFINING • PLASTICS PROCESSING

Cocoa Manufacture

Cocoa powder has evolved from the chocolate drink first discovered in Central America, which became very popular in Europe in the 17th century. This chocolate drink was rather sickly compared with the cocoa that is used today because cocoa beans contain a large amount of fat (all plant seeds contain fats or oils), and the original drinking chocolate was simply ground up cocoa beans. However, in 1828, the Dutch chocolatier Coenraad van Houten discovered a way of pressing out the excess fat, which paved the way for making cocoa as we know it today.

Cocoa beans

It is extremely important that cocoa beans are picked when they are neither immature nor over-ripe. They are taken from their pod and fermented to develop flavor. Drying, which follows fermentation, is also important for ensuring the quality of the beans. They are then ready for processing. Around 90 percent of the world's crop is harvested in West Africa and Brazil, but these beans, known as Forasters or consumer-quality beans, have a less pleasant taste than superior-quality Criollo beans used in top-quality chocolate. These are harvested in Trinidad, Ecuador, Venezuela, and Java.

Processing the beans

Essentially cocoa is cocoa bean, from which the excess fat has been expressed, ground to an extremely fine powder. There are three main methods of manufacture; all start with the fermentation and subsequent drying of the cocoa beans as soon as they have been harvested followed by roasting, and then removal of husks or shells. The higher the roast, the darker the color and the stronger the flavor of the finished cocoa. The three processes that follow this preliminary preparation are the liquor, Dutch, and expeller processes. In the liquor process, the beans are ground until they become a liquid brown mass, the liquid being due to the presence of cocoa butter in the beans. This mass is then pressed to remove most of the fat, resulting in a product called cake. The cake is ground and sieved to give cocoa powder.

In the Dutch, or alkali, process, the beans are soaked in alkaline solutions until soft and wet. They are then dried and treated as in the liquor process. According to the degree of alkalinity, both the flavor and the color of the cocoa can be altered, and a much darker color can be obtained.

The roasted beans are treated with steam in the expeller, or extrusion, process, which softens

◀ Cocoa bean pods ready for harvesting. The tree can grow to a height of 24 ft. (7 m).

but does not wet them. The softened beans are easier to press, and a much greater proportion of fat can be expelled from them. The resulting cake is therefore very low in fat content compared with cake made by the other two methods, and the particle structure of the final cocoa is different.

In all three processes, the final stage is the reduction of the cake to an extremely fine powder by grinding. Cakes that are low in fat content are very hard and are usually passed through a breaker with intermeshing teeth, after which the resulting lumps are treated in a hammer mill. The final grinding is extremely critical since the quality of the cocoa, apart from its flavor, is usually judged by its particle size. The pulverization is carried out by two disks, one rotating at very high speed.

Types of cocoa

Cocoa to be used for drinking is commonly blended with vanillin, cinnamon, salt, and sometimes other powdered spices. These additives are pulverized so that their particle size is the same as that of the cocoa powder.

This staple cocoa drink was popular for many years until after World War II. A cheap, nourishing drink, it was very palatable, even if made with water and sugar alone. The onset of greater affluence produced a demand for more convenient foods, and cocoa tended to lose its popularity as it was too much trouble to make—ordinary cocoa powder is difficult to dissolve and does not disperse readily in hot milk.

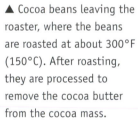

In order to improve the dispersion of the cocoa powder in milk, it is necessary to add to it an edible wetting agent. Soya lecithin has traditionally been used for this purpose, but it unfortunately imparts a slightly off-flavor to the cocoa. Various companies have tried to overcome this problem and they have developed a flavorless phospholipid based on rapeseed oil. Various methods are employed to add the lecithin. One of the most common methods is to spray it in liquid form into a large vessel, where the cocoa powder

▲ Cocoa beans leaving the roaster, where the beans are roasted at about 300°F (150°C). After roasting, they are processed to remove the cocoa butter from the cocoa mass.

◄ After the cocoa butter has been extracted, the cake is ground to a fine powder and packed automatically into cans.

is suspended in air. By this means, each individual particle of cocoa comes into contact with the lecithin, and the maximum surface coating of the particles is ensured. Alternatively, there is a process in which the cocoa powder is cooked and agglomerated with sugar, giving a product that will instantly dissolve in hot milk. Cocoa is sold as a flavoring ingredient for use in compound drinks, ice cream, cakes and cookies, and especially in icings and candy coatings.

In the United States, there are three classes of cocoa: breakfast cocoa, with not less than 22 percent cocoa butter; cocoa, which is never less than 10 percent cocoa butter; and low-fat cocoa, containing less than 10 percent cocoa butter. In the EU countries, there are only two main categories of cocoa powder: one with a minimum of 20 percent fat and a fat-reduced cocoa with a fat content typically between 10 and 12 percent.

The consumption of cocoa has a mildly stimulating effect as it contains the alkaloids theobromine (2.2 percent) and caffeine (0.1 percent). Concentrated cocoa has an approximate composition of 40.3 percent carbohydrate, 22.0 percent fat, 18.1 percent protein, 6.3 percent inorganic ash, plus small quantities of water and fiber. It provides about 2,214 calories to the pound.

SEE ALSO: AGRICULTURAL MACHINERY • CARBOHYDRATE • CONFECTIONERY • FAT • FOOD PROCESSING

Coffee

The stimulating effect of the coffee berry was originally discovered in the third century in Abyssinia. According to legend, a shepherd noted that his flock became livelier after eating the fruit of a certain plant. But it was the Arabs during the 13th century who first used the roasted seed, or bean, to make a beverage. The habit was perpetuated by Middle Eastern pilgrims and nomads and gradually spread to Europe.

The plant flourishes in a warm, dry climate at heights between 1,500 and 6,000 ft. (450–1,800 m) and is indigenous to Abyssinia and Arabia. Until the 17th century, Arabia was the only source of supply, but during the 17th and 18th centuries, when coffee houses became fashionable among Europeans, the plant was transplanted to their colonies in the Indies and the Americas. Coffee is now grown successfully between the Tropics of Cancer and Capricorn, and principal producing countries include Brazil, Colombia, the Ivory Coast, Kenya, and India.

The coffee plant is an evergreen that can grow to a natural height of about 20 ft. (6 m), but when cultivated commercially, it is pruned to a height of 6 to 8 ft. (about 2–2.75 m) to encourage a fuller bush and allow easier harvesting.

The two botanical species normally cultivated are the arabica and the robusta. The latter is considered inferior as it produces a coarser-tasting coffee compared with the finer flavor of arabica. The stimulating effects of coffee beans are caused by the organic compound caffeine.

The fruit develops from a fragrant flower and when ripe turns a deep-red color and is called the cherry. The cherry contains a yellow pulp called the mucilage that surrounds the parchment skin, covering a fine silver skin that protects the bean. Generally in each cherry, there are two female beans that lie with their grooved, flattened faces together. In about 5 percent of the cherries, there is only one bean, the male bean, known as the peaberry. After harvesting, the cherries are processed by the wet or dry method to produce the dried green coffee beans used in the preparation of the coffee beverage.

Curing the beans

The dry method, which is generally favored in countries where water is in short supply, involves drying the cherries either by artificial means or by spreading them on the ground to dry in the sun. Frequent raking is necessary to ensure the cherries dry evenly. A hulling machine is then used to remove the cherry skin, the parchment, and some of the silver skin, thus revealing the green beans.

▼ Diagram of instant coffee manufacture. Hot water is pumped through the roasted and ground coffee to brew a liquid of the required strength. Coffee is extracted as a powder by spray drying, or as granules, by freeze drying.

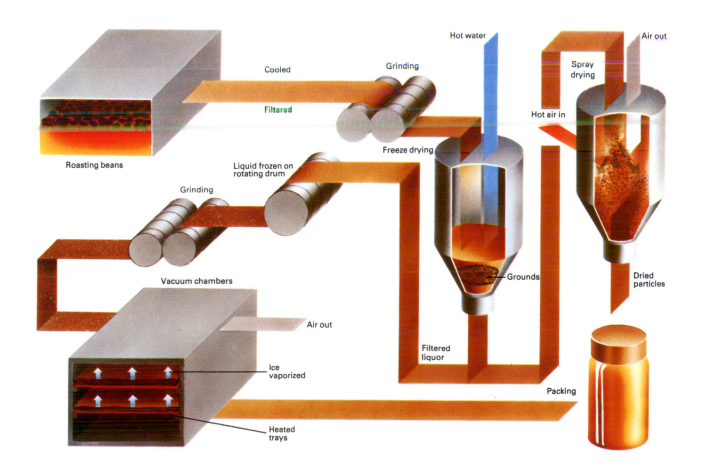

Roasting beans

Cooled

Filtered

Grinding

Hot water

Spray drying

Air out

Hot air in

Freeze drying

Liquid frozen on rotating drum

Grinding

Vacuum chambers

Air out

Ice vaporized

Heated trays

Grounds

Filtered liquor

Dried particles

Packing

◀ Brazil is one of the world's major coffee growers. A local worker can pick over 100 lbs. (45 kg) of coffee cherries in a day. After harvesting, the cherries are processed into coffee beans.

When the cherries are cured by the wet process, the red cherry skin is first removed by a machine, then the beans, which are still in their mucilage and protective parchment, are soaked in water for up to 72 hours to ferment any pulpy sugar still left. After the water is drawn off, the beans are thoroughly washed until the parchment is quite clean. The beans are then dried, and the remaining parchment skin and some silver skin is removed by a milling machine. The result of either of these processes—cured beans—is generally called green coffee.

When the curing process is completed, the coffee is tested, graded, and marketed. Supplies of green coffee can be bought either direct from the country of origin or from the warehouse stock of a coffee broker. As the flavor of the bean varies according to type, growing conditions, method of drying, and other factors, coffee buyers require a very specialized knowledge in order to choose the right beans for their standard blends.

The international coffee trade is affected by natural, political, and economic factors; for example, crop damage in 1953-1954 resulted in record prices and extensive new planting. When the fruit of the new plants reached the market in the late 1950s, the supply exceeded the demand. In order to allocate supplies and stabilize the market, an International Coffee Agreement was signed in 1962 and an International Coffee Organization set up with headquarters in London.

▼ Raking over coffee beans in Sudan to ensure they dry evenly in the sun. The process takes two to three weeks, during which time the beans must be raked frequently.

Green coffee is sometimes further processed to remove the stimulating properties of caffeine. This process, known as decaffeination, involves the removal of caffeine by steam or supercritical carbon dioxide or by an accepted chemical that dissolves the caffeine out of the bean. The coffee is then further processed to remove any remaining residual solvent and is then dried.

Roasting

After blending, the beans are roasted, a process that requires accurate timing to ensure that the porous cells will transfer their flavor and aroma more readily during the brewing stage. There are a number of methods by which coffee can be roasted. One is by placing the beans in rotating drums, which are usually gas heated but which allow no direct contact with the heat source. The beans are then released into a large circular perforated metal tray where they are stirred by revolving metal arms. Rapid cooling helps preserve the aroma of the coffee by closing the outer skin pores of the bean.

Before the beans can be brewed into a beverage, they must be ground so the full flavor is extracted. Grinding can be done by the consumer but is often done by the manufacturer, who then packs the finished product into vacuum-sealed containers to preserve freshness.

Instant coffee

An American chemist invented a practical soluble coffee, today called instant coffee, in 1909, but it did not become a commercial success until World War II, when it was widely issued to U.S. troops in the field. Between 1946 and the early 1960s, instant coffee rose in popularity in the United States until it captured 25 to 33 percent of the coffee market, and it has remained at this level since then.

There are three methods of producing instant coffee, and the initial stages of roasting, grinding and brewing are similar in all the processes. First the green beans are cleaned and blended. Blending brings together the qualities of different varieties and enables manufacturers to produce a more economical

product. Supervision by the blenders and meticulous quality control ensures that required standards are met.

Instant coffee manufacture

The selected blend of beans is roasted and cooled before being fed into a granulizer, which is adjusted to give the type of grind required. A suitable particle size ensures the full flavor will be extracted (brewed) from the cells without crushing them. The ground coffee then goes to the extraction plant, where water at high temperature and pressure is pumped through it. When the required strength is obtained, the brew is pumped through a clarifier and cooler, leaving the spent grounds to be ejected. The liquor is then ready to be processed into instant coffee.

The spray-drying process is the cheapest and most common processing method. The coffee brew is injected as a fine spray into a chamber through which a stream of hot air is blown. The water in the droplets evaporates and the vapor is removed, leaving behind the particles of dry coffee, which are then conveyed to the packing machinery. Soluble coffee must be sealed as quickly as possible into moisture-proof containers; otherwise it will quickly deteriorate.

Agglomeration

In a more recently developed process, after spray drying is completed, the product is partly wetted by steam, water, or a mixture of both to bind the powder together in large granules. It is then subjected to a further drying process, which alters the appearance of the coffee but not the taste.

◄ These workers are sorting the dried beans to remove any that are moldy or otherwise unsound.

▼ Part of the freeze-drying process. Trays of frozen coffee granules are exposed to low heat in a vacuum. This process dries the coffee without it becoming liquid again.

Accelerated freeze-drying

Freeze-drying is the most expensive method of producing soluble coffee, but one which retains more of the coffee flavor. Thus even though it provides a more expensive product, it has led to an increased consumer acceptance of instant coffee, particularly in the United States.

After extraction, the liquor is foamed with gas to produce the right bulk density in the finished product. It is then frozen on a belt or drum in the form of a ribbon. While still frozen it is broken, ground, and sieved into the desired particle size and placed on trays, which are conveyed into a vacuum chamber and lowered onto heated plates. The combination of applied heat and vacuum conditions causes the coffee to dry without returning to a liquid state. After drying, the product is returned to normal pressure and temperature conditions and packed.

Manufacturers are continuing their research, which has been going on since at least World War II, in the hope of producing better instant coffee at the lowest possible price.

SEE ALSO: AGRICULTURAL SCIENCE • COFFEE-MAKING EQUIPMENT • FOOD PROCESSING • VENDING MACHINE

Coffee-Making Equipment

In the aftermath of World War II, the lack of coffee in the southern European marketplace and its consequent high cost drove coffee machine manufacturers to experiment with different ways of obtaining the maximum results from a minimum amount of coffee. It was discovered that forcing hot water at high pressure through a small amount of coffee produced a beverage with a pleasant, full aroma and an attractive creamy top. The espresso drink and espresso machine were thus simultaneously invented, and this Mediterranean way of drinking coffee has since spread around the world.

Espresso machines

The main component of a professional espresso machine is the boiler, which is normally made of copper, a material whose characteristics do not alter over time. Water, at a working temperature of 240 to 250°F (115–120°C) occupies the lower two-thirds of the boiler, with the upper third being taken up by steam.

The machine is heated by an electric element that is immersed in the water contained in the boiler. The heating element power ratings range from 1,500 watts (W) on the smaller "one group" machines to 5,000 W on the larger "four group" machines. Some machines are heated by an external gas burner underneath the boiler.

Another key element of the espresso machine is the group head. This part of the machine is where the filter holder containing the coffee powder is placed and where the espresso is brewed. Water at a temperature of 200°F (90°C) and at a pressure of 9 bars forced through the 6 to 7-gram dose of ground coffee for a period of 25 to 30 seconds. Each group head is connected to a heat exchanger, which is immersed in the boiler water. The water that flows from the heat exchanger is used to brew the espresso and keep the group head warm. The water circulates by the thermalsiphon effect: hotter water, being less dense, rises and flows to the group head. It heats the group head, loses temperature, gains density, and thus flows back to the heat exchanger.

To make the frothy top required for cappuccinos and lattes, a steam tap is provided. This tap is connected to the upper part of the boiler and releases the steam required to heat and froth milk. A water tap is connected to the bottom of the boiler. It is used to draw off hot water to prepare other beverages such as tea.

▲ Coffee bars, found all around the world, are places to sit and relax. A range of flavorings can be added to ordinary black coffee to give almost endless permutations on a simple cup of coffee.

Types of machine

There are various types of espresso machines available in the marketplace. The most common ones are lever-actioned machines, in which the pressure to force the water through the coffee is generated by pushing down a piston. This method was used in the first espresso machines produced in Europe in the late 1940s and 1950s.

In another type of machine, the semiautomatic espresso machine, the water pressure to brew the coffee is generated by an electric pump, which is controlled by an on/off switch on each group head on the front of the machine. In electronic machines, the water pressure is similarly generated by an electric pump, but the dose of water to each group head is electronically controlled.

▶ This elaborate Gaggia espresso machine makes a prominent display of the water boiler that is central to its operation. A pressure gauge tells the operator when there is enough steam to froth the milk for a cup of cappucino.

The most sophisticated machine is the fully automatic type, which is also known as a bean-to-cup machine. These fully programmable devices produce espressos, cappuccinos, and lattes at the touch of a button. No operator intervention is needed: the grinding of the beans, the brewing of the coffee, the warming and frothing of the milk are all handled by the machine.

The aroma of a coffee drink is created by the volatile substances trapped inside the roasted coffee beans. To obtain a good cup of espresso, the coffee beans must be correctly ground and used immediately. The coarseness of the grind and the quantity of powder placed in the filter holder depend on the coffee blend. Coffee is 98 percent water. To obtain a good quality beverage, the manufacturers of machines sometimes include a water softener and a filter to remove chlorine from the water. Ideally, the water hardness should not be higher than 8 degrees.

Filter coffee machines

Filter coffee machines are much simpler in their operation: cold water is poured into a small holding tank at the top of the machine. The water then flows by gravity from this tank through a hole in its floor and into a tube that relays the water, again by gravity, through a one-way valve into an aluminum tube that curls round the heating plate at the bottom of the filter machine. This tube is part of an aluminum casting that also contains the machine's heating element.

The resistive heating element is simply a coiled wire, very much like the filament of a light bulb or the element in an electric toaster, that heats up when electricity is passed through it. When the machine is switched on, the heating element's proximity to the tube containing the water ensures the water inside is quickly brought to boiling point.

As the water boils, the bubbles inside it force the boiling water up a second, vertical tube (it cannot return the way it came because of the one-way valve). The water then drips out of the open end of the tube, which lies on top of a perforated plate situated above the filter containing the coffee grounds. From here, the water drips into the coffee below. Once the coffee is made, the heating element serves the further purpose of keeping the coffee warm by heating the warming plate, which it presses against—a conductive grease is used to ensure a good electrical connection.

To ensure the heating element does not overheat, three solid-state temperature sensors are included in the machine. The first, attached directly to the coil, is the primary temperature sensor. When the coil goes beyond a predeter-

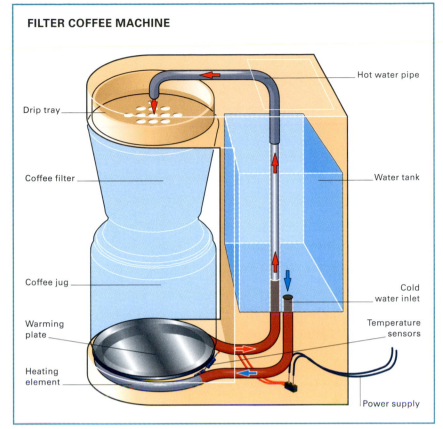

FILTER COFFEE MACHINE

Hot water pipe

Drip tray

Coffee filter

Water tank

Coffee jug

Cold water inlet

Warming plate

Temperature sensors

Heating element

Power supply

mined temperature, it cuts off the current. Then when the coil cools down, the sensor switches it back on. This process of cycling on and off ensures that the coil remains at an even temperature. The other two devices are thermal fuses acting as fail-safes in case of failure in the main sensor. They simply cut power if the temperature rises too high.

Plunger coffee maker

The plunger method of coffee making, also known as the French press, or Cafetière, was developed in Italy during the 1930s but first became popular after World War II in France, where it became a favored domestic coffee-making method. Before then, coffee was simply brewed in a jug and strained or left to settle.

The pot is a narrow glass cylinder with a fine mesh filter that fits snugly inside. A rod connected to the filter fits through a tightly fitting hole in the lid of the pot. Coffee grounds are placed in the cylinder and near-boiling water is then poured over them. After the grounds have brewed for about four minutes, the rod is pushed down, driving the filter through the coffee, forcing the grounds to the bottom and leaving the filtered brew on top, ready to be poured into a cup.

▲ The filter coffee machine found in most homes is essentially a simple piece of equipment. It makes use of the natural force of hot water, which rises up a tube in a siphon effect to produce a jug of coffee.

SEE ALSO: COFFEE • FOOD PROCESSING • PRESSURE • VENDING MACHINE

Cog Railway

Railways in their normal form are not suitable for climbing steep hills, and main lines are limited to gradients no steeper than about 2.9 percent (1 in 35) and on branch, or narrow-gauge lines, where train loads are lighter, about 5 percent (1 in 20). At 2.9 percent, a railway can climb no more than 150 ft. in one mile (29 m/km). In hilly or mountainous areas, this rate of climb might not be sufficient to carry a line high enough to keep pace with the rise of a valley or the slope of a mountain. A sufficient rate can, however, be achieved by making the railway much steeper at 12.5 percent (1 in 8) or more and using rack-and-pinion (cogwheel) propulsion to ensure that the wheels do not slip on the rails when under power or, more importantly, when braking.

The rack-and-pinion system dates from the pioneering days of the steam locomotive between 1812 and 1820 and coincides with the introduction of iron rails. One British engineer, John Blenkinsop, did not think that iron wheels on locomotives would have sufficient grip on iron rails, and on the rail line serving Middleton colliery near Leeds, he laid an extra-toothed rail alongside one of the ordinary rails, which engaged with a cogwheel on the locomotive. The Middleton line was relatively level, and it was soon found that on railways with only gentle climbs, the rack system was not needed. The driving wheels grip the rails by friction.

Little more was heard of rack railways until 1869, when the system was used for a line built up Mount Washington in the United States. Two years later, Nicholas Riggenbach opened the first cogwheel mountain railway in Europe almost to the top of Mount Rigi, near Lucerne in Switzerland. Since then, numerous rack lines have been built up or through mountains in various parts of the world, but mainly in Europe. A few industrial railways have also used rack-and-pinion systems to rise from one level to another.

For the last 100 years, the rack system has used an additional toothed rail that meshes with cogwheels under locomotives and coaches. There are four basic types of racks varying in details: the Riggenbach type looks like a steel ladder, and the Abt and Strub types use a vertical rail with teeth machined out of the top. One or other of these systems is used on most rack lines, but they are safe on gradients no steeper than 25 percent (1 in 4). One line in Switzerland up Mount Pilatus has a gradient of 48 percent (1 in 2.1) and uses the Locher rack with teeth cut on both sides of the rack rail instead of on top.

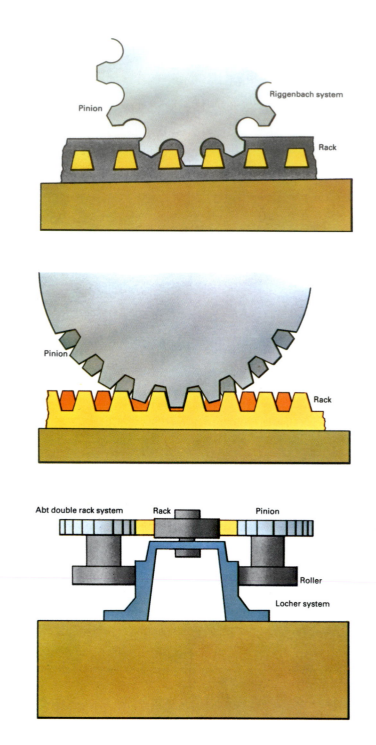

The first steam locomotives for steep mountain lines had vertical boilers, but later locomotives had boilers mounted at an angle to the main frame so that they were virtually horizontal when on the climb. Today steam locomotives have all but disappeared from most mountain lines and survive in regular service on only one line in Switzerland, on Britain's only rack line up Snowdon in North Wales, and on a handful of others. Most of the remainder have been electrified, and a few have converted to diesel.

▲ Three types of rack-and-pinion systems, which give a train extra drive and braking power on steep gradients. The rack consists of teeth that engage in cogwheels on the locomotive.

SEE ALSO: LOCOMOTIVE AND POWER CAR • RAILROAD SYSTEM

Coins and Minting

The earliest known coins in the Western world were made about 700 B.C.E. in western Asia Minor from a naturally occurring alloy of gold and silver known as electrum. Four hundred years before that, however, the Chinese were making "spade and key" coins; the spade was shaped like the digging implement, and the key was similar in appearance to a modern latch key.

The Chinese coins bore a denomination but, unlike coins of Asia Minor, they were cast from molds that carried the design. Examples of the Asia Minor coins show that they were stamped on one side with a tool bearing the design, rather than cast. The Asia Minor practice, therefore, was the true forerunner of modern coin-minting techniques.

Modern minting methods

The coinage acts of many countries set rigid legal requirements on the composition of coins as well as on the size and weight. For this reason, modern minting methods begin with standard nonferrous industrial techniques.

The alloys used are melted in furnaces and poured into molds of rectangular cross section. Some modern installations include horizontal continuous and vertical semiautomatic casting plants, which allow the stock to be molded in continuous lengths and cut off as desired.

Next the stock must be rolled under pressure to make it the right thickness for the particular coin. Stock of thick cross section is hot rolled, while thinner stock is cold rolled. The rolling process causes work hardening of the stock, which then has to be annealed. Annealing is a process of heating and cooling that makes the stock soft enough for further rolling and cutting.

Once the rolling has been completed, the stock, which can be in long lengths or in coils, is passed to machines with multiple cutting tools that cut it into blanks at a rate of up to 10,000 blanks per minute. Because of the annealing process and the use of lubricants during rolling, the blanks are stained and oxidized on the surface. They must now be pickled in dilute acid, usually in revolving barrels that also allow them to burnish one another, giving a brightness to the chemically treated surfaces. The blanks are washed and then dried in hot air.

Some coins are difficult to shape from flat blanks, particularly when there is a wide step, or rim, around the edge. In this case, the blanks are rolled in grooves

◀ One of thousands of pieces of eight recovered in 1978 from the *Concepción*, a Spanish galleon wrecked in 1641. Coins like this were hand stamped onto roughed-out blanks, often making them uneven and the stamp miscentered.

▲ Many "silver" coins today are made of cupronickel alloys or, in the case of Canadian coins, pure nickel.

▼ Minting silver coins with hand tools in the 18th century.

under pressure to force the metal around the edge up until the edge has a greater thickness than the center. This process is called rimming or upsetting. When coins have security designs on the edge, the design is rolled into the edge of the blank after rimming.

Minting tools

Pairs of dies are required for the striking of the designs into the blanks, one die each for the head and the tail of the coin (obverse and reverse in minting terminology). The manufacture of the die begins with an artist's model of the design six to eight times the size of the finished coin. A nickel-plated replica of the design is produced and then mounted in a reducing machine. A reducing machine is a tracing device that machines an exact copy of the design in tool steel to the scale of the coin to be produced. Tool steel is a very high-quality steel that can be hardened by heat treatment, a heating and cooling process similar to annealing except that it makes the

metal hard rather than soft. The steel must be heated to a precise, very high temperature and cooled at a specified rate in a certain type of bath. The exact specifications of the process depend on the particular type of steel that is being treated.

From the finished tool, known as the reduction punch, a series of tools is made by hobbing (striking one design into a new die steel). These are the matrix, working punch, and working die, one made from the other in succession.

The coining process

Coining presses are capable of producing coins one at a time or up to four at a time. Those that strike singly can work at a rate of up to 650 coins a minute where pressing loads of up to 180 tons (160 tonnes) are required. Heavier presses used for larger coins or harder metals normally work at 120 coins a minute at pressing loads of 250 tons (225 tonnes).

A collar is installed in the press. This is a block of steel which has been bored out to the size of the finished coin. If necessary the collar has grooves cut in it to give the coin a milled edge. The sequence of striking is carried out by the press pushing the blank into the well of the collar

▲ In a modern minting process a large-scale model of the design for the coin is first molded in a hard resin and placed in a reducing machine (left). A press then stamps out the metal coins from long metal sheets (right). The waste metal, known as scissel, is returned to the furnace to be rolled out into sheets again.

▼ The blanks are prepared for striking with the design (left). The metal is annealed to soften it and cleaned in acid to remove any stains. The finished coins (right) are checked for flaws in the material and for surface scratches and discoloration as the move along a conveyor belt for packing.

at the bottom of which is installed one of the dies. The other die then travels down from above and, on impact, causes the design to be impressed on both sides of the blank. At the same time, the pressure is sufficient to cause the metal blank to spread out to fill the collar.

Bimetallic coins

Some countries have introduced bimetallic coins as a means of making a new coin distinctive, such as the two-pounds coin introduced in the United Kingdom in the 1990s. Two different alloys are used for this coin—a nickel–brass outer ring and a cupronickel center. Blanks are cut for each alloy and annealed and burnished in the usual way. The outer blanks are placed into the rimming machine, where they are given a raised edge and the decorative lettering used as a forgery countermeasure is applied. At the same time, a central hole is punched out to take the cupronickel center. The inner blanks also undergo rimming to key the edge of the blank for bonding.

The two parts of the coin are joined in the coining press. A pierced outer blank is fed into a dial plate segment and rotated to the next stage, where an inner blank is dropped into the central

▲ A coin-validating machine uses three different sensors. Sensor 1 compares the coin's thickness with a reference stored in a memory chip, sensor 2 checks its material content, and sensor 3 measures size and shape. Ceramic snubbers make the coin roll smoothly. Vending and ticket machines use similar sensors to check inserted coins.

hole. The two parts are passed over the lower half of the die, whose upward movement pushes the blanks into a restraining collar. It meets the upper half of the die with a force of 100 tons (90 tonnes), impressing the coin on both sides simultaneously. The squashing action of the die spreads the metal outward and forces the raised edge of the center blank to fold over the inner edge of the outer blank, effectively locking the center blank in place. The completed coin is ejected from the collar by the downward motion of the upper die.

Inspection

Surface conditions are very important in coining, so the blanks are usually held to a maximum center line average that limits surface irregularities. Mints with modern equipment use X-ray fluorescent spectrometers to analyze alloys; otherwise chemical analysis is used.

After coining, the diameters of coins are checked with micrometers or other types of gauges. The weights are checked by measuring the weight of a specified number of coins against a stated weight, to which is added an allowable tolerance. Sometimes coins are accidentally double stamped or have other defects. Such coins rarely get through the inspection process, but when they do, they quickly become valuable collectors' items because of their irregularity.

SEE ALSO: ALLOY • COPPER • COUNTERFEITING AND FORGERY • METALWORKING • NICKEL • SHEET METAL

Colorimetry

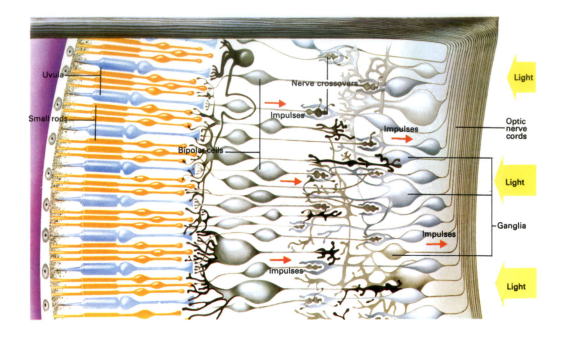

Labels on image: Uvula, Small rods, Bipolar cells, Impulses, Nerve crossovers, Impulses, Impulses, Impulses, Light, Light, Light, Optic nerve cords, Ganglia

◀ The retina is the part of the eye responsible for light sensitivity. Light passes through the eye to the surface of the retina, which consists of two types of cells—rods and cones. Only the cones are capable of discriminating colors. At night, only the rods are used and all colors are seen as shades of gray.

Colorimetry is the study of the measurement of color. In order to discuss this subject, it is necessary to understand just what color is. Color is based on the fact that the eye is able to detect and distinguish between certain wavelengths of electromagnetic radiation. These wavelengths constitute the visible spectrum, or rainbow, and range from 780 nm (nanometers) for red light down to 380 nm for violet light. When a human being sees a color, he or she is sensing one or a combination of wavelengths of electromagnetic radiation.

The part of the eye responsible for light sensitivity is the retina. Although the retina consists of two types of cells, the rods and the cones, it is the cones that determine color. There are three types of cones, each sensitive to a different part of the visible spectrum, with maximum sensitivities at 445 nm, 535 nm, and 565 nm, corresponding to blue, green, and red areas of the spectrum, respectively. It is therefore possible to produce a range of colors by mixing appropriate proportions of these three color ranges, which are called the primary colors.

Other colors produced by mixing primary colors are said to be produced by an additive process. White light can be produced by mixing all the colors of the spectrum or equal proportions of the primary colors.

Conversely, if a primary color is removed from white light, the complementary color is obtained. This is a subtractive process, and the primary colors are yellow (white minus blue), magenta (white minus green), and cyan (white minus red).

When an object appears colored, it does so because the object itself is absorbing certain wavelengths of the spectrum and reflecting others. The color reflected results in the color seen. Thus, colored pigments, such as paints, filter color from white paper; the color seen results from the subtractive process. The primary colors used by an artist are therefore magenta, cyan, and yellow.

Color blindness is thought to be due to a lack of function in one or more sets of cones, so that some individuals can see only certain colors. Monochromatism occurs in people with no functioning cone system, so that they have no perception of color and can see only shades of gray.

Color perception can also be affected by the intensity of illumination. Blue and green objects appear brighter than red ones at low light levels compared with their relative brightness under stronger illumination. A related shift in hues occurs as more light is shone onto an object, with colours appearing less red and green, and more blue and yellow.

An instrument that allows the observer to match a patch of light by a combination of the three primary colors is called a trichromatic colorimeter. Although this method relies on the perception of the eye, it is a useful device for color measurement. The monochromatic colorimeter does not measure types of color but more specifically measures the intensity of a particular color. Unlike the trichromatic colorimeter, it does not depend on the perception of color by the eye.

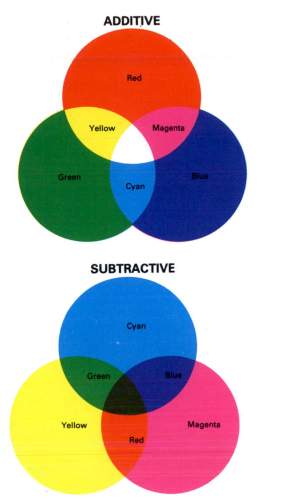

ADDITIVE

SUBTRACTIVE

◀ Additive colors (top) combine to give yellow, cyan, and magenta or, using all three, white. Subtractive colors (bottom) such as pigments combine to form red, green, blue, and black.

The CIE standard observer is defined by three distribution curves that are related to the responses of the three different detectors in the retina, showing the peak sensitivity of each one. To measure the tristimulus values of a sample, either of two basic methods can be used. The simplest device is a type of light meter in which suitable colored optical filters match the response of the instrument to each of the distribution curves in turn. This device is called a trichromatic colorimeter and enables the direct reading of the tristimulus values of a reflecting sample. A densitometer can be used for this purpose.

Monochromatic colorimeter

Because the monochromatic colorimeter measures the intensity of color, it has become an extremely important tool for chemists. Many solutions are colored, and, as the intensity of the color is dependent on the concentration of the colored species in the solution, this device can be used as a measure of concentration. The colorimeter consists basically of a light source, a tube containing the test solution, and a photocell.

Trichromatic colorimeter

Any color may be specified by the amount of the three primary colors that are required to match it: these are called the tristimulus values X, Y, and Z, for red, green, and blue, respectively. The Commission Internationale de l'Eclairage (CIE), in 1931, was able to specify the results of such measurements for a standard observer, or average person.

A graph of three variable factors ought to be depicted in three dimensions—stereoscopic. So that colors can be represented on a two-dimensional piece of paper, two chromaticity coordinates, X and Y, are calculated from the tristimulus values. These are the proportions of red and green lights in white light. By plotting a graph of X against Y, all colors can be shown on a set of diagrams.

Pure colors plot near to the colors of the spectrum on such a graph and are said to be saturated. Colors may be desaturated by addition of white light or, in the case of colorants such as dyes and pigments, by addition of white or black colorant. These colors plot near the white point in the middle of the diagram. The hue of a color can be denoted by the wavelength nearest to it—its dominant wavelength.

▶ A TV picture uses additive colors. The screen is made up of many small dots that give the illusion of continuous color. Color printing uses subtractive combinations so that a wide range of colors can be printed using only cyan, yellow, magenta, and black inks.

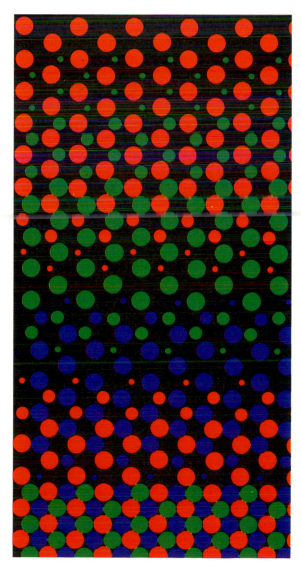

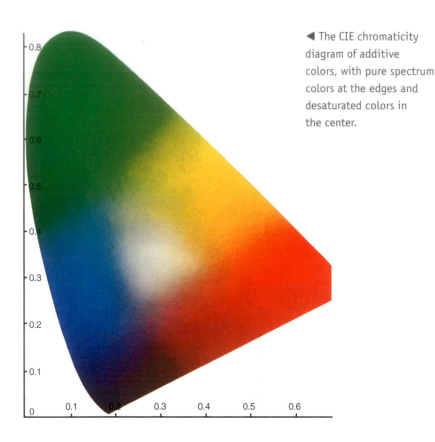

◄ The CIE chromaticity diagram of additive colors, with pure spectrum colors at the edges and desaturated colors in the center.

Thus the filter should absorb wavelengths not absorbed by the solution. The filter that has a color complementary to the test solution is therefore usually the one to use and gives the highest absorbency and lowest transmission. For example, a blue filter would be most suitable for measurements of red solutions as it strongly absorbs red light.

Spectrophotometry

As the monochromatic colorimeter does not depend on color perception of the eye, it provides a reasonably accurate method for determining intensities of color and thus concentrations of solutions. However, a more accurate instrument than a colorimeter is a spectrophotometer, which operates in a similar way to a colorimeter except that the required wavelength to be measured is more accurately determined. Instead of filters, a grating is used to select the wavelengths. The range of wavelengths transmitted—the bandwidth—is greatly improved and may be used to produce an absorption spectrum of a test solution.

A narrow beam of light from the light source passes through the test solution and is detected by a light-sensitive photocell. The current generated in the photocell is proportional to the light transmitted through the test solution. This current is detected by a meter and can be read as either light transmitted or light absorbed by the test solution. The more colored or concentrated a solution, the more light is absorbed (less is transmitted).

Usually it is the practice to standardize the colorimeter using a blank. This blank may consist of a colorless liquid such as water or the test solution minus the colored species. An identical tube containing an identical solution plus the colored species is then measured relative to the blank.

The absorbency of a colored solution is often referred to as its optical density (OD). The colorimeter can be used for measuring sample concentrations of solutions or following chemical reactions. If two chemicals react to produce a color, the rate of reaction can be followed by watching how fast the OD, or concentration of products, increases.

As only the intensity of the color is measured by a monochromatic colorimeter, only one color is being measured. It is therefore necessary to choose an appropriate light filter to improve the accuracy of colorimetric work. This filter is placed between light source and test solution. The most suitable filter for an experiment is one that selects the band wavelengths of light that are most strongly absorbed by the colored solution.

► An abridged spectrophotometer being used to check the tint of sunglass lenses. This machine measures more accurately than the tristimulus colorimeter.

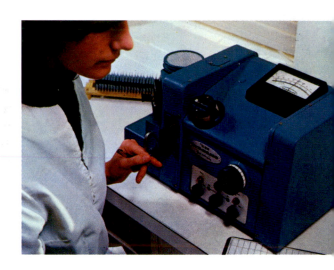

► A reflection densitometer is commonly used as a colorimeter in printing works. The inks (cyan, magenta, yellow, and black) will already be of the correct hue, but it is necessary to check their strength when printed.

SEE ALSO: Light and optics • Photoelectric cell and photometry • Printing • Spectroscopy

Compact Disc, Audio

In 1877, Thomas Edison achieved a remarkable feat of recording and playing back a recital of "Mary had a little lamb" on his newly invented phonograph. Edison's cylinders eventually gave way to discs—shellac 78s—which in turn gave way to microgroove long-playing records, but the basic principle remained the same—sound wave patterns were stored as undulations, or wiggles, in a groove traced by a stylus, or needle.

Now, with compact discs, there are records without grooves and there is no stylus. Compact discs are played by optical means and do not wear out, because there is no contact between the laser-scanning head and the disc. The clicks, pops, and cracks caused by dust and scratches on conventional LPs are a thing of the past. And despite its small size—only 4¾ in. (12 cm) diameter—a compact disc can offer an hour of uninterrupted music on only one side.

All this has been achieved by dispensing with that basic principle of representing sound waves as undulations in a groove, undulations that form a direct physical representation, or analog, of the sound wave form being recorded. The compact disc is a digital audio system in which the sound wave signals are processed in an entirely different way. To understand digital recording and replay, it is easier to look first at conventional analog audio.

Analog audio

When we hear sound, our ears are detecting more or less subtle cyclical changes in air pressure. The alternating compressions and rarefactions of air set in motion by a vibrating object are sound waves. These can be visualized as resembling the ups and downs of ripples traveling across the surface of a pond. In analog disc-cutting equipment, the audio signal is amplified to several hundred watts in order to drive the cutting head, which carves the groove on the master lacquer disc.

When a record is played, the stylus sitting in the groove is set in motion, and its movements are used to produce an electrical signal. When fed to a suitable amplifier and loudspeakers, this signal reappears as a fairly close approximation to the original sound. It is inevitable that every stage in the recording and replay process will cause some degradation of the musical signal.

The record-cutting process imposes quite severe limitations. For example, very loud bass notes have to be reduced in level because otherwise the wiggles in the groove would become unacceptably large. If the engineer tries to over-

come this problem by reducing the overall level of the music, then another problem arises—background noise. The recording system contributes a certain amount of unwanted background hiss to the sound, and the lower the level of the music the more obvious the hiss will be.

The level of background noise inherent in an audio system or component is defined as its signal-to-noise ratio, and allied to this is the concept of dynamic range. The dynamic range of the system is the difference between the loudest sound that can be recorded without unacceptable distortion and the quietest that can be recorded before disappearing into the noise floor. Both these limits are always expressed in decibels (dB). Although very useful to the engineer, decibels are often confusing to the layman because they are not an absolute unit—like meters or degrees Centigrade—but express a ratio between two levels of acoustic or electrical power, and so any figure in dB is a relative figure. We can say that if the threshold of hearing is taken as 0 dB, then the threshold of pain is something over 120 dB.

The reproduction system ought therefore to be capable of reproducing sounds in the range from 0 dB to about 95 dB. The 95 dB ratio between the quietest and loudest sounds is the desirable dynamic range of the hi-fi reproduction

▲ Compact disc players are now a common feature of home hi-fi equipment. As well as requiring less storage space, CDs are immune to scratches, dirt, and grease.

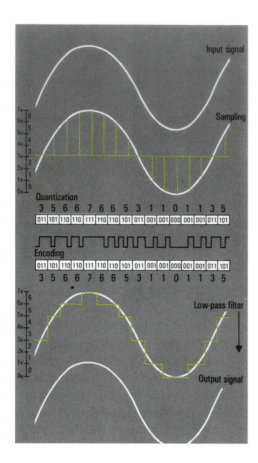

◀ An analog recording signal (top) is converted to a digital code (center) and then back to analog form as an output to the amplifier.

chain. However, the actual dynamic range achievable by conventional systems—disc or tape—is limited to perhaps 60 or 70 dB.

Disc-cutting engineers have to bear in mind that the groove they cut must not be too difficult for the playback stylus to follow—there is no point in producing a perfect recording if no one can play it back without distortion spoiling the sound. It is possible for some musical instruments to produce extremely steep transient wavefronts, a good example being the trumpet. The initial attack of a trumpet note, if reproduced accurately by the cutter, could appear as such a sharp bend in the groove that no stylus could follow it without losing contact with the groove walls to produce breakup, or mistracking distortion. Instead of a clean piercing transient, the listener hears a nasty buzz of distortion.

Space problems

In any case, the task of the stylus in following the groove becomes more difficult as it reaches the end of the record side, because although the record turns at constant speed, the length of groove per unit time becomes shorter as the stylus follows the inward spiral. So some signals that would be quite trackable in the relatively spacious outer grooves become real obstacle courses for the stylus when packed into the last band of a disc.

One last drawback with conventional audio systems is the tendency, however slight, to suffer

▶ Compact discs being manufactured. Clean-room technology is used to prevent any particles or other impurities that might affect the playback qualities of the recorded sound from contaminating the surface of the disc.

from cyclical pitch fluctuations, usually described as wow and flutter. Audible rising and falling of pitch is caused by variation in the (supposedly constant) speed of a turntable or tape drive capstan. On the best hi-fi systems, these effects have been reduced to virtual insignificance, though even a very slight warp in the disc will produce enough wow to upset a musical ear.

Skilled recording engineers and hi-fi designers can overcome or disguise the limitations of conventional disc-playing equipment to a remarkable extent, and good discs on a good system can sound natural and lifelike. With digital recording, it is theoretically possible to sweep away all the analog system's limitations. Recording studios have gradually been replacing their analog tape mastering recorders with digital tape systems.

Digital recording

In digital recording, once the sound has been converted by microphones into electrical signals, there is no attempt to replicate the shape of those signals by recording them continuously, as with analog tape or disc. Instead of recording the waveform continuously, it is sampled, that is, measurements are made of the instantaneous value of the waveform, and these measurements, taken at frequent regular intervals, are then recorded as numerical values. As in all microprocessor and computer technology, the numbers are in binary code. For example, if a measurement at a certain moment in time is found to be 6 volts, it will be converted to the binary equivalent, which is 110. The big advantage of making recordings in binary code is that it has only two,

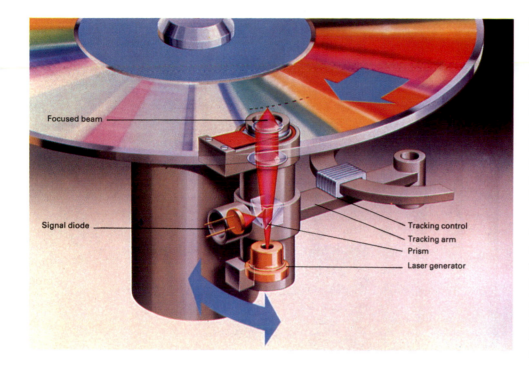

Focused beam

Signal diode

Tracking control
Tracking arm
Prism
Laser generator

bumps 0.5 microns wide, a minimum of 0.97 microns long and 125 nanometers high pressed into it from the side that will contain the label in a single, continuous, and lengthy spiral data track. Once the polycarbonate disc has been formed, a thin, reflective aluminum layer is added to provide a coating for the bumps. Finally a thin acrylic layer is sprayed on top to protect the aluminum layer beneath.

A CD has a single spiral track of data that winds from the inside of the disc to the outside—the reverse of the vinyl disc. Because the spiral track starts at the center, a CD can be smaller than 12 cm, and there are even plastic baseball and business cards that can be read in a CD player. CD business cards hold around 2 megabytes (MB) of data in the amount of spiral track available.

It is the compactness of the bumps that makes the spiral track on a CD so long. If the track on a conventional CD could be unwound into a straight line, it would be five miles long.

Reading this extremely small data track is achieved by reflecting the signal from the disc to a photodiode, which reacts electrically to the light signal received—the output from the photodiode is thus a series of electronic ones and zeros. It does not matter exactly how much light is received because anything above a certain predetermined level can be defined as a one and anything below that level, a zero. Here we can see the fundamental benefit of working with digits—only on or off conditions have to be detected to reproduce the original input. In an analog system, the playback device is expected to trace accurately the infinite variations of signal level, an action it can never do perfectly.

Playback

To play the disc back, a drive motor spins the disc at between 200 and 500 rpm. A laser and lens system then focus on the bumps and reads them. A tracking mechanism capable of moving at micron accuracy moves the laser assembly so that its beam can follow the spiral track. The CD player utilizes computer technology to form the data into understandable blocks and to send them either to the CD player or to a computer's CD-ROM drive.

The CD player's task is essentially to focus the laser on the track of bumps. The laser beam passes through the polycarbonate layer, reflects off the aluminum, and bounces back to an opto-electronic device that can detect alterations in

unambiguous conditions—a zero and a one or, electrically, on and off. So numbers in binary code retain their intrinsic accuracy no matter how often they are processed and no matter how complicated the processing may appear to be.

The accuracy of the measurements or quantization of the signal values is related to the number of bits (binary digits) used. In the compact disc system, 16 bits are used. Consequently, the measurement error cannot be greater than 1 bit in 2 to the power of 16 bits (2^{16}), which equates to 1 part in 65,536. In practice, the sampling of the signal is performed 44,100 times a second, ensuring signal detail is not lost between samples. This sampling rate is theoretically adequate for a signal frequency up to 20,000 cycles per second (20 kHz), which is conventionally taken as the highest audible frequency. When converted into digital form, the sound signal is just a series of numbers—44,100 numbers of 16 bits each second per channel. Since each bit is nothing more than a zero-or-one condition, it can be replicated reliably.

The silvery reflective surface of a compact disc carries the signal information in the form of a series of pits, etched into the reflective layer, that can be read by optical equipment. When light from a small laser is focused precisely on the pattern of pits, a reflected signal is received from the flat parts of the surface while little or no signal is received back from the pits, where the laser beam is scattered.

Materials

A CD is formed from injection-molded clear polycarbonate plastic about 1.2 mm in thickness. During manufacture, the plastic has microscopic

▲ Part of the CD player's servomechanism that keeps the laser tracking the disc correctly. The laser generator supplies a beam that is focused by the head of the tracking arm deep into the disc. It renders dust and grit particles on the surface out of focus and thus incapable of affecting the output of the beam.

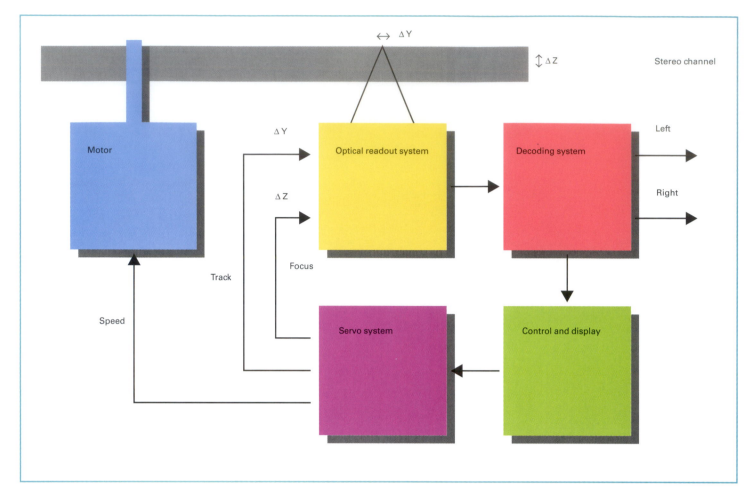

light levels. The bumps have a different reflectivity from the remainder of the aluminum layer, and the opto-electronic sensor can detect that change. The electronics in the drive interpret these changes to read the bits that make up the bytes.

The tracking system performs the difficult task of centering on the data track. The tracking system, as it plays the CD, has to continually move the laser outward. As the laser moves outward, the spindle motor slows the speed at which the CD is revolving so that the data coming off the disc maintains a constant rate.

Play starts from the inside of the disc at a speed of approximately 500 rpm, slowing down to 200 rpm as the laser tracks across to the outside, allowing a constant linear speed past the laser head. Although small scratches or specks of dust on the CD are happily ignored, larger scratches or foreign objects can cause data to be misread (this is known as a burst error).

This problem is solved by interleaving the data on the disc, so that it is stored nonsequentially around one circuit. The drive reads data one revolution at a time and un-interleaves the data to play it. A compact disc player can be regarded as a dedicated computer, the disc itself being an extremely high-density form of storage.

Compact discs are more expensive than conventional records and basic players but can claim

▲ Marantz uses a complicated tracking and focusing system to feed the signal from the disc to the decoder electronics. Controls allow any combination of tracks to be played in any sequence simply by entering the track numbers on a keypad. Other systems use similar electronics.

FACT FILE

■ *The surface of a CD often reflects rainbow patterns similar to those seen in soap bubbles. This effect is created by constructive and destructive interference of light as it strikes the top layer. The angle a CD is held at controls the colors seen, since the angle at which white light hits the reflective film alters the wavelength of light reflected into the viewer's eye, and hence the color seen.*

■ *Because the laser has to be able to move between songs, there is data encoded within the music telling the drive its precise location on the CD. This coding is achieved without interfering with the music using "subcode data." Subcode data can encode the absolute and relative position of the laser in the track and also information, such as song titles.*

■ *There are several different formats used to store data on a CD. The most common are CD-DA (audio) and CD-ROM (computer data).*

the twin benefits of improved sound quality and durability. The player can be added to an existing system simply by connecting it to the auxiliary, tape, or tuner socket of the amplifier.

Dynamic range

The dynamic range from a CD can comfortably exceed 90dB, and this range is usable because distortion does not tend to rise with increasing signal level. Distortion remains far lower than that produced by pickup cartridges or even loudspeakers. Wow and flutter cannot be created on a CD because the output of bits is controlled by a quartz crystal clock rather than being at the mercy of mechanical parts. Channel separation is extremely high since the two channels are recorded and replaycd as two alternating data streams, and this, combined with the system's inherent pitch and phase stability, allows a very good stereo image—instruments and voices can be pinpointed very accurately on the imaginary stage between the two loudspeakers.

With no physical contact between playback head and disc, compact discs are not susceptible to wear and the resulting deterioration of sound quality or to the dirt and grit particles that lodge so easily in the grooves of vinyl discs and that are so difficult to remove.

▲ The laser techology used for playing compact discs has had great success in portable CD applications. Unlike the needles used to play vinyl records, the laser in a personal CD player is not susceptible to bumps or movement, making it ideal for carrying around.

SEE ALSO: Hɪ-Fɪ sʏsᴛᴇᴍs • Lᴀsᴇʀ ᴀɴᴅ ᴍᴀsᴇʀ • Mᴜsɪᴄᴀʟ sᴄᴀʟᴇ • Pʜᴏᴛᴏᴇʟᴇᴄᴛʀɪᴄ ᴄᴇʟʟ ᴀɴᴅ ᴘʜᴏᴛᴏᴍᴇᴛʀʏ • Sᴏᴜɴᴅ

Compressor and Pump

Compressors and pumps are used to enable the transportation of gases or fluids from one point to another by utilizing mechanical pressure. The compression of air as a source of energy goes back to the early development of primitive humans, who used air compressed in their lungs to blow onto cinders to make them burst into flame. Adult human lungs, in a healthy state, can deliver 3.5 cu. ft. (100 l) of air a minute at a pressure of 0.3 to 1.2 psi (0.02–0.08 bar).

The Egyptians in 1500 B.C.E. used foot-operated blow sacks made from animal stomachs to increase furnace heat for smelting metals. From this developed the bellows, which remained the main form of air compression until as recently as the 17th and 18th centuries. From this period onward, industrial needs required more advanced devices to perform a wide variety of functions; compressors are used in tunneling machines, pneumatic delivery systems, passenger elevators, and the operation of machinery for mass production. Even the earliest compressor required a basic energy: muscle power. Once compressed air has been produced and stored, it is a source of power, but first of all a prime mover is required to operate the compressor. It may take the form of water power, a gas engine, an electric motor, a gasoline (petrol) or diesel engine, or even a gas turbine. Using compressed air as an energy source enables high output powers to be obtained from small motors—the bulky prime mover and compressor can be remote from the work area.

There are several different basic types of compressor, but the simplest is the bicycle pump, the most elementary form of reciprocating piston compressor: a leather cup piston moving by hand power up and down a long cylinder—the barrel of the pump. As the handle is pulled out, air is drawn in past the piston until the cylinder is full of air at normal pressure. As the handle is pushed in, the leather cup is spread by the resistance of the air in the barrel, which is compressed until it has sufficient pressure to pass through the nonreturn valve at the far end and into the bicycle tire.

Not all of the energy goes into air pressure: lost energy appears in the form of heat. Most cyclists will have noticed that the air in their pump is hotter when compressed, with the end of the pump sometimes becoming too hot to touch.

TWO-STAGE COMPRESSOR

In the low-pressure cylinder of the two-stage compressor, air is compressed from ambient pressure to a pressure equal to the square root of the final pressure in atmospheres. The second stage takes the air to its final pressure. At these ratios, power requirement is at a minimum.

The low- and high-pressure stages can be combined in a single cylinder with both sides of the piston acting to compress the air. This design is known as a two-stage double-acting compressor.

As mentioned before, compression produces heat, and in order to reduce temperature problems, which particularly affect lubrication, a cooling stage is normally included between the low- and the high-pressure cylinders in the form of a water or air cooled heat exchanger.

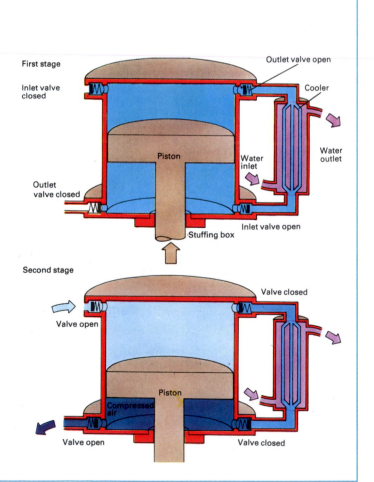

First stage
Inlet valve closed
Outlet valve open
Cooler
Piston
Water inlet
Water outlet
Outlet valve closed
Inlet valve open
Stuffing box

Second stage
Valve open
Valve closed
Valve open
Piston
Compressed air
Valve closed

screws rotate. This design is very compact and can operate at a high speed, both features being well suited to larger air requirements.

The rotary vane compressor comes in numerous forms, but basically it comprises a rotor eccentrically placed in a cylinder, the rotor being fitted with a number of vanes that, as the rotor turns, are flung outward by centrifugal force against the cylinder walls. The sliding in and out of the vanes against the lining of the cylinder forms a seal assisted by lubrication. Because the rotor is offset within the cylinder, air is taken in between the vanes at the point of maximum distance between the rotor and the cylinder wall and is compressed during rotation toward the pressure chamber where the rotor is at its closest to the cylinders.

Up to 72 psi (5 bar) pressure, rotary vane compressors tend to be single stage, but above this pressure they have to be built in two or more stages. This type of compressor is well balanced but is more suited to lower pressures and, in comparison with reciprocating types, is rather less efficient in relation to the energy consumed.

Where very large volumes of compressed air are needed, turbo compressors—sets of rotating and fixed blades similar to jet engine mechanisms are used. The kinetic energy given to the air by the moving blades is converted into pressure as the moving air is slowed by the fixed blades.

▲ A Broom Wade V Compact compressor is designed to operate in subzero temperatures.

Reciprocating compressor

The reciprocating compressor, the most common type used in industry as a permanent installation, is powered by an electric motor. It may be mounted on two or four wheels for use on construction sites or road works, and it is powered by either a gasoline or diesel engine. The main components are a crankcase, crankshaft, piston rod, piston, and cylinder, the last incorporating suction and discharge valves. For pressures up to 72 to 87 psi (5–6 bar) a simple single-stage design is sufficient, but above these pressures, two stages of compression are usual, low pressure and high pressure (see box at left).

Various cylinder arrangements and multiples are available, as numerous as in the internal combustion engine, but often a further cooling stage is required in the form of an aftercooler. Air or water cooling can be incorporated according to the size or needs of the installation. The compressed air is normally fed into a pressure cylinder or air receiver to smooth the pulses in the flow from the compressor caused by the piston's cycles.

Rotary compressors

Two other types of compressor design are common, both on the rotary principle. The screw compressor comprises one or two pairs (stages) of intermeshing screws that rotate together without touching, taking the air in at one end and compressing it as the

▶ Aerostyle rotary vane compressors have sliding vanes to maintain contact with the walls.

Use of compressors

Applications for compressors are numerous, but in simple terms, stationary compressors are used mainly for industrial purposes, from small garage types for inflating tires, spraying, and powering certain tools to the larger units used for operating air power drills and screwdrivers on assembly lines, for paint-spray shops, for powering presses, for pumping beer and other liquids, and for

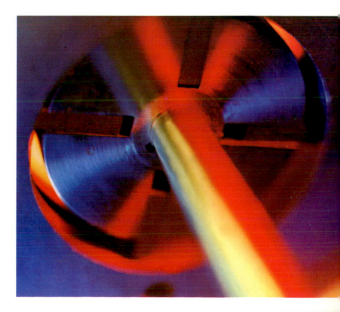

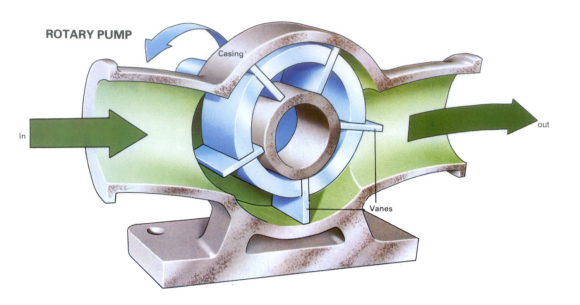

ROTARY PUMP

Casing

In

out

Vanes

▶ The rotary pump. The fluid is speeded up as it goes through by the action of the spinning rotor. The rotor is offset and the vanes slide in and out (or bend if they are made of rubber) on the inner circumference of the casing.

pneumatically controlling advanced production machinery. Portable air compressors can be seen on most construction and civil engineering sites operating paving breakers, pumps, and drills.

Pumps

A pump is a device for raising a fluid from a lower to a higher level. More generally, it is a device for imparting energy to fluids (including gases).

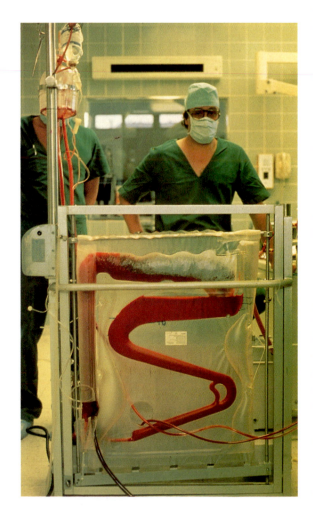

▶ An external blood pump, which is being developed to circulate blood during surgery for the implantation of an electric-hydraulic heart.

In ancient times, crop irrigation was carried out by gravity; irrigation channels had to be lower than the water source, which would usually be a river. When water had to be raised to irrigate high land or to remove it from a mine, it would be carried in buckets.

The earliest account of a pump appears in the literature of the scholars of the museum at Alexandria and is credited to Ctesibus's fire engine— a kind of double-action pump. The first known pump, however, was used in the Roman Empire after 100 B.C.E. It was a positive displacement pump, having a cylinder with a plunger in it and valves at each end. It is also called the Bolsena pump because an almost complete example was found at Bolsena, Italy.

Positive-displacement pumps

The Bolsena pump is called a positive-displacement pump because with each stroke of the piston a fixed amount of fluid is displaced. The valves are of the nonreturn type, so-called because the fluid is allowed to flow in one direction only. Such pumps are reciprocating—that is, the action of a piston, plunger, or diaphragm moves the fluid in bursts. A bicycle pump is a good example; with each stroke of the pump, air is pushed into the tire and a nonreturn valve keeps it from coming back out; with the return stroke of the piston air is pulled into the cylinder in front of the piston to be pushed into the tire on the next stroke. This principle has been the most widely used throughout history, from hand-cranked models to the giant pumps used to drain mines and keep up the water level in canals in the 18th and 19th centuries. A reciprocating pump can also be designed as a double-action pump, moving the fluid on both sides of the piston with the addition of extra valves and a seal where the piston rod enters the cylinder.

Rotary pumps are also positive-displacement types, but they are not reciprocating pumps and have no valves. The fluid enters an inlet and is pushed by rotating vanes, gears, or lobes through an outlet. The amount of displacement depends on the clearance between the vanes or the gear teeth.

Positive-displacement pumps are more suitable for pumping clean fluids because of the small clearances necessary in construction; an exception is the diaphragm pump, in which the piston or connecting rod is connected to a diaphragm. The movement of the diaphragm causes the displacement, and because the fluid cannot pass the diaphragm to contact the working parts, this pump can be used to move solids in suspension, if the valves can pass the material without becoming clogged.

Peristaltic pumps are valveless rotary pumps, moving fluid by use of a continuously squeezed flexible tube. These are also suitable for pumping fluids containing small solids in suspension as well as thick liquids. Blood in a heart-lung machine is pumped by a peristaltic pump.

The reciprocating Bolsena-type force pump is still widely used for raising water. Fuel and oil pumps on cars and trucks are usually of the piston and diaphragm type. Hydraulic pumps, which operate aircraft controls (such as the undercarriage and flaps), jacks to lift cars for repairs, and earth-moving equipment, are also positive-displacement pumps. They must have some means of relieving pressure on the pump delivery, such as a pressure valve, because excessively high pressures will cause damage to the working parts.

Centrifugal pumps

The centrifugal pump began development in the mid-19th century. It comprises a wheel with vanes or blades called an impeller in a housing or case. The fluid is led into the "eye" or center of the impeller through an inlet and pressure is created as the fluid is rotated by the impeller at high speed.

The centrifugal force providing pressure in the fluid can be understood by imagining a bucket of water at arm's length; if it is swung fast enough, centrifugal force will keep the water in the bucket. The shape of the outlet changes the low-pressure, high-velocity fluid stream into a high-pressure, low-velocity stream.

The total pressure of a particle of fluid is made up of static pressure—measured on a pressure gauge—and dynamic pressure, which depends on its speed. The dynamic pressure is the pressure exerted on an object suddenly introduced in front of the moving particle. This dynamic pressure increases as the square of the velocity. It is not pos-

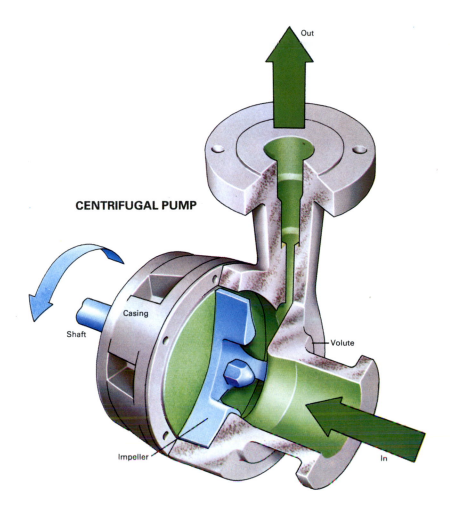

CENTRIFUGAL PUMP

Out

Casing

Shaft

Volute

Impeller

In

▲ The centrifugal pump. The rotor is called an impeller. It impels the fluid around the inner circumference of the casing, applying centrifugal force to it; the casing is called a volute and is graduated in size from the impeller to the outlet, so that the flow of the fluid is changed from a high-velocity, low-pressure stream to a low-velocity, high-pressure stream.

sible to convert all the dynamic pressure in a flowing liquid to static pressure, but the pressure recovery can be 0.5 to 0.8 that of the dynamic pressure. The simplest method slowly increases the delivery channel area (at no greater taper than 8 degrees) with a device known as a diffuser, often used on small pumps. On most larger pumps the volute—outer part of the housing—has a cross-sectional area that increases toward the outlet; the fluid is thrown into the volute by the impeller.

Unlike the positive-displacement pump, the centrifugal pump requires no pressure-relief device because, given a certain impeller and a certain rotational speed, a predictable maximum pressure is achieved. In effect, such a pump is a velocity machine or a hydrodynamic pump.

Self-priming pumps

Many applications call for the pump to prime itself. If the water level is below the pump inlet, only a positive-displacement pump will move the column of air from the suction pipe first, followed by the normal pumping operation, that is, providing the height the water is to be lifted does not exceed the equivalent height of water whose weight produces one atmosphere of pressure. For fresh water the height is 34 ft. (10.4 m); it would

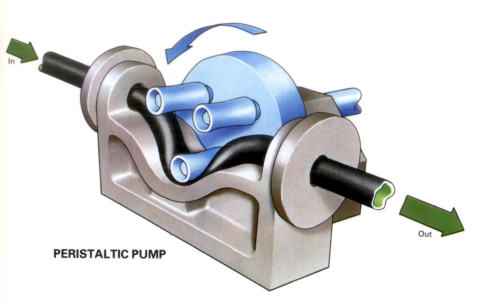

PERISTALTIC PUMP

be impossible to lift higher than this as a perfect vacuum would exist above the water column. In practice water can be lifted only about 28 ft. (8.5 m).

An ordinary centrifugal pump, when empty, cannot remove air from the suction pipe, but once the air is removed by other means, it is primed and pumps normally. The wet self-priming pump is the most common type and is used extensively in construction. The body of the pump is filled with water, which is kept in place by a nonreturn valve. Circulation of this water removes air from the suction pipe and allows water to rise into the pump.

Normal centrifugal pumps will not cope with snore—large amounts of air mixed with water. Vacuum pumps and air-operated ejectors are used to prime these pumps. Such units are used in construction where work has to be done below groundwater level. In air ejectors, air from a compressor, usually operated off the pump motor, is passed through a jet across an opening connected to an air-separation chamber on the suction side of the pump. A vacuum is created in the separation chamber, and water is drawn up to the pump, which then operates normally. Air that comes up with the water is removed from the water in the separation chamber and blown through the ejector.

High-pressure pumps

The pressure produced by a centrifugal pump is roughly proportional to the square of the tip velocity of the impeller, so for a given pressure requirement, the impeller diameter can be large and the speed low or vice versa. The highest rotational speed available from an electric motor (the usual means of driving a centrifugal pump) is 2,900 rpm on 50 cycles electric frequency or 3,400 rpm on 60 cycles; at these speeds higher pressure can be obtained using larger-diameter pumps.

▲ The peristaltic pump, a common type of positive-displacement pump, imitates the action of the intestines during digestion (peristalsis) by squeezing a length of flexible tube.

There are limits, however, one being the strength of the materials used to make the pump; a more important limitation is that the fluid friction produced by the impeller rotation affects the horsepower required to drive the pump, and it increases more rapidly above a certain impeller diameter. For pressures much above 100 psi (6.9 bar), centrifugal pumps are normally built in stages with the impellers arranged in series all mounted on a common shaft, the liquid being led from the output of one stage to the inlet of the next. Owing to experience gained building rocket pumps and multistage compressors for jet engines, commercial pumps now run at speeds higher than cycle speeds, enabling a single stage to be used to obtain higher pressures. These pumps are simple, having a gear drive or a belt drive with high-speed belts, and represent savings in space and cost.

Other types of pumps

Some pumps are neither centrifugal nor positive-displacement types. The air ejector can also be used to lift fluids. The main advantage is that there are no moving parts, but efficiency is low, at most 30 percent. The most common use of a jet pump, as it is known, is in conjunction with a centrifugal pump to raise water over 34 ft. (10.4 m) and as much as 150 ft. (45.7 m).

SEE ALSO: CENTRIFUGE • ENERGY RESOURCES • FIREFIGHTING • GAS LAWS • GAS TURBINE • HYDRAULICS • PRESSURE • REFRIGERATION • TURBINE • VENTURI EFFECT • WATER RAM • WATER SUPPLY

Computer

A computer is a machine that can accept and store information, carry out operations in accordance with stored sets of instructions called programs, and display and store the results. In the case of numerical information, computers can add, subtract, multiply, divide, and compare numbers, but a computer is far more than a high-grade calculator. The range of manipulations that a computer can perform on information is limited only by the imagination of the person who writes the program. This makes the computer by far the most versatile tool ever invented.

Computers work only on numbers, but because all information can be represented by numbers, computers can process information of any kind. One of the most commonly processed classes of information is text. Word processing is possible because when text is entered into a computer, each letter is immediately converted into a number, in accordance with an internationally agreed code.

Development of the computer

Historically, there were two classes of computer—analog and digital. An analog computer was a machine that received and represented information in terms of continuous quantities, such as a distance along a line on a surface, the angle of rotation of a wheel, or a continuously changing voltage level. Analog computers were mechanical or electrical and were usually designed to perform a particular function. In World War II, for instance, analog computers were used as antiaircraft gun-aiming predictors. The now obsolete slide rule is an analog device. Digital computers—the kind now familiar to all—operate on a different basis. They represent information in terms of a series of distinct numbers. Input to the internal functioning parts of a digital computer is always in the form of a stream of numbers.

The idea of providing a machine with instructions (a program) for its operation seems to have been originated by the French inventor Joseph-Marie Jacquard. In 1805, Jacquard showed how a weaving loom could be programmed to produce different patterns of cloth by means of a series of cards punched with holes in different positions. Different card sets could be used to create different weave patterns.

This ingenious idea was developed further in 1822 by the British mathematician Charles Babbage, who was working on an analog computer that used trains of gear wheels to perform

repeated additions. Babbage saw the value of Jacquard's idea of using punched cards to input data and developed a machine he called the Difference Engine. A remarkable Englishwoman, Ada, Countess of Lovelace, the daughter of the poet Byron, wrote the program for this machine and was thus the first person to write a program for a general-purpose computer. Her name is remembered in the programming language ADA.

Babbage was too far ahead of his time and never saw his machine in action. After many years of labor, the project was abandoned and most of the 12,000 parts were melted down for scrap. But in 1991, he was proved to have been working along the right lines. His machine was built in the London Science Museum and worked perfectly, doing exactly what he had intended.

The punched card idea still had some potential and was taken up by the American inventor Herman Hollerith. Hollerith developed a range of electromechanical machines using packs of standard cards, each with one corner cut off to ensure proper orientation and printed with 80 columns of 12 rows of small boxes. Each of these 960 boxes represented a unit of information and could be punched with a hole or left unpunched. As the cards moved rapidly through the machines, they were read by spring-loaded needles that passed through the holes to make electrical contacts. This new and important way of storing and reading large quantities of data, was quickly taken up by the International Business Machines (IBM) company and other companies. For more than 50 years, until around 1960, these noisy punched-card machines provided governments

▲ The personal computer is increasingly found in homes as a tool for information and recreational activities. Access to the Internet has opened up a wealth of information sources, and sophisticated graphics and video capabilities have led to the rise in interactive game playing and educational programs.

and large-scale businesses with information storage and processing.

In the meantime, new ideas had emerged that would eventually make possible the modern digital computer. By the end of the 19th century, it had become apparent from the work of the British mathematician George Boole that it was possible to represent any number using only the numbers 1 and 0. The use of these numbers to perform arithmetical functions is called binary arithmetic. It was then appreciated that any device that could exist in two states, such as "on" and "off," could represent and store the two numbers. Several such devices could be combined to perform functions such as addition and subtraction.

Prior to the development of the transistor, all electronics required vacuum tubes, and these were used almost exclusively as amplifying devices for radio and audio purposes. Vacuum tubes could also be switched very rapidly from a conducting state (on) to a nonconducting state (off), and in 1942, the U.S. physicist John Atanasoff produced a calculating device using vacuum tubes. Four years later, the U.S. engineers J. Presper Eckert and John Maunchly switched on a remarkable machine weighing several tons and containing 18,000 vacuum tubes. This was the general-purpose computer Electronic Numerical Integrator and Calculator (ENIAC), and it could perform 5,000 calculations a second.

ENIAC could be programmed only by changing the internal connections, and the U.S. mathematician John von Neumann pointed out that the set of instructions (the program) could be entered into the machine in exactly the same form as the numerical data. Eckert and Maunchly saw the advantages of this way of programming and built the first commercial electronic digital computer using stored programs, a machine known as UNIVAC (the universal automatic calculator).

The breakthrough that was to lead to a computer in almost every home was the invention of the transistor in 1947. Vacuum tubes were bulky, fragile, ran very hot, and consumed large quantities of electricity. Transistors require tiny currents and simple power supplies, are highly reliable, and can be switched very rapidly from on to off, so they were ideal for the purpose. One of the earliest computers using transistors was designed by Seymour Cray who later built the first supercomputer. Progress was rapid and machines were designed using plug-in printed circuit boards with many transistors and miniaturized versions of the other necessary components. These boards could be changed quickly for repair if faults developed. The second generation of computers had arrived.

▲ An early test for the UNIVAC computer was to compile an index for the Bible, a long and complicated task that required a great deal of careful programming. Today, publishers can code text as it is typed in using specialist mark-up languages. From this code, they can generate an index for a short book in a matter of seconds.

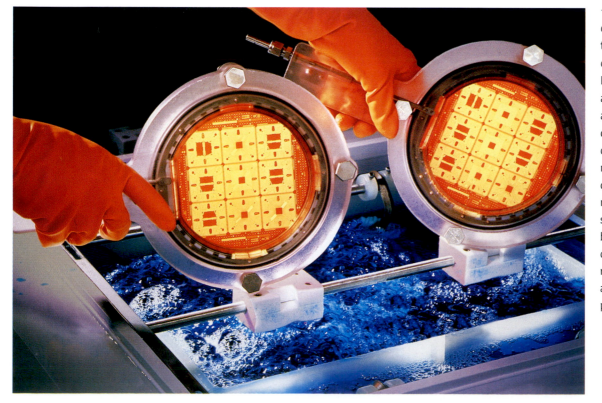

◄ Computers are set to get cheaper and faster with the development of IBM's copper chip technology. Existing chips use aluminum, which is cheap and a good electrical conductor, but copper carries electrical signals more quickly. A single chip can incorporate a quarter mile of copper wiring and speed up a microprocessor by 40 percent. Use of these chips will make a whole range of equipment, such as cameras and mobile phones, smaller and faster.

The rise of the integrated circuit

When it became clear that very large numbers of transistors would be required for each computer, the idea arose of combining several connected transistors and encapsulating them into a single device. This idea was rapidly developed and led to integrated electronic circuits in which many transistors were combined with resistors and capacitors and their associated connections on a single silicon chip. Although many such chips were necessary, the advance made for a remarkable increase in compactness and introduced the third generation of computers. The most notable of these were the IBM System 360 computers, introduced in 1964, which put IBM in the forefront of computer production worldwide.

Chip development proceeded rapidly as ever larger numbers of transistors were incorporated into integrated circuits (ICs). Plug-in boards were still necessary, but these now featured rows of integrated circuits, usually sealed into small blocks of black plastic. The earlier ICs were now described as "small-scale integration." Medium-scale integration, with as many as 1,000 components per chip, followed and was succeeded by large-scale integration (LSI), with up to 10,000 components, very-large-scale integration (VLSI), and ultra-large-scale integration (ULSI), with over a million components.

A machine, known as a minicomputer, that was smaller than the large mainframe machines and that was of such a size as to be suitable for business and administrative purposes appeared in 1965. When large-scale integration advanced, in the mid-1970s, to the point at which a complete microprocessor could be accommodated on a single chip, the fourth-generation computer, or microcomputer—later to be known as the personal computer (PC)—was born.

In the earliest personal computers, the operating system, typically the Microsoft disk-operating system (MS-DOS), required that instructions—such as those to load or open programs—should be typed in at a prompt on the screen, known as a command line. This task had to be done exactly, and this necessity was daunting to many non-technical people and delayed the expansion of PC use. Operating systems were therefore developed, principally by Apple and later Microsoft, that featured screen displays containing small symbols, or icons, which could be used to open programs and effect other functions by pointing and clicking with a movable device called a mouse.

The most successful of these graphical user interfaces (GUIs) was the version 3.1 of the Microsoft Windows operating system, which also introduced other important elements, such as the

▲ Supercomputers like this Cray TE 3 use thousands of microchips to parallel-process millions of pieces of information simultaneously. This model has been installed at the U.K. Meteorological Office, which receives data on weather conditions all around the world, and displays the results in graphical forms that can be used to predict global weather patterns up to five days ahead.

ability to run several different programs simultaneously (multitasking). The graphical user interface was the turning point that converted a rather specialized activity into one accessible to almost anybody, and it led to an enormous expansion in personal computer use. With each upgrade in operating system, the scope of the machine has been enlarged and the relationship between the user and the machine facilitated. Multimedia computing with music, synthesized speech, animated displays, modem communication, electronic mail, and quick access to the Internet have been developed and are now commonplace.

Television viewing in a window, teleconferencing using miniature TV cameras, speech-recognition systems, and a very large number of programs performing a wide range of functions are currently features of personal computing, both for private and business purposes. Personal computers are now so powerful that the average desktop machine can perform almost all of the functions that 20 years ago would have required a mainframe computer.

Types of computer

The remarkable speed of development of the personal computer has made any system of classification of computers difficult. Traditionally, computers have been graded by physical size, cost, processing speed, and word size into supercomputers, mainframe machines, minicomputers, and microcomputers. They have also been classified by the number of users that can simultaneously access them. But comparisons are confusing because today's micro can, in almost every respect, outperform yesterday's mini; today's mini can outperform yesterday's mainframe, and so on. In addition, every class of computer from the PC upward can be arranged to be accessed by a number of individuals. These categories, however, remain convenient as indications of relative power and of relative physical size and cost.

The supercomputers of today are large machines with facilities that make them appropriate for handling very big problems. They are accessible by hundreds or thousands of operators using remote terminals. They are found most commonly in scientific and technological research; major industrial and manufacturing enterprises such as the automotive, aerospace, chemical, and electronic industries; large governmental and administrative organizations; weather forecasting bureaus; very large database applications; and any application involving modeling of phenomena with very large numbers of variable factors.

Supercomputers may be regarded as combinations of large numbers of smaller machines, all working together. This parallel processing may involve many hundreds of microprocessors that share the work between them. One of the largest current machines, produced by the Thinking Machines Corporation, uses 64,000 processors and has a price tag of $5 million. Supercomputers are also made by firms such as the Cray Research Company, Silicon Graphics, IBM, Fujitsu, and Intel. Parallel processing on this scale involves very elaborate programs to keep everything in order.

▼ Almost every office now uses computers to process the vast amount of information and records an average business generates. Computers can be linked using networks, allowing users to access centrally held files and send documents to other workers electronically.

Mainframe computers are smaller, slower, and cheaper than supercomputers but are still capable of being accessed simultaneously by hundreds of users. They will usually have up to eight parallel-operating processors and are commonly divided into subunits with different functions. The growth of enormous databases of information has somewhat revived the fortunes of the mainframe computer, many of which are now being designed as servers for Internet databases. If an Internet service provider (ISP) offers every customer ten megabytes of storage space, a lot of computing power is needed, and this is ideally provided by mainframe machines designed for this purpose.

Minicomputers, which are intermediate in size, power, speed, and capacity between mainframes and microcomputers, have served many useful purposes since the late 1960s, when they were introduced. They have been used, typically, in medium-to-large business and industrial organizations, hospitals, warehouses, local administration, police departments, and other venues where up to 200 operators require access. Many functions once served by minicomputers are now easily handled by microcomputers.

Personal computers

By far the greatest number of computers in the world today are microcomputers, usually known as personal computers. Today these are numbered in the hundreds of millions. Desktop microcomputers for business purposes are often subclassified as workstations. These are personal computers of more than average power and often use microprocessors that differ from those in regular PCs. Many workstations use reduced-instruction-set computer (RISC) processors. These are less versatile but significantly faster than the microprocessors in common PCs.

For business purposes, microcomputers are commonly joined by cables forming a local area network (LAN). In this case, one machine with a large storage capacity is nominated as the server, to which all the other machines, known as the clients, are connected. The server will often contain the main database storage of information required by the clients.

Laptop and palmtop computers are essentially the same as desktop machines but use liquid-crystal flat-screen displays and a high degree of compactness in the fitting together of the various components. This packing density makes for higher manufacturing and retail costs. Even smaller pocket machines, such as the Psion or Palm organizers or the computing facilities now available in mobile telephones, necessarily limit the scope of the machine.

Anatomy of the personal computer

The hardware of the personal desktop computer varies slightly from model to model, usually depending on the cost, but there is a basic minimum structure without which the machine would be of little use. A computer requires an input device that allows the entering of instructions, or data, or other information, such as text. There are several input devices, but the most obvious is the keyboard. This usually has a standard alphabet key layout, known for obvious reasons as qwerty, but occasionally arranged in other ways. The Dvorak keyboard is more efficiently laid out but is fighting long tradition and is not widely used. In addition to the alphabet and the numerals, keyboards have keys that perform particular tasks, either alone or in combination with other keys.

Another input device is the microphone, used with a special, highly advanced program that converts speech into numeric code that the computer can use. Both the keyboards and the microphone usually provide visual confirmation on the monitor screen of what has been entered. Typed text or numbers appear as such on the screen, and spoken words appear as text. A scanner is a peripheral input device that converts images into code. If text is scanned, it will appear on the screen, but such text is not immediately editable because it is not in the form in which a number exists for each individual letter. It is known as a bit-mapped image of text. Such an image can, however, be converted to editable text by an optical character recognition (OCR) program.

The mouse is also an input device that conveys information to the computer. Movement of the mouse on a surface sends signals to the machine that cause a cursor (indicating the typing point) or an arrow or other pointer to move over the screen. If the cursor or pointer is positioned over one of various screen icons, the clicking of one of the switches will bring into action one of a wide range of functions. Clicking the right-hand button will often cause a menu of functions to appear from which a selection can be made. Tracker balls serve the same function as the mouse.

The floppy disk drive, usually known as the A-drive, is both an input and an output device. The original floppy disks were larger and were enclosed in a floppy flexible case, hence the name. Present-day disks have a more rigid case. The floppy disk drive is used to input programs, data, and text, but it is also used to make copies of stored material for backup and distribution purposes. The CD-ROM (compact disc read-only memory) or DVD (digital versatile disc) drives are input devices, widely used for the commercial distribution of large programs or collections of

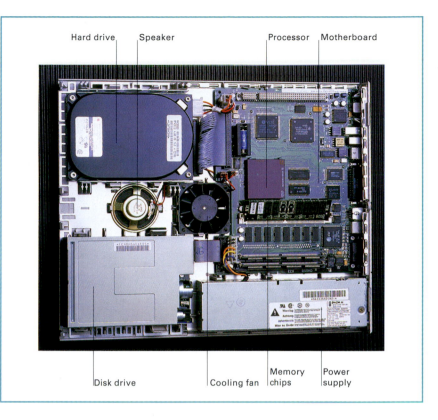

All personal computers are very similar inside and consist of a number of standard components. The hard disk drive is where most of the program and data files are stored permanently. The disk drive, which can take floppy disks, CDs, or DVDs, allows users to install new programs or information from another computer and output data for storage. The central processing unit is the brain of the computer and carries out all the computing tasks. It sits on the motherboard, which is covered in electrical circuits that connect it to other specialized chips that carry out specific functions. A number of expansion slots are included so that the user can customize the computer by adding extra graphics or sound cards or extend its memory capacity to run bigger programs.

programs, reference works, encyclopedias, and so on. Recordable CD drives are also output devices. Various supplementary external disk drives, such as the Iomega Zip drives, function as both input and output devices.

Other computer input devices include bar code readers; joysticks (used mainly for games); touch-sensitive screens that respond differently to touch at different points; digitizing tablets that allow drawings to be directly entered; and pen-based devices that allow normal writing to convey information to the computer.

Output devices

The most obvious output device is the monitor, sometimes called a visual display unit (VDU). It may be a cathode-ray tube of the type used in television receivers or a flat panel display using liquid crystal or other systems. Color monitors are now standard. Monitors are driven by graphics cards (video cards or adapters) that plug into slots in the main computer board (the motherboard) and, like other cards, offer an external connection for the cable behind the machine. In some cases, as in many of the Apple PCs, the monitor is integral with the rest of the machine so that no external cable connection is necessary. Graphics cards convert computer code for images and text into a form that the monitor can display. They will usually incorporate memory allowing rapid change of image on the monitor.

Whatever is displayed on the monitor can immediately be sent to another important output when it is first switched on and before any other programs are loaded. This is a nonaccess, read-only memory (ROM), and its contents are retained when the machine is turned off.

The motherboard also has special multiconnection slots for the random-access memory (RAM), which is contained on small memory boards that are inserted into the slots. It is thus possible to change the size of the RAM. Currently, for most purposes, a RAM of about 128 megabytes is adequate. Many PCs, however, have 256 or 512 megabytes of RAM. During machine operation, the random-access memory temporarily stores programs that are in use and data that are being input. RAM functions only when provided with a power supply. It is a volatile memory, and if the machine is switched off without first storing the content of RAM in the hard drive or elsewhere, it will all be permanently lost, thus frequent backing up is mandatory.

The hard disk drive, commonly designated the C-drive, is the principal storage device of the machine. It is used to store a range of programs and other material along with work in progress. Programs are copied to the hard drive from CD-ROMS (usually the D-drive) or floppy disks, and any data from the keyboard or elsewhere can also be permanently stored there. Information stored on the hard drive can also be instantly removed (deleted, or erased).

Hard drives consist of stacks of circular plates coated with an iron compound that can be magnetized. The plates are on a common spindle and rotate at speeds up to 10,000 revolutions per minute. Read/write heads lie just above the surface of each plate and can be moved, on an arc, from edge to near-center so as to scan the whole working surface. Pulsed currents passed to the heads produce tiny spots of magnetization on the surface, and they can later be read by the head. Some drives use separate write and read heads.

The capacity of hard drives has risen impressively in recent years. One megabyte is the amount of storage required for the text of a long book without any text compression. Most books require less than a megabyte. War and Peace can be stored in 4.4 megabytes; the whole of the Bible in 10.7 megabytes. In 1980, a hard drive might have had a capacity of 5 megabytes and cost $500. Today a typical hard drive has a capacity of 100,000 megabytes (100 gigabytes) and costs about $300. Multiple hard drives, each of this capacity, may be fitted and will be designated E, F, G, and so on.

device, the printer. Earlier printers were noisy and operated on the line-printer, dot-matrix, or daisy-wheel principle, but these are now all obsolete. They have been replaced by laser printers and ink-jet printers. Mass demand and mass production have resulted in sharp reductions in price. Most laser printers are still monochrome, and color laser printers remain expensive. Plotters are large-area printers used to draw architectural and other design plans.

Inside a computer

The remainder of the hardware is usually hidden within the case of the computer. The microelectronic components are accommodated on a large printed circuit board called the motherboard. This carries the microprocessor, also known as the central processing unit (CPU), which is the heart of the machine. The CPU has three main parts: an arithmetic and logic unit (ALU) that performs all the logic and calculations, a control unit that reads and carries out the program instructions, and an immediate access memory that holds data and current instructions. The motherboard carries expansion slots for additional plug-in cards such as modems, sound cards, and special graphics cards. It also carries some memory chips containing a start-up program that energizes the computer, telling it what to do

▲ Laptop computers are now an essential part of business life, providing employees with the ability to carry work around with them and to be able to connect with the office from anywhere in the world. Key to this rise in portability was the development of flat-screen technology, long-life batteries, and miniaturization of components, enabling manufacturers to build compact yet powerful machines.

In one rear corner of the computer case is a large metal box, the power supply unit (PSU). This is enclosed because electricity supplies at full power-line voltage enter it from behind. The PSU contains a transformer that changes the supply voltage to 12 volts for the drive motors and 5 or 3 volts for the electronics. All cables emerging from the power supply within the machine carry current at these low voltages and are safe.

How a computer works

Soldered to the motherboard is a tiny can containing a quartz crystal. This crystal is part of a small electronic circuit that generates a rapid stream of square-wave electrical pulses that pass right around the motherboard, keeping all its functions in step with each other. The number of pulses per second, known as the clock speed, determines the speed of the machine. The earliest PCs ran at 4.77 million pulses per second (4.77 MHz). The fastest machines that became available at the beginning of the 21st century have a clock speed of 1,000 MHz.

Information entered into a personal computer is coded as numbers using a code known as the American Standard Code for Information Interchange (ASCII). Like other computer codes, this is a binary code using only 1 and 0. The ASCII code contains numbers corresponding to all the letters of the alphabet as well as numbers, blank spaces, and punctuation marks. The code also contains some commands.

A binary digit (1 or 0) is called a bit. For each letter or number in the code, there is a binary number consisting of eight bits called a byte. So when the key for letter A is pressed, the machine generates the binary code 01000001. All the ASCII symbols, including some that are not on the keyboard, are the only common language shared by different makes of computer.

Sequences of binary numbers from the keyboard, or from a program or data store, are moved around the PC at clock speed. These sequences are stored in RAM until needed, taken from RAM to the CPU, manipulated in accordance with the instructions of the program, returned to RAM, retained or deleted as required, and if instructed, copied from there to the hard disk or floppy for permanent storage. Movement of these numbers is effected along parallel narrow conducting strips of copper on the printed circuit. Each set of such parallel strips is called a bus. Typically, there are three internal buses: a data bus connecting the CPU to the RAM and the various components of the computer including the expansion slots; an address bus, which selects the route for data to follow between the CPU and the

millions of addresses in the memory; and a control bus, which determines whether data is taken from or sent to the data bus. The buses on the motherboard have to be linked to the drives. Linking is done by flat, flexible, cables with 40 or 34 parallel insulated conductors.

The word length of a computer is the number of bits that are handled at one time. An 8-bit computer has words 1 byte long, and the data bus will have 8 parallel copper strips. A 16-bit computer has 16 lines in its buses and words two bytes wide. Some PCs have 32-bit buses, and a larger machine may have 64-bit words. The speed of the machine is greatly affected by the word length.

Programming

The term *software* can be used either as a noun or as an adjective. Software is the intangible but essential part of a computer system including the programs and the data. Originally, it was applied only to the contents of the programs or the data, but software has been extended to include the physical media on which programs and data are recorded and distributed. The term is also used for the stream of electrical pulses, coded as programs and data, that passes around the computer or along any digital channel of communication. Without software, a computer is useless, and the purpose of programming is to produce software that, when executed by a computer, will carry out a useful function.

▼ Who says robots have no feelings? Kismet is a special robot that has been programmed to respond to actions by changing its facial expression. Developed for the study of action recognition and learning, Kismet displays several "moods" in response to visual stimulation, such as waving hands or moving toys. When there are no stimuli, it has a sad face. During play, Kismet looks calm and happy. Over-stimulation causes distress, in a similar manner to a baby. Surprise, as shown here, results in Kismet lifting its eyebrows and ears, widening its eyes, and opening its mouth.

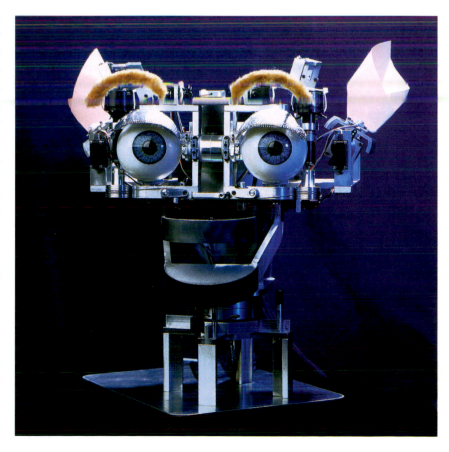

Programmers may write complete operating systems such as MS-DOS, Unix, Linux, Windows NT, and Windows 2000—which make the running of other programs easy—or they may write application programs for purposes such as word processing, accounting, database management, design, page layout, desktop publishing, and so on. Many thousands of application programs have been written.

Computer central processing units (CPUs) can operate only on binary numbers, and the instructions they respond to must also be binary numbers. The number of instructions a CPU can obey is limited and is called the instruction set. The set includes instructions such as add two numbers together; check which of two numbers is larger; check whether two numbers are equal or not; and take a number from a particular memory address and put it somewhere else. So programs have to be organized in such a way that they only call for instructions that are in the instruction set of the CPU for which the program is being written. Each instruction is a string of numbers.

Computer languages

Programmers always write programs on computers using an editor like a simple word processor. In theory, a programmer might simply write a very long string of binary numbers and save these as a file. This "writing machine code" would be impossibly tedious and time-consuming. If each instruction is given a unique short name, this name can call up the instruction just as a file name can call up a file. The set of names for the whole instruction set for a particular chip is

▼ Personal organizers, such as this Psion model, are highly sophisticated and can offer many of the functions of personal computers. Most can run word processing, spreadsheet, and database programs and can offer Internet access via a mobile phone. They can also hook up to office or home computers to download or print information.

called an assembly language, and the program that converts assembly language to machine code is known as an assembler program.

Early programmers found they were writing the same sequences of instructions over and over again. This repetition was wasteful, so they saved these sequences as short, named files so that they could be recalled again and again when required. By proceeding in this way, programmers were able to build up increasingly higher-level programming languages, which greatly simplified their task. Most programs for PCs are now written in languages such as C++ or Java.

Writing Windows programs is greatly facilitated by the use of programs called development tools, which run under Windows. The familiar shrinkable windows and their iconic control contents, menus, and so on can be produced in minutes with no more trouble than dragging objects from a palette onto a form and then modifying their properties by attaching the appropriate code in a high-level language such as C++ or Java.

Programs written in a high-level language must be translated into the appropriate sequence of machine code instructions before the machine can use them. This translation is done by a program called a compiler, the output of which is an executable program. Compilers stop when they encounter a syntax error and usually indicate the nature of the error. New programs almost always also contain logic errors. Eliminating errors is called debugging and may take longer than writing the program. Large new programs are sent out to hundreds or thousands of "beta testers" who try to find bugs.

Computer security

Information is valuable. Often its value depends on limiting or denying other people's access to it. Information is also often personal and private to the individual concerned, and privacy must be respected and protected. So computer security can mean all the measures taken to ensure that information stored in a computer cannot be read or copied by any unauthorized person. Computer security has another meaning. Because nearly all machine are now linked to all other machines by the World Wide Web, there is a constant possibility that any machine that opens such a link may be vulnerable to damage by short destructive programs known as viruses released into the Internet and spread by e-mail.

Information security is maintained by limiting access to stored data by means of unique passwords; by limiting access to sensitive machines by requiring personnel to wear active badges that emit radio or infrared signals; and by physically securing computer equipment so that it cannot be used or removed. Passwords, if well-chosen and unidentifiable as related to the individual, are of value within an organization but must be more carefully selected if access is possible via a network. Programs can quickly run through lists of every known word, including names, until the right one is found, so systems should arrange that after three or four attempts all further access is denied. Arbitrary sequences of alphanumeric characters can also be used as passwords.

The avoidance of viruses calls for strict computer discipline. Viruses are often carried on floppy disks containing games and other unauthorized software. These should never be used. Internet access by business machines can be prohibited except for electronic mail. No e-mail message should ever be opened unless the recipient is sure of the source. A good policy is immediately to delete any e-mail message of uncertain provenance without looking at it. Unsolicited offers or advertisements (spam) should be deleted at once.

Backing up important files is an essential element in avoiding loss. It must be done systematically and will usually involve a rotating sequence of sequential copies on disk, tape, or other storage medium.

The future of computing

Extrapolation from the present rate of development suggests that the desktop microcomputer of 2010 will have the power of current supercomputers. Equipment will continue to become smaller, more portable, and more indispensable so that the term *personal computer* will acquire a whole new meaning. Verbal, textual, visual, and voice communication from any site between any two people in the developed world will become commonplace.

The principal software development is likely to be in the realm of artificial intelligence (AI) and robotics. The computer has already far outdistanced the human being in its power to provide accurate information; artificial intelligence will ensure that knowledge is constantly updated and refined by experience. Unless the propagation of scientific advance is blocked by commercial motives, scientific and technological developments of all kinds will be accelerated by AI. Medical diagnosis and prescription of best treat-

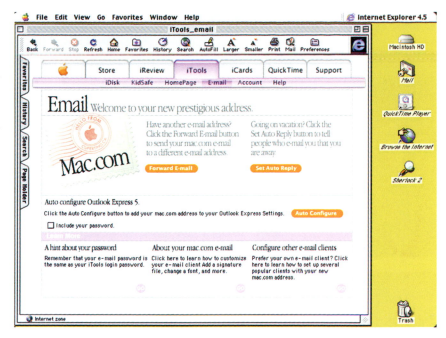

▲ Apple computers were the first to use a graphical user interface (GUI) as a means of instructing the machine to perform tasks. The idea made Apple computers very popular, particularly in the design and publishing fields, as it meant that users could simply point and click to achieve the effect they wanted, without having to write complicated command instructions.

▶ This PC is small and light enough to be used anywhere. The head-mounted display enables the computer to be carried around without any need for a screen, and is activated by a handheld device instead of a mouse.

ment may one day be better provided by AI systems on computers than by individual doctors.

The question remains whether the future of computing will make any significant contribution to human wisdom. This is a serious question that, in a context of rapid development of artificial intelligence and instant access to virtually the whole spectrum of human knowledge, will have to be addressed. The exercise of such immense power without the insertion of a controlling ethical dimension into the equation will be very dangerous. The philosophers and the computer scientists must get together before it is too late.

SEE ALSO: ARTIFICIAL INTELLIGENCE • BINARY SYSTEM • COMPUTER GRAPHICS • COMPUTER NETWORK • COMPUTER PRINTER • DATA STORAGE • INTEGRATED CIRCUIT • INTERNET • MODEM AND ISDN • MOUSE AND POINTING DEVICE • MULTIMEDIA • VIRTUAL REALITY • WORD PROCESSOR

Computer Graphics

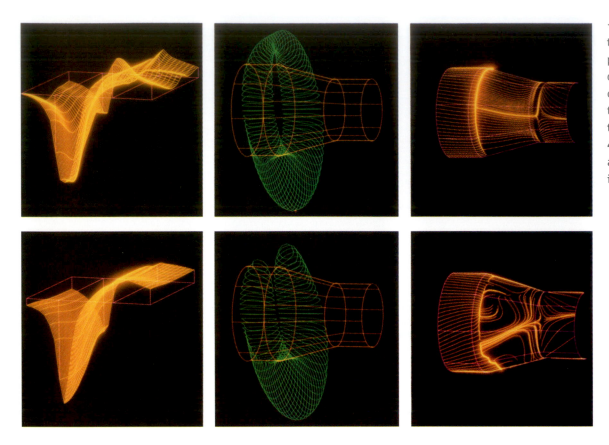

◀ These graphics portray the flow of air around a part of a missile. The flow details are calculated by computer simulation. In the upper set of images, the missile is flying at 4 degrees to its central axis; in the lower set it is flying at 12 degrees.

Computer graphics are the public face of high technology. They are familiar from the screens of home computers, from arcade games, and from a growing number of blockbuster films. Printed computer graphics appear in newspapers and magazines and on advertising billboards. Engineers use computer-aided design (CAD) to create virtual models of new objects, and these designs can be used to create instructions for machines that produce real objects in a technique called computer-aided manufacture, or CAM.

The most usual medium for computer graphics is the high-resolution monitor, in which hundreds of thousands of pinpoints of light make the image visible on screens. One type of monitor is based on the cathode-ray tube, or CRT. In such a monitor, beams of electrons strike dots of phosphor compounds on the reverse of the screen, causing them to glow. The other main type of monitor is the liquid-crystal display, or LCD. In an LCD, the alignment of liquid crystals in cells between two light-polarizing filters determines whether or not light can pass through each minute cell. The pattern of opaque and transparent cells forms the image on the screen.

Virtual-reality goggles have a separate screen for each eye. The images in the screens are "viewed" from slightly different angles, as happens when a person looks at a solid object.

As well as being viewed on monitors, computer graphics can be printed onto paper or onto transparencies that can then be projected so that they can be seen by large audiences.

Raster graphics

Raster scanning is used to display computer graphics on monitors. It can be likened to weaving: when weaving a rug, for example, the pattern in the rug is built up from many strands aligned in one direction. Individual lines are divided into segments of color, and patterns are created by coordinating the segments of color in each line.

In a color CRT monitor, the weave is created by electron beams that scan along lines of phosphors on the screen. Working from the top of the screen to the bottom many times per second, separate beams zigzag across three sets of phosphors—red, green, and blue. The intensities of the beams vary according to the variations in each color along each line of the raster pattern.

The phosphors or liquid-crystal cells are grouped in sets of three—one for each color. Each of these groups is a pixel, or picture element. The pixels of a screen are the smallest units that can produce the full range of colors available to the monitor. A standard type of monitor, called a super video graphics array (SVGA), has almost 800,000 pixels in 768 rows that have 1,024 pixels each.

Monochrome displays

At one time, a monochrome display was the only means of viewing information from a computer without having to resort to printing. Owing to advances in technology, high-resolution full-color monitors are now the standard for all but a few applications, such as the displays of mobile telephones. Nevertheless, an understanding of monochrome screens helps in the explanation of more sophisticated color monitors.

In the most basic type of monochrome screen, each picture cell has one of two possible conditions: on or off. In the "on" condition, the pixel might glow white, green, or orange, or it might be dark gray for an LCD screen; in the "off" condition, the pixel would be black for a CRT screen or light gray for an LCD monitor. Note that a basic monochrome screen is capable of producing only full-contrast images with no shades between the "on" and "off" colors.

The on and off conditions translate as 1 and 0 values of a binary digit, or bit, of computer information. Hence a basic monochrome monitor that has 200 rows of 320 pixels requires 200 x 320 = 64,000 bits or 8,000 bytes of memory to describe an image (1 byte = 8 bits).

Gray scale

Gray-scale imaging introduces the possibility of shading by allowing each pixel to have a number of intensity values between "on" and "off." In a simple gray-scale image, each pixel may have intensity values from 0 to 7, which translates to a range of 000 to 111 in binary code. Hence, three bits are needed to describe each pixel in a gray-scale image, compared with one bit per pixel for a basic monochrome display, so this type of image is said to have three bit planes.

If the number of bit planes is increased to eight—corresponding to 256 possible levels of gray per pixel—it is almost impossible to differentiate computer graphics from a photograph. However, the memory required to store such an image with 200 rows of 320 pixels is a little less than 64 kilobytes: eight times the requirement for a basic monochrome image of those dimensions.

Color displays

Color images are created in a similar way to gray-scale images. However, the three colors of each pixel have separate information bits that define their intensities. A color image might have eight bit planes divided between the three colors, giving a capability of 256 colors. Red and green intensities are defined by three bit planes each; blue can be defined by only two, since the human eye is less sensitive to variations in blue.

A more complete range of colors can be achieved in the 24-bit color system, in which each of the three colors has eight bits, or one byte, of definition per pixel. This type of image is called a bitmap. Bitmaps have 256 levels of intensity for each shade, giving a total of $(256)^3 = 16,777,216$ colors. The disadvantage of bitmaps is the amount of memory they use: a 640 x 480 pixel image—a standard monitor desktop size—requires 900 kilobytes (921,600 bytes) of memory.

Color mapping and compression

Since computer memory is an expensive commodity, it is desirable to use techniques that reduce the sizes of image files without reducing the perceived quality of their images. Such techniques include color mapping and compression, and they have the added advantage of reducing the time taken to transfer images through network connections, such as links to the Internet.

While the human eye can discern far more than the 256 variations in shade of the eight-bit color system, any given image is unlikely to require more than 256 of the 16 million or so shades in the 24-bit color system. In color mapping, each image has a palette of 256 colors selected from the full range of the 24-bit system and stored with the image. Each pixel in the image then has an eight-bit description that identifies one of the shades in the palette.

In a technique called dithering, the number of colors in an image palette is reduced by allowing combinations of colors in adjacent pixels to

▼ Creative artwork can be created from ready images, called clip art. In this design, a simplified image of a human head has been colored, copied, and pasted many times over in a regular pattern.

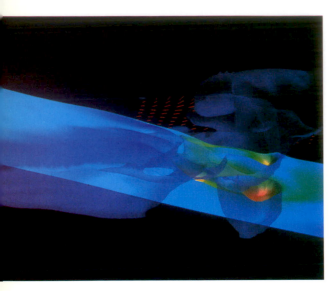

◀ A virtual reality simulation of a thunderstorm. This image combines data on cloud water density (shown as a translucent blue surface), wind direction, and magnitude (shown as red arrows of varying lengths and directions). Generating images of weather processes requires highly sophisticated graphics programs and a great deal of computer processing power.

five-second clip would require 0.9 x 60 x 5 = 270 megabytes of information—clearly a huge demand on memory resources.

In the Moving Picture Experts Group (MPEG) format, the memory requirement is reduced by letting the processor do more work. Relatively few frames are used as the basis for an MPEG image: the software identifies common elements in subsequent frames, and the processor creates intermediate frames by a process called interpolation. The intermediate frames create the impression of smooth motion. They exist only in a temporary memory and must be created each time an MPEG movie is played on screen.

replace pure colors. This technique depends on the eye not seeing the individual colors of pixels but perceiving them as a different color.

The JPEG (Joint Photographic Experts Group) compression technique eliminates subtle gradations of color and shade that are not discernable to the human eye. The resulting file size for a 640 x 480 pixel image is around 140 kilobytes—around one-seventh the size of an equivalent bitmap image. JPEG is mainly used to compress photographic images.

In the graphics image format, or GIF, files are compressed by grouping together large areas of pixels that all have the same color. For this reason, GIF compression is mainly used for icons and other simple computer-generated images that include large blocks of single colors.

Color-register encoding

Color-register encoding is a variation on color mapping. It allows images to be edited by color, so all the blue regions of a photographic image can be changed to orange by changing the blue shades of the color palette to orange.

Photographic editing software, such as Adobe's Photoshop, enable an operator to select a region of pixels whose colors fall within a certain range. Once selected, a region can be cut from an image or modified by changing its color or texture or by replacing it with a predefined pattern.

Moving pictures

There is no fundamental difference between the ways that still and moving images are displayed on a monitor—the image on screen is in any case refreshed between 50 and 60 times per second. In the case of a moving image, however, the image gradually changes from one frame to the next. If a 640 x 480 pixel moving image were to be created by showing 60 different bitmaps per second, a

Hardware requirements

The core components of any computer are the central processing unit (CPU), a read-write memory (random-access memory, or RAM), a read-only memory (ROM), internal storage devices, and an input-output section (I/O) that allows the computer to communicate with external devices, such as keyboards, printers, scanners, and digital cameras and video recorders.

The information for a graphics image is held in read-write memory that may be part of the computer's RAM. In general, however, the graphics memory forms part of a dedicated graphics card, so the general RAM does not become overburdened by the demands of graphics processing. The image that should be displayed on screen at any one time is held in the screen memory, and the size of this memory is related to the number of pixels and the color quality of an image. Computers that are designed for multimedia applications generally have some form of accelerated graphics port, or AGP, which provides a fast link between the graphics card and the computer's

▶ Computers can generate space-filling models of molecules using atomic radii and coordinates for the atoms in a given molecule. The resulting image can be viewed using goggles that create the impression of a three-dimensional object by showing projections from two slightly different angles. These models help molecular biologists to design drugs, since the shape of a molecule has a strong influence on its pharmacological activity.

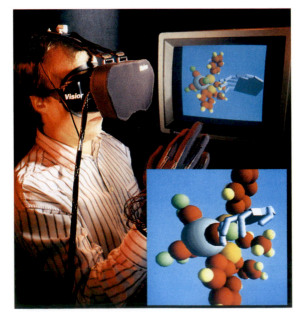

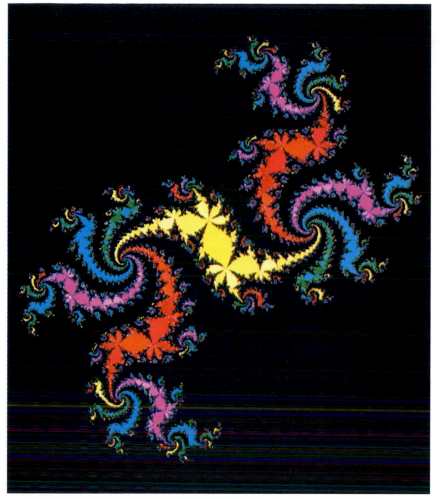

light is then detected and converted into digital signals that correspond to variations in color and shade along lines that cross the image.

The resolution of a scanned image depends on the number of times the detector head scans the image per unit length. Low-resolution scans are a fast means of producing rough images that can be used in formulating the page layout of a magazine, for example. High-resolution scans take longer, but they provide top-quality images for publishing that are faithful to the original copy when viewed close up. The level of resolution has a direct bearing on the size of the image file.

Manipulating graphics

The main purpose of a computer keyboard is for the entry of text, but keyboards are of limited use for manipulating and creating graphics on screen.

The most widely used device for manipulating graphics is the mouse. At the heart of a mouse is a trackball that rolls as the mouse moves over a mouse pad or desktop. Two sets of rollers, set at 90 degrees to one another and in contact with the roller, detect the motion of the trackball. The computer translates the motion of the rollers into the motion of a cursor—a position marker on the screen. Up to three buttons allow the operator to give instructions that relate to images under the cursor, so he or she can "press" an onscreen button by positioning the cursor over the button and clicking one of the buttons on the mouse.

Portable computers generally have a trackball or a trackpad instead of a mouse. A trackball rolls in a cradle of rollers in the computer casing, and the motion of the ball causes the cursor to move. A trackpad is a flat pad that detects the motion of an operator's finger over its surface; the cursor then mimics the motion of the finger.

A graphics tablet is a flat surface on which a designer can "draw" images using a stylus or pointer. A mark appears on screen in a position that corresponds to the position of the stylus on the tablet. Graphics tablets are sufficiently sensitive to allow freehand onscreen drawing with an accuracy that would be near impossible using a mouse, trackball, or trackpad.

Light pens can be used to point directly at onscreen objects on a CRT. A lens and photocell in the pen detect when the electron beam hits the pixel under the pen; the photocell produces a pulse of current that passes down a wire connected to the computer. The software then identifies the targeted pixel by the timing of the pulse.

Joysticks are mainly used for steering onscreen objects in computer games. A joystick consists of a hand-sized pivoting upright shaft with a thumb-operated "trigger" button at the top.

main memory. This link gives the graphics card access to sufficient memory to store the large numbers of images generated in a movie.

A computer's video I/O section includes scanning circuits, or multiplexers, that feed information to the monitor. They look through screen memory at a speed synchronized with the raster scanning and count through the memory addresses, reading each one in turn. For a CRT monitor, the stream of digital information from the multiplexers passes through digital–analog converters—one for each color—that feed control signals to the three electron guns.

A similar scanning procedure feeds picture information to a printers when a hard copy of an image is required. In this case, however, the final image is composed of black, cyan, magenta, and yellow dots whose areas vary with color intensity.

Importing graphics

Image files can be imported from a number of sources, such as CD-ROMs, the Internet, and the memories of digital cameras and camcorders. Digital versions of hard-copy images, such as printed photographs, can be obtained by use of devices called scanners. A scanner has a light source that moves across an image. The reflected

▲ This design is an example of a fractal—a geometric form made up of elements that have the same geometry but different sizes. Fractals have an unusual property —if a small part of the design is magnified, it resembles the larger design.

Three-dimensional images

While television screens and movie screens are essentially flat surfaces, television and film images can create the impression of three dimensions for a viewer. The challenge for computer-graphics designers is to create the same impression using computer-generated images. Designers use a number of visual effects to trick the brain into seeing a third dimension—depth—that does not exist in the computer screen.

In general, the first step in creating a three-dimensional image is a wireframe—a set of linked points with relative coordinates in virtual three-dimensional space. The distances between these points diminish as the supposed distance from the screen increases. This gives the illusion of single-point perspective—the effect by which the ties in a straight railroad track appear to get smaller with distance and vanish to nothing at the horizon.

Next, the wireframe is covered by a surface. The surface is built up from simple polygons (many-sided flat shapes) that link the points of the wireframe. The greater the number of polygons for a given object size, the smoother and more natural the appearance of the object.

The surface of the object is then given colors, textures, opacities, and reflectances that suggest familiar materials: opaque matte black for slate, diverse skin tones with a slight sheen for body parts, shiny silver for chrome, and so on.

Finally, the object is "illuminated" using ray-tracing. The designer selects the positions and intensities of light sources—the Sun, candles, artificial lights—in the virtual three-dimensional image. The software then calculates the amount of light that would be reflected to an observer at the screen by each point on the surface of every object in view. The ray-tracing software must calculate where shadows fall, the angles at which rays of light hit each surface, the amount of incident light that will be reflected by a given surface material, and so on. Raytracing places huge demands on the processing power of a computer.

Three-dimensional games and movies

Introducing motion into a virtual world adds to the challenges that exist when creating static three-dimensional images. Perhaps the first of these challenges is the recreation of natural motion. Where the object is a humanoid figure, the information used to build the wireframe is provided by actors. The actor wears a black suit with white reflective markers attached to their joints and other locations that are key to motion, such as the feet, hands, and head. The actor then performs the actions of the animated character, and cameras detect the motion of the markers.

The coordinates of the moving markers form the points of the moving wireframe, on which the surface is imposed and refined by surface effects.

The whole virtual world in which the action of a game or movie takes place must have a pre-programmed map, since the surroundings must change as the viewer moves through the landscape. Furthermore, objects that are opaque must completely obscure other objects that are "behind" them in the view, while semitransparent objects, such as dirty windows, merely modify the appearances of the objects behind them. Highly sophisticated virtual worlds also account for further object properties, such as the bounce of a rubber ball or the splash of water when a car drives through a puddle.

Finally, every object in every scene must be raytraced to form an accurate impression of changes in lighting as objects in the scene move in and out of shadows and cast their own moving shadows on the objects around them.

▲ This computer-generated image shows an Earth-like planet in the sky over a lunar surface. The basic forms in the image were created as meshes of simple polygons. The appropriate colors, textures, and reflectances were imposed on the surfaces, and the whole was "illuminated" by tracing rays from a virtual sun beyond the top right-hand corner of the image.

SEE ALSO: ANIMATION • CAMERA, DIGITAL • MOUSE AND POINTING DEVICE • MOVIE PRODUCTION • SPECIAL EFFECT • VIRTUAL REALITY

Computer Network

In the simplest terms, a computer network is a functioning connection between two or more individual computers so that some measure of communication is possible between them. The connection between machines may be by wiring or by a combination of wiring and other forms of communication linkage. Networks are divided into local-area networks (LANs) and wide-area networks (WANs).

Networks greatly add to the power and usefulness of individual computers because any machine on a network can share data held on any other machine. If, for instance, a group of people are all working on different but related parts of the same project, each of them will have immediate access to additions, changes, and updating carried out by another person in the group. Individual computers may have limited storage capacity relative to a very large project, but if they are on a network that also includes a large-capacity machine, known as the server, they can all access the storage of this machine. The effect is as if each of the computers has the power of the server. A properly organized local-area network of standard personal computers can rival the power of a minicomputer.

One of the advantages of computer networks is person-to-person communication. In the early days of local-area networking, management-to-employee communication was quickly adopted. However, it soon became apparent that the real power of the system lay in its ability to provide two-way communication between any two people on the network. This was the beginning of electronic mail. E-mail has since become an indispensable tool, and in recent years, it has expanded hugely from local area networks to the largest wide area network of all—the Internet. E-mail use in the United States is now about ten times greater than the mail service. Wide-area networks can cover millions of individuals—the majority of homes in the United States are now part of such a network, and its advantages are familiar to all.

To send information via a network requires an agreed upon set of rules that must be complied with by the sending and the receiving machine, that is, the protocol. The protocol lays down the way of indicating the end of a message by the sending machine and the way of indicating by the receiving machine that a message has been received. Protocols also lay down the method used to check for and deal with errors.

▲ Networking computers has made communication of information in an office much easier. Files can be accessed from a central server and worked on by different employees.

Local-Area Networks

Local-area networks are linked computers occupying a relatively small area, often a single building or a small group of buildings. The smallest and simplest of all networks consist of two or three machines linked together with no central server or controlling machine. Such arrangements are known as peer-to-peer networks because each member of the network is able to decide what resources on his or her machine can be shared with the others. In most cases, a LAN will be the principal internal communication system for a single organization.

The LAN may be confined to a subdivision of the organization, or it may extend throughout the whole company. In some cases, it may be connected to other LANs within the organization. Computers on a LAN need not be identical nor even of the same type. Apple machines and Windows PCs can work together on the same LAN so long as the programs and files they are using are compatible. The number of machines that can be connected to a single LAN varies with the hardware and the controlling software used. Some have a limit of as few as 15 machines; other may have as many as 500 machines.

In a LAN, each individual computer is called a node. Most of the nodes will be regular personal computers (PCs) and each of these will be able to work normally using its own stored programs held on its hard disk drive and functioning with its own central processing unit (CPU). A LAN, however, allows computers to be used in a way that increases the computing power of an organization. All the CPUs in a network can be combined functionally so that they can all execute a single program. This is called distributed processing.

Economies can be effected in small LANs by allowing the sharing of an expensive printer or other peripheral device between all the members of the LAN. A minor disadvantage, however, is that individuals may have to wait until a device, such as a printer, is free. They will also have to walk a greater distance or go to another floor of the building to retrieve the printed material. There is another way in which a LAN can effect economy. Only one of the machines on a network need be fitted with a hard disk drive. This machine, the server, can provide all the other (client) machines with storage capacity and with the necessary programs. In this method, the client machines are called diskless PCs or workstations, and they can access data more rapidly than would be possible if they had their own slower disks. This method is often adopted to improve security and to make backup of data easier. It has the notable disadvantage, however, that

LOCAL-AREA NETWORKS

Local-area networks are commonly found as internal communications systems in offices and homes where two or more computers need to transfer data between themselves without having to copy files onto a portable storage device such as a floppy disk. The simplest devices just use cabling and connecting devices to transfer data, as traffic on the system is intermittent and users can restrict which files can be accessed. As the system grows more complicated, a series of protocols needs to be used to direct the flow of traffic around the system and prevent two operators from trying to work on the same file at the same time, a situation that would crash the system.

Bus network

▲ A bus network is the simplest LAN, in that all the computers and output devices are linked by a single cable. Each computer has a network interface card installed that manages communications between the computers. All the computers on the network can see the packets of information that are being sent, but only the one it is addressed to can pick it up.

▶ Ring networks transmit data sequentially from one computer to the next by circulating a token that is captured to gain the right to transmit data onto the ring. Once the data has been copied to a destination computer, a new token is transmitted.

Ring network

▶ In a star network, each computer is connected to a central hub by an individual length of twisted pair cable. Files sent from one computer to another are repeated to all ports on the hub, allowing all computers to see each data packet sent on the network, but only the computer the packet is addressed to pays attention to it.

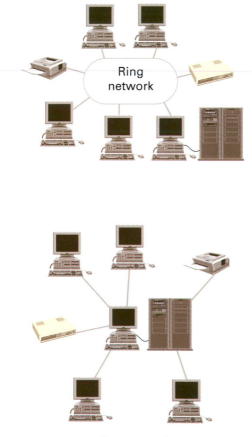

Star network

if the network suffers a fault—a not-infrequent event—all work may have to stop until the breakdown has been corrected.

Local-area networks can be arranged in a number of different ways. The pattern of the diagram showing how they are connected together is called the topology of the LAN. The arrangement may be a simple straight line (bus network) to which all the machines are connected; a circular arrangement with all the machines connected to it (token ring); or a series of lines radiating from a central controller, or hub, to the separate machines and devices (star network). The hub of a star network is a small boxed device that refreshes and amplifies any signals received before sending them on to the radiating lines to the other machines. A switch is a hub that can check the destination of an incoming packet of data and ensure that it is sent only to the hub port to which the recipient machine is connected. Switches are sometimes called intelligent hubs.

Connecting computers

Computers in a local-area network may be connected with a variety of conducting media. Many LANs require only a single pair of insulated copper wires twisted together, called a twisted pair. Such a cable is cheap and easy to use but has a limited top rate of digital conduction and is susceptible to electrical interference. Others use a special cable with a central conductor surrounded by and insulated from a sheathlike cylindrical conductor called a coaxial cable because the two conductors have the same axis. Coaxial cables allow much faster transmission than a twisted pair and are less affected by interference. Fiber-optic cables are very fast and are not susceptible to electric or magnetic interference but are expensive and hard to set up. In the most sophisticated LANs, cables are eliminated altogether and the connection between the machines is by radio.

Every desktop machine connected to a LAN requires a special network interface (adapter) card to be plugged into one of the expansion slots. Plug-in cards are so arranged that when they are in place, their outlet panel with its connector sockets appears at a vertical slot at the back of the case of the machine. In the case of laptop machines, there may be a card slot at one side for a special miniaturized connection.

LANs require special software, but networking has become so important that PC operating systems now usually incorporate networking software. MS-DOS had no intrinsic networking capacity, and separate software was needed. The same problem applied to the earliest widely successful Windows operating system, Windows 3.1. This system was, however, quickly followed by Windows 3.1 for Workgroups, which did have networking facilities. All subsequent Windows systems have incorporated networking software.

Currently the most commonly used LAN system is the Ethernet, a bus network that is now so popular that Ethernet adapter cards can be purchased for as little as $20 each. These cards allow communication via the local-area network at a much more rapid rate than is possible over regular telephone lines. Standard Ethernet communication runs at 10 million binary digits, or bits, per second (10 Mbps), and fast Ethernet runs at 100 megabits per second. In the token ring network, a pattern of binary pulses known as a token travels around the connection circle to which all the machines are connected. If one machine wishes to send a message, it picks up the token and attaches the message to it. The combination then travels around and can be taken up by other machines. FDDI is the fiber-optic digital device interface, a set of protocols used to send digital data over a fiber-optic channel.

Networks within a company that are limited to the use of company employees but that otherwise have all the features of the Internet are called Intranets. These allow any kind of personal computer to be linked to any other, enable additional members to join without adjusting the network, and provide standard facilities such as e-mail, voice mail, fax, and the use of regular browsers. Intranet use is expanding rapidly.

Wide-Area Networks

A wide-area network (WAN) is a computer network connecting machines separated by long distances. The most familiar WAN is the Internet, which now connects tens of millions of people in all parts of the world. For domestic and most business purposes, a connection to a WAN is usu-

▲ More complicated computer networks operate through a controlling system known as a hub. Hubs amplify signals from the central computer before sending them on to the receiving terminal.

WIDE-AREA NETWORKS

Wide-area networks are a means of connecting unrelated computer systems. Information from a personal computer is sent to a central mainframe computer, such as an Internet service provider, via a modem and a standard or digital telephone line. This information can then be passed on using conventional telephone links, or it can be beamed long distances using geostationary communication satellites orbiting Earth. Advances in palmtop computer and mobile phone technology in recent years have eliminated the need for any land-based cabling and use a wireless link known as wideband code-division multiple access, which is expected to significantly lower access times in the future.

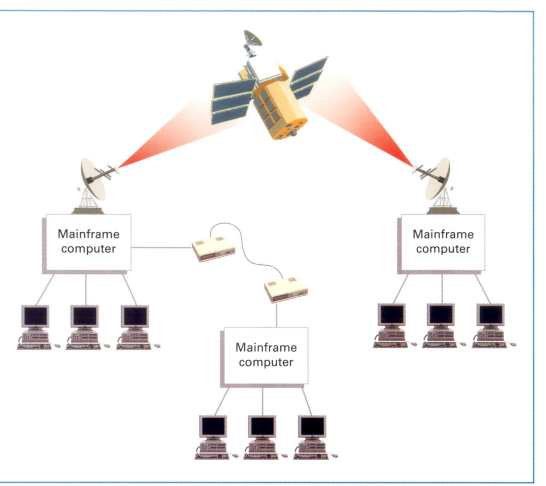

ally made by the regular telephone lines via a modem. The modem (modulator-demodulator) first converts the electronic digital pulses into sounds that phone lines can transmit and then reverses the process. At the digital telephone exchange, the sounds are converted to full digital form. The best current modems are limited to a speed of about 56,000 bits per second (56 kbps).

An improvement on the modem is the integrated services digital network (ISDN). This is a service that allows fast digital communication over phone lines with two 64,000 bit-per-second (64 kbps) channels as well as normal phone use. PCs using ISDN need to have a special terminal adapter. Even higher speed access that allows downloading of massive quantities of Internet material in short periods of time is a recent development. Digital subscriber lines (DSLs) use existing telephone lines but allow speeds of 256,000 bits per second (256 kbps). Cable modems, provided as an extra by cable TV companies, allow access speeds of up to 1,500,000 bits per second (1.5 Mbps).

Wide-area networks are also accessible without any wire connection by making use of two advances: direct satellite download via a home satellite dish antenna and wireless links direct from handheld computers, such as those currently

being sold by the Palm Computing Company, or recent models of mobile cellular telephones. Mobile phone Internet access developed in the last year or two of the 20th century and by the year 2000 had become a fast-growing application. This success was based on third-generation cell phones using a system known as wideband code-division multiple access (WCDMA). Systems of this kind promise transmission rates of up to 348,000 bits per second (348 kbps).

Network connections

Internally, computers move data around in parallel mode, a "word" at a time. This means that at least 8 bits, but more usually 16 or 32 and sometime 64 bits, travel together along multiway parallel pathways called buses. Parallel mode is fine for connecting computers to printers but is unsuitable for long-distance transmission because of the cost of the multiway cables and because the bits in a word would tend to get out of line with each other and break up the words. So, all network traffic travels in what is called serial mode, in which the bits move in a single stream, one after the other. This mode allows computers on a net to connect to each other with only two wires, but each machine requires hardware to convert its parallel data to serial form.

Asynchronous transfer mode is a standard for high-speed serial transmission of data. It is used in both private and public networks and is the basis of transmission on the Internet. All movement of data within a computer is synchronous and is controlled by an electronic clock that emits a stream of pulses. This is not a suitable system for long distance transmission, which is almost always asynchronous.

When separate local-area networks are joined together to produce a wider network, special hardware is necessary. When the two networks are virtually identical, the device used is called a bridge. Two Ethernet networks might, for instance, be linked by a bridge to form a network larger than the allowable physical limit of one Ethernet. Bridges transfer data between the networks, making no change in the data. If dissimilar LANs such as Ethernet and Token Ring are to be connected, a router is used, but the LANs must have a common protocol. Routers work with packet-switching and can be programmed to find and use the most cost-effective route to take between the LANs. When LANs with different protocols are to be linked, it is necessary to use a different device, called a gateway. Gateways are also necessary if a LAN that does not charge a fee for its use has to be connected to a wide-area network that does.

Transmitting data

Information transmitted over the Internet and other public data networks is sent by packet switching. This is a widely-used method of digital communication between multiple points. Messages are divided into segments of fixed size, and each segment carries a code identifying the sender and the addressee. Packets also carry error-control information. A large file might be cut up into numerous separate packets, and these may be sent by different routes. They are sent serially, without regard to the location of the addressees, so as to fill up the communication time and space available and avoid wastage. The identifying code ensures that addressees receive only the appropriate packets. These are then reassembled in the correct order to build up complete messages. A breakdown in part of a wide-area network does not result in loss of data because there are always alternative routes that the packets can use.

Before successful serial transmission can occur, it is necessary that the machines at each end of the link should agree on a system of transmission. They must, for instance, agree on how fast the bits should be sent (the baud rate) and on whether data are to be sent only in one direction

at a time (half duplex), as in a walkie-talkie, or in both directions simultaneously (full duplex), as in a telephone conversation. Computers will also have to agree on the technique used for detecting errors and for correcting them (parity bit checking), and they may also have to agree on how data are to be coded and decoded. These various agreements are all included in a set of rules known as a communications protocol. Before transmission can occur, the two machines must pass messages to each other confirming the communications protocol. This preliminary process of agreement over the mode of the subsequent data transmission is called *handshaking*.

Serial transmission occurs at very high rates, and it is imperative that some system of checking should be adopted to ensure that every bit sent is transferred correctly. This ingenious system is known as parity checking. The parity of a number is its state of being either even or odd and in binary numbers refers to whether the number of 1s is even or odd. In parity checking, each set of eight bits (1 byte) is made to have an even number of 1s. This goal is achieved by using only seven of the bits for data and, when necessary, adding an extra bit—the parity bit. As each byte is sent, the

▼ An artist's impression of the two Astra communications satellites. An increasing number of these satellites are being put into space to cope with the demand for mobile phones and other services that operate on wide-area networks.

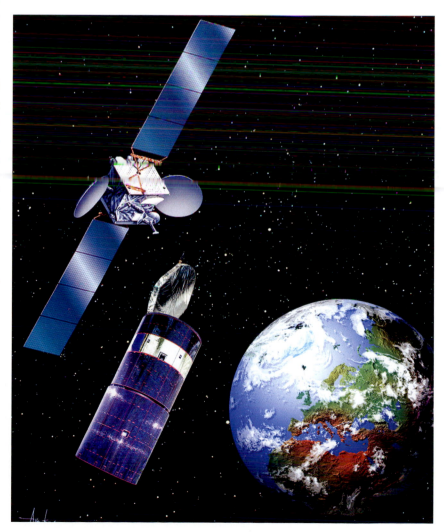

◄ Remote sensing via a wide-area network enables this gas company to monitor the status of equipment along the length of its pipeline from a central control room. Monitors can be programmed to report at specific intervals through telephone or radio links, and the central computer can send new instructions to pumping stations or distribution points hundreds of miles away.

sending machine counts the number of 1s in the seven data bits. If this is an even number, the computer adds a 0 parity bit; if the total of 1s is odd, the computer adds a 1 parity bit. So every byte sent has an even number of 1s, and this number is checked by the receiving machine. If the receiving machine finds any byte that does not have an even number of 1s, it knows that an error has occurred in the course of transmission, and it immediately asks for that byte to be repeated.

Parity-bit checking is highly effective but is not able to detect the unlikely coincidence of either two or four bits being changed in transmission. When 100 percent accuracy is essential, more sophisticated protocols are used. Parity-bit checking is not confined to communications use. Accuracy of data movement and recording is so vital to effective computer function that parity checking is constantly used within computers. Every time a personal computer is switched on, the internal memories are tested by a parity-bit check.

Optical fiber and radio communication systems

The most efficient and rapid physical medium for the transmission of information is a hair-thin fiber of high-quality glass. A light beam passed along a fine glass fiber does not escape unless the fiber is sharply bent, but remains in the cable by total internal reflection. It is easy to convert electrical pulses to light pulses using devices such as semiconductor lasers. The current through the device determines its light output,

and, by rapid switching, light signals are readily converted to digital form.

Light has a very short wavelength but a constant speed and thus a very large number of waves per second (a very high frequency). This means that the device that converts electrical signals into light pulses can do so at a very high rate. Optical fibers can carry as many as 5,000 million bits per second (5,000 Mbps)—a speed at which the entire text of the *Encyclopaedia Britannica* could be transmitted in about a tenth of a second. In engineering terms, the bandwidth of an optical fiber channel is very high—much higher than a normal radio or TV channel. By a method known as multiplexing, a large number of different signal channels can be accommodated simultaneously along a single optical fiber. In multiplexing a number of channels, the first bit from each channel is sent, then the second from each, then the third, and so on. In this way, many channels are combined to form a single stream of data. At the other end, the successive bits are separated and sent each to its appropriate channel.

The carrying capacity of fiber-optic channels has recently been multiplied by using laser light of different colors, thus increasing their commercial attractiveness. Their use is expanding rapidly. They are quickly replacing existing long-distance telephone lines and now run across the Atlantic and Pacific Oceans. So far, the cost has precluded widespread fiber-optic connections to domestic locations, but the advantages are so great that such connections are inevitable.

In large wide-area networks, an indispensable element in the connections between physical networks is the use of radio microwave links. Microwaves are radio waves of very short wavelength. Since all electromagnetic propagation is at the speed of light, the frequency is very high so that a very large number of pulses can be transmitted per second. Microwaves can be transmitted over any line-of-sight distance. Terrestrial transmission requires towers to avoid obstruction and is limited by the curvature of Earth. But three satellites traveling at the same rate of rotation as Earth (geostationary satellites) remain above fixed points and, for purposes of transmission of microwaves, can cover the entire surface of the globe. This fact has contributed enormously to the success of the WAN and, in particular, the Internet.

SEE ALSO: ANALOG AND DIGITAL SYSTEMS • BINARY SYSTEM • CELLULAR TELEPHONE • COMPUTER • FIBER OPTICS • INTEGRATED CIRCUIT • INTERNET • MODEM AND ISDN • SATELLITE, ARTIFICIAL • TELECOMMUNICATIONS • TELEMETRY

Computer Printer

With the increasing use of computers to process large amounts of data, the development of printers became necessary to output the information from the computer at high speeds.

Laser printers

The black-and-white laser printer is the most commonly used output device in offices and works in a similar manner to a photocopier. The laser printer's main element is a rotating metal drum coated with a photoconductive material that is initially negatively charged and that cannot conduct electricity unless exposed to light.

The output from the computer is normally assembled into page format in an internal memory and then transferred to the page. When a command to print is sent from the computer, the microelectronics in the printer target a laser beam of variable intensity towards a mirror that reflects infrared light to parts of the drum's surface. Those areas on which light is shone begin to conduct electricity, and therefore, the negative charge escapes. By the time the laser has stopped moving, the drum is covered in a pattern of negatively charged areas, which remained unlit, and uncharged areas, where the laser light shone. These areas precisely match the nonprinting and printing areas of the original computer document.

To develop the image, positively charged toner particles are brought into contact distance with the drum. Because like charges repel, no toner will stick to the negatively charged areas—those that have not been exposed to the light. However, toner does bind weakly to the uncharged areas, where the laser light was transmitted. This process translates the charge image into a positive print image.

When the toner has adhered to the drum, the printer positively charges a sheet of paper, which is then rolled across the drum. Because of its stronger charge, the paper attracts the negatively charged toner particles from the drum. As the paper moves through the printer, a heated roller melts the plastic toner, fusing it permanently to the paper. Chemicals can also be used to fix the ink, and some printers use cathode-ray tubes or light-emitting diodes to write the image onto the drum.

Color laser printers work in a similar manner to four-color printing presses. The image is scanned through four separate filters—magenta, cyan (a light blue), yellow, and black. Each layer of color is deposited on the paper in sequence, building up a color image. Color laser printers are quite slow to print because of the number of steps involved and cannot give more than an approximation of the true color of a document, as the colors are sealed on top of each other.

Ink-jet printers

An ink-jet, or bubble-jet, printer fires extremely small droplets of ink onto paper to create an image. The dots of ink are extremely small—between 10 and 30 dots per millimeter—and are positioned very precisely. In color printers, the dots are composed of multiple colors made from four ink cartridges in the basic printing colors—cyan, magenta, yellow, and black. From mixtures of these four colors, any other color can be easily created.

Ink-jet printers are extremely inexpensive compared with the more sophisticated laser printers and significantly less expensive than color laser printers. Different types of ink-jet printers form their droplets of ink in different ways. There are two major technologies in use. Most ink-jet printers, including the popular bubble-jet machines, use thermal technology, in which heat is used to squirt ink onto the receiving paper through tiny nozzles. In a bubble-jet printer, tiny resistors create heat, which is used to vaporize the ink, thus creating a bubble. The pressure created by the expansion of the bubble causes a droplet of ink to squirt from the print head. A bubble-jet print head will typically contain 64 or 128 tiny nozzles, all able to simultaneously fire a droplet of ink.

Ink-jet printers operate under a continuous stream of ink droplets or by drop-on-demand. In continuous-stream models, the ink is emitted at high pressure through one or more nozzles so that the ink breaks up into droplets at a fixed distance from the nozzle. At the breakup point, the droplets are charged according to digital signals from the computer and pass through an electrostatic field, which adjusts the trajectory of the droplet to make it fall in a particular place on the paper or into a gutter for recirculation.

Most bubble-jet printers use drop-on-demand, which produces high-velocity droplets from closely spaced nozzles situated at the end of ink-filled channels. A current is pulsed through a resistive layer in the ink channel causing a bubble to form at the end of the nozzle. The bubble swells until it has absorbed all the heat, drawing a droplet of ink out of the channel. The bubble collapses onto the resistor, propelling the droplet toward the paper. The ink channel then refills by capillary action. The whole process takes less than 10 microseconds from bubble formation to collapse.

Epson uses a slightly different technology in its Stylus range. Instead of using thermal technology to fire the ink, these printers contain a piezoelectric cell that exerts mechanical pressure on the ink to force it out onto the paper.

The piezoelectric actuator head in the Stylus printers consists of multilayered piezoelectric elements behind a vibrating plate that sits against the ink chamber and has a small nozzle at one end. When a short electrical pulse is applied to the piezoelectric element, it expands and immediately contracts. The vibrating plate translates this motion to the curved surface (meniscus) of the ink held at the end of the nozzle leading to the ink chamber. The meniscus consequently expands and contracts as a result of the firing at high speed and pressure, so the droplet of ink ejects cleanly.

In thermal printing, the inks used must be heat-resistant. Piezoelectrics allow more control over the shape and speed of ink droplets since charging the chamber and firing the ink is a simple electrical process. The use of heat in thermal printers also creates a need for a cooling process, so they are slightly slower and more energy intensive than modern piezoelectric types. A particular advantage of the laser or ink-jet printer is that type sizes and faces are controlled by software, so can be varied almost indefinitely, and graphics added as desired.

Line printers

Conventional line printers print a complete line at a time and work at speeds of over 2,000 lines per minute. The two main types of line printers are barrel printers and train, or chain, printers. Page printers, such as the laser printer, effectively print a complete page at a time; the fastest of these have an output of more than 200 pages a minute.

A row of small hammers, one for each print position, is mounted behind the paper on the opposite side to the type slugs (letters or symbols)

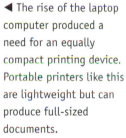

◀ The rise of the laptop computer produced a need for an equally compact printing device. Portable printers like this are lightweight but can produce full-sized documents.

and the inked ribbon. There can be up to 160 print positions, although most printers use only 132. All the characters are moved rapidly past the print positions, and where a character is required to be printed, the hammer for that position is operated electromagnetically just before the character arrives in front of it.

The hammer then has time to move the paper toward the ink ribbon and the character, so that when the paper and ribbon hit the character and the imprint is made on the paper, the alignment is correct. Because the characters are always moving, the duration of contact is in the region of ten microseconds, so smudging and blurring are kept to a minimum. When each hammer has been given the chance to operate for each character, the paper is moved up for the next line.

Barrel printers

The main difference between barrel and train printers is the way in which the type characters move across the print line. The barrel printer, an earlier design than the train printer, uses a row of wheels, one for each print position, mounted vertically on a horizontal shaft that is rotating continuously. Each print wheel carries 64 characters, so for each revolution of the barrel, every print position is presented with every character.

Train and chain printers

Train and chain printers differ from barrel printers in that the characters are moved horizontally across the print line. The configuration usually consists of five sets of 48 characters. Generally, the type slugs on a train printer are cast as groups of three letters or symbols, but the slugs of a chain printer carry two characters each.

The assembly that carries the slugs is called the cartridge. In a chain printer, the slugs are fixed to an endless chain by small screws, and the chain is driven at high speed by a small wheel. The train printer has a hardened steel rail along which the slugs can slide, and teeth cut into the rear of each slug engage with the drive wheel. The slugs next to the drive wheel are pushed along the rail and in turn push the rest of the slugs around the cartridge at a speed of more than 11 mph (18 km/h).

The advantage of the train cartridge compared with the chain cartridge is that the slugs are held more rigidly for printing, and the problems arising from a loose or stretched chain are eliminated. Also, worn or damaged characters can be replaced easily by lifting the slug off the rail.

SEE ALSO: COMPUTER • INK • PRINTING • PHOTOCOPIER

Concrete

Concrete is the most widely used structural and civil engineering material today. Its applications range from small objects like fence posts and street light standards to roads, dams, cathedrals, and massive offshore oil production platforms. The raw materials used for making concrete are found in abundance throughout the world, and its technology is as suited to labor-intensive and low-technology applications in the developing world as it is to the capital-intensive and highly mechanized technology of the industrialized nations.

Basically, concrete is a conglomerate of strong but chemically inert aggregates, that is, natural sand and small stones or artificial mineral materials bound together by a matrix of mineral cement. Cement hardens and gains strength over a period of time as a result of chemical reactions with water, but before it hardens, the concrete can be mixed into a plastic mass and cast or molded into any shape.

History

The ancient Egyptians used hydrated lime and gypsum (calcium sulfate) cements. The Romans discovered that the addition of pozzolana, a natural volcanic ash found near Mount Vesuvius, produced a concrete that was not only stronger and more durable but would also set and harden under water, making it valuable for building bridges and aqueducts. Lime and pozzolanic concretes continued to be used after the Romans by builders in the so-called Dark Ages (from about the 5th to the 11th century C.E.). However, it was the invention of Portland cement by Joseph Aspdin in England in 1824 that created new possibilities for concrete as a structural material.

Modern concrete

The key to concrete's wide structural use is its inherent strength under compression. This attribute is still the major controlling factor in modern concrete construction, and it depends mainly on two factors: the proportion of cement to aggregate in the mix and the proportion of cement to water. In the broadest terms, the more cement in proportion to aggregates and the less water in proportion to the cement, the stronger the concrete. The proportioning of the mix, however, depends on the application and the materials most economically available.

A standard method of testing concrete for compliance with its specification is the comprehensive strength, or cube, test; a 4 in. (10 cm)

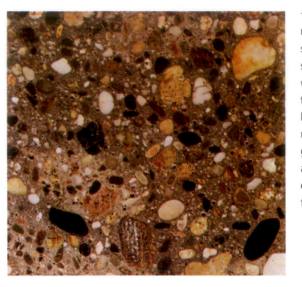

◀ Concrete made with river gravel, showing the structure with rounded stones. Cement paste and water bind the particles together and their lubricant action at first reduces internal friction, giving the fresh concrete a pliant consistency that enables it to fit the framework more closely.

cube cast and cured under controlled conditions is crushed until it fails in standardized testing press, most commonly at an age of 28 days. The material must be able to withstand pressures from 2,900 psi (20 N/mm^2) for lightly loaded floor slabs to 7,250 psi (50 N/mm^2) for ordinary structural concrete and even higher pressures for some applications.

Durability is an important attribute of concrete and is achieved by keeping the ratio of water to cement sufficiently low for the expected exposure conditions. Durability is also enhanced by entraining microscopic air bubbles in the concrete: all modern concrete roads have 3 percent to 6 percent entrained air by volume. A typical cubic meter of concrete with 2 cm maximum size aggregates would consist of 46 percent (by weight) coarse aggregate, 33 percent sand, 13 percent cement powder, 8 percent water and 4.5 percent (by volume) air. Only 45 percent of the water is needed to react chemically with all of the cement;

◀ A hardened cement paste, which has been reinforced with fine polypropylene monofilament fibers. The cement itself has been polymer modified, that is, a polymer emulsion of polyvinyl acetate (PVA) has been added during the mixing. It is used in making window frames and panels and for other high-strength applications.

◀ Aerated concrete in a mold. It is next put into an autoclave, where aluminum powder reacts with the cement, lime, and water to produce hydrogen gas, which swells the mass into a cellular structure. Then, by use of high-pressure steam, it is turned into a low-density concrete that floats on water.

ported through pipelines and placed by specially designed pumps. In some applications, such as in tunnel or swimming-pool construction, it may actually be sprayed into place.

Thorough compaction is necessary to ensure complete filling of the formwork and, more importantly, to expel all the unwanted air from the mix. For relatively thin concrete slabs—building floors and sidewalks—the concrete can be compacted by vibrating beams across the surface: internal poker vibrators are used for larger and deeper sections. In both cases, the vibration fluidizes the concrete, allowing trapped air to rise to the surface.

Whether the concrete is finished smoothly by hand or mechanical troweling or left with the texture imparted by the formwork, it requires careful curing. Contrary to what many people think, concrete does not harden by drying out; if it is allowed to dry too fast in its early life, it is likely to be ruined. Preventing it from drying too fast, by slowing evaporation, is a key part of the curing process. It may be done by sprinkling the newly hardened concrete with water and covering it with polyethylene sheeting, or sometimes in the case of small objects such as blocks, pipes, and so on, high-pressure steam curing in an autoclave is used.

Reinforced concrete

Although concrete by itself is very strong in compression, it is only a tenth as strong in tension. Until methods were developed for reinforcing concrete in tension toward the end of the 19th century, the material was limited to foundations, footings, block masonry, and other uses where the stress was almost entirely in compression. Today, roads and dams are usually made in unreinforced concrete.

Where more tensile strength is needed, steel is embedded in the concrete; 80 percent of reinforcement is by high-yield ribbed or deformed bars. Round bars of mild steel are less economic but are still used where high strength is not required. Fibers, often steel, can be added to the mix, not necessarily to give strength but to give impact resistance. Durable concrete has the very important property of chemically preventing any rusting of the steel, provided there is sufficient cover on the steel.

Precast concrete

Concrete does not need to be cast entirely on the construction site. One of its great advantages is that individual beams, planks, blocks, or whole wall units can be cast away from the actual site.

Besides reducing on-site work in congested locations, precast construction permits casting

the rest is needed to make the concrete sufficiently fluid and workable. A recent development involves replacing 15 to 20 percent of the water with a silica 100 times smaller than cement grains. It is similar to, but much more reactive than, the volcanic ash used by the Romans and, in conjunction with water-reducing chemicals, doubles or even quadruples strengths.

Mixing, placing, and curing

As important to the strength, durability, and appearance of the finished concrete is the care that goes into the mixing, placing, and subsequent treatment of the mix while it is fresh and plastic. The various ingredients must be thoroughly mixed, and for all but the very smallest quantities this means machine mixing. Mixing is done either on-site or in central batching and mixing plants. The fresh concrete is taken from the point of mixing to the site in trucks fitted with a revolving drum to prevent the mix from setting.

Once delivered, the concrete must be carefully placed in its formwork, so as to fill the forms properly and prevent separation of the ingredients. Traditional methods of placing by wheelbarrow or crane-handled skips are still widely used, but increasingly the fresh concrete is trans-

◀ Mobil's Statfjord B oil rig is one of the biggest concrete structures ever installed at sea. It is strong enough to take the stresses of heavy ocean waves in the harsh conditions of the North Sea.

itself, finishing, and detailing to be carried out under factory conditions, affording standards of quality control that would be virtually impossible on-site. Also, standardized beams and other units can be formed in long-life, high-precision steel molds for use in structural and architectural applications.

Prestressed concrete

Of all the various techniques employed in concrete construction, the only 20th century development was prestressing. Used in limited applications from World War I onward, prestressed concrete has only approached its full potential in the last 50 years.

Prestressing is a logical extension of reinforcement. The difference is that instead of merely passively resisting tensile and bending stresses as reinforcement does, prestressing counters them actively, allowing a lighter element to carry the same load. High-tensile steel bars, strands, or cables are tensioned and anchored at the ends or at points along their length so that they keep the prestressed concrete element under constant compression within the limits of its design loading.

There are two basic forms of prestressing. In pretensioning, the concrete element is cast around tendons, prestressing wires that have already been placed under heavy tension between permanent anchors at each end of the casting bed. When the concrete has reached the desired strength and is bonded firmly to the tendons, the ends are cut off the prestressing wires and their elasticity places the whole unit under compression. Because of the way it is done, pretensioning is for practical purposes limited to precast units, but within those limitations, it has various uses

from fence posts and lintel beams a few feet long to bridge beams measuring up to about 150 ft. (46 m) and weighing many tons.

The other form of prestressing—posttensioning—involves the use of tendons, or bars, which are tensioned once the concrete has hardened by means of hydraulic jacks and specially designed

▶ Reinforced concrete being used to lay the foundations of a high-rise office complex in the clay of central London.

anchorages. Posttensioning can be used with pre-cast elements, but its most widespread use is in on-location concrete structures. Preformed ducts are cast into the concrete during construction, and the tendons are threaded through them and tensioned once the concrete has reached a pre-determined strength.

Another use of posttensioning is in segmental construction, especially suited to bridges and viaducts, where site conditions prevent the use of complex falsework (temporary supports) between piers. The actual bridge deck structure is made up of slices, sometimes cast on-site but more often today cast and cured in advance either in a yard near the site or in a precasting factory farther away. As each segment is completed or posi-tioned, it is tied back to the structure by post-tensioned tendons; the whole structure is held together like a row of books picked up by pressing in on the end volumes.

Lightweight concrete

Volume for volume, ordinary concrete is lighter than most other structural materials, but strength for strength it is heavier. In many cases, this char-acteristic does not matter, but where large spans are concerned or in other uses where weight is a critical design factor, it can be a problem. The logical answer, and one the Romans discovered, is to use lightweight aggregates. For the dome of the Pantheon, slightly larger than that of St. Paul's in London, the Romans used a concrete

▶ Laying a new main sewer in a town is a major operation. The men here are working with concrete pipe sections 54 in. (1.4 m) in diameter. The pipes have to be big enough to dispose of millions of gallons of sewage each day in a large city, and strong enough to be buried underground.

with natural pumice aggregate, probably the first lightweight concrete in history.

Pumice aggregate is still used where it is easily available, mainly in lightweight blocks for house construction. But there are many other forms of lightweight concrete. Perhaps the most widely used is concrete made with lightweight aggre-gates such as clay, shale and slate, sintered pulver-ized fuel ash, and foamed blast furnace slag.

Another form of relatively lightweight con-crete is no-fines—concrete made with normal dense aggregates but without fine material so that empty spaces are left between the coarse aggre-gate particles. Finally, there is aerated concrete, actually a sand-cement mortar, which is foamed chemically, either on site or during the manu-facture of precast building units and blocks, to produce a very light cellular material that has reasonable structural strength, a high thermal insulation value, and such a light weight that it will actually float in water.

All of these different forms of concrete have their specific applications. Besides these, there are special concretes with extra-hard aggregates for use under highly abrasive conditions and other concretes with radiation-absorbing aggregates for use in nuclear power plants.

FACT FILE

- Because concrete ships are heavier and less fuel efficient than steel ships, future concrete seagoing vessels may well take the form of submarines, with everything apart from the bridge under water while traveling, thus reducing water and wind resistance and increasing fuel efficiency. The ship's water friction will be further reduced by the use of polymer impregnated concrete (PIC).

- The DAM-ATOLL ocean energy conversion system developed by the Lockheed Missiles and Space Co. changes wave power into electricity by means of a large concrete dome with a vertical central core containing a turbine. Waves ride up over the dome and are then channeled by vanes down through the core to power the turbine, which in turn drives a generator.

SEE ALSO: Bridge • Building techniques • Cement manufacture • Civil engineering • Dam • Tunneling

Condensed-Matter Physics

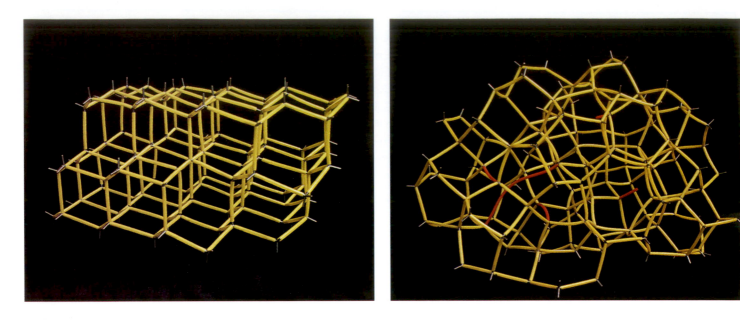

Condensed-matter physics studies the properties that substances have only when they are liquids or solids. The liquid and solid states are collectively known as the condensed states; a description that distinguishes them from the gaseous state, in which matter is relatively sparse.

Metallic conduction is a good example of a condensed-state phenomenon, since it only occurs when large numbers of metal atoms combine in a solid or liquid mass. (The metal vapors in mercury and sodium discharge lamps conduct electricity by the formation of metal ions, a different mechanism of conduction to that which occurs in metallic liquids and solids.)

Condensed-matter physics was called solid-state physics when it first emerged as a distinct field of study; this name reflected the almost exclusive interest in the solid state at that time. For a while, the "solid-state" description was applied to the miniaturized electronic devices that were made possible by the greatest development in condensed-matter physics to date: the semiconductors used in transistors. Since then, increasing interest in the properties of liquids has prompted the adoption of the current name.

Condensed-matter physicists are interested in the responses of solids and liquids to changes in temperature, mechanical stresses, light and other forms of electromagnetic radiation, and electric and magnetic fields. Some of the phenomena that they observe are spectacular: superfluidity, for example, is a fluid's complete loss of resistance to fluid motion, a loss that allows a superfluid to flow over the edges of its container. Superconductivity is a similar loss of a material's usual resistance to the passage of an electrical current.

▲ These diagrams show the difference between crystalline and amorphous solids. A crystal (left) has a structure that can repeat regularly over thousands of formula units. By contrast, an amorphous solid (right) has no such long-range order. The immediate environment of each type of atom is similar in the whole structure, however, so there is a degree of short-range order.

Crystalline solids

Crystalline solids are the most easily described type of condensed matter, since they consist of regular assemblies of atoms or molecules. They are formed by metals, semiconductors, insulators, and many molecular materials, ranging from dry ice (solid carbon dioxide, CO_2) to enzymes. Perfect crystals—those without a single deviation from a regular structure throughout—are a condensed-matter physicist's ideal, since their regularity allows their properties to be calculated from the quantum mechanical descriptions of the atoms that compose them. The permitted energy bands for electrons in conductors and semiconductors are calculated in this manner, for example.

A perfect crystal may be formed by seeding an extremely pure liquid sample with a small crystal at the melting point of the liquid. The crystal must form slowly enough for the atoms and molecules in the liquid to become perfectly arranged in the crystal structure of the solid.

Perfect crystals are rare, however, and most crystalline materials have boundaries at which the orientation of the crystal structure changes abruptly. These imperfections influence properties such as conductivity and flexibility.

Conventional liquids

A conventional liquid consists of molecules—or, rarely, atoms—that are held together by intermolecular attractions. Groups of molecules in a liquid can influence one another's orientation to some extent, but the molecules are free to move and the structure of a liquid is not ordered over the long range. This structure allows a liquid to flow in the characteristic manner of a fluid.

Liquid crystals

Liquid crystals differ from ordinary liquids in that they have a structure that is ordered in two of the three dimensions of space. Substances that exhibit a liquid-crystal phase have rod-shaped molecules that stack like logs. They form structures that are ordered across what would be the cut faces of the logs in a pile, but the individual molecules remain free to move along their longer dimensions.

Above a certain temperature, thermal energy becomes great enough to overcome the order in a liquid crystal; the substance then becomes a true liquid. Where the molecular rods have opposite electrical charges at their two ends, however, an electric field can cause a liquid crystal to form below that critical temperature. In this way, the elements of a liquid crystal display are turned on.

Amorphous solids

Amorphous means "without form," and amorphous solids were so named because physicists were unable to detect distinct structures for them. Modern techniques for determining structures have filled this gap of knowledge to some extent, so condensed-matter physicists now have a greater understanding of their structures.

Amorphous solids are rigid because strong forces hold their constituent atoms in fixed positions, although those atoms can vibrate. In one respect, however, they are like liquids: they have short-range order but no long-range order.

Glass is an example of an amorphous solid. Normal glass consists mainly of silicon dioxide, in which each silicon atom is surrounded by four oxygen atoms in a tetrahedron. Each oxygen atom connects to two atoms of silicon through bonds that are at an angle of approximately 100 to 110 degrees to one another. The short-range order of these bond geometries is maintained, but there is no regular pattern in the structure over greater dimensions: there is no long-range order.

▶ The display of a scanning tunneling microscope reveals the individual atoms in the surface of a sample. The colored scale helps reveal the "height" of the surface above a fixed baseline.

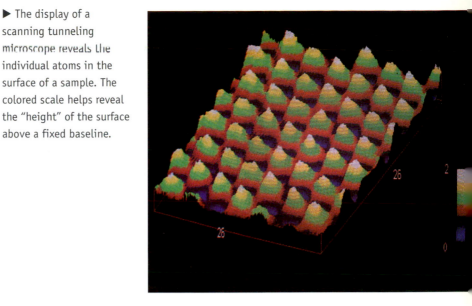

"Seeing" atoms

Atoms are too small to be seen using a light microscope, since the photons that make up visible light have wavelengths longer than the diameter of an atom. X-ray photons have much shorter wavelengths than visible photons, so they can be put to use to probe the structures of solids.

In X-ray crystallography, a beam of X-ray photons irradiates a sample of the material under investigation. X-ray photons that strike atoms bounce off them at an angle that depends on the position of the strike. The reflected X rays then interfere to form a diffraction pattern that can be detected as spots on photographic film.

If the material is crystalline, the diffraction pattern is simple, and the geometry of the atoms or ions in the crystal can be calculated from the positions of spots on the film. A highly disordered amorphous solid produces a blurred pattern that gives little information. Partially ordered materials that have crystalline regions, such as linear polyethene, can be spun in the beam so as to blur out the background from disorderly regions and produce a pattern of rings whose radii are used to determine the structure of ordered regions.

Although computers help calculate structures from complex diffraction patterns, X-ray crystallography is still a rather indirect way to "view" the structure of a material. A further weakness is that it gives a structure that is averaged for the whole of sample, obscuring details of imperfections.

Images of individual atoms first became possible with the invention of the scanning tunneling microscope, or STM. "Tunneling" is a quantum-mechanical expression for the ability of subatomic particles to pass through space in a way that is not possible according to classical physics. In an STM, a pointed stylus with a tip that is one atom wide probes the surface of a conducting material.

◀ Inside a semiconductor laser, now widely used for optical fiber communications and in such devices as CD players. Solid-state electronics has led to increasing miniaturization of components that exploit the thermal, electrical, and optical properties of materials in new ways.

As the tip gets close to the surface of the material, a voltage drives a current between the stylus and sample as electrons start to be able to tunnel through the gap between the atom at the tip of the stylus and an atom in the surface. The current increases sharply as the gap decreases.

As the tip of the stylus scans over the surface, the mechanism of the microscope adjusts the position of the stylus to keep the electron flow constant. In doing so, it traces out the profile of atoms and molecules in the sample surface.

An adaptation of the STM is the atomic-force microscope (AFM). In this case, the tip of the stylus is brought close enough to the sample surface for electrons in the tip and the sample to start repelling each other. As the stylus scans the sample, its position is adjusted to maintain a constant repulsive force, so an AFM traces the surface profile in the same way as an STM. The advantage of AFM is that it can be used to study insulating materials, since no current passes between the tip and the sample during the scan. One application of the detailed images produced by STM and AFM is in catalyst research, since the nature of ridges and imperfections in the surface of a catalyst can influence its activity.

A future application of a technique related to STM might be in the field of data storage. If the voltage of an STM is increased, atoms start to fly from the tip onto the sample surface; reversing the voltage picks them off again. In this way, an adapted STM can write and erase patterns in the surface of a metal. In 1991, a researcher at the University of Basel, Switzerland, wrote the word "Heureka" in the pits of a compact disc. Each pit is a bit of information—a "yes" or "no" that is one-eighth of a byte—so this technique could be used for the extremely dense storage of information.

▶ A glass memory switch consists of a thin slice of semiconducting glass with metal electrodes vacuum-deposited on opposite faces of the glass (inset). In the "off" state, the resistance of the switch is high (lower line). Above a threshold voltage—slightly over 10 V in this case—the resistance suddenly drops and the current rises (upper line). This is the "on" state of the switch.

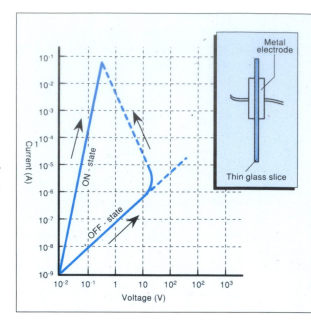

◀ Solar panels are arrays of silicon photodiodes, which cause a current to flow when light shines on one of their surfaces.

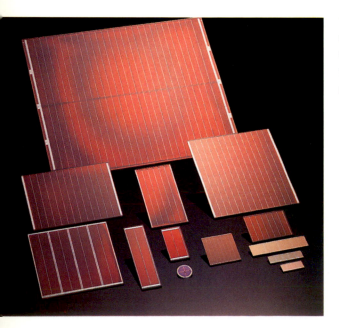

Glass switches

Glass memory switches can be made using a thin layer of a glass that contains such materials as copper phosphate or silicon–tellurium–arsenic–germanium (STAG). The glass layer is as little as 5 to 20 micrometers thick and has metal electrodes deposited on either side in a vacuum chamber, creating a metal–glass–metal sandwich.

At low voltages and small currents, the switch is off—the glass has a resistance as high as several thousand megohms. Above a critical voltage, the current suddenly rises, and the resistance of the sandwich to current drops to just a few tens of ohms. The switch is now on and remains so, even if the voltage drops to zero. To turn it off again requires a pulse of heavy current.

Semiconductors

Silicon is an example of a semiconductor that, when pure, has too few free electrons to conduct electricity like a metal. By adding traces of materials called dopants, condensed-matter physicists can enable silicon to conduct by the motion of electrons or their vacancies (holes). Layers of silicon with different dopants form the switches that are the working parts of microchips.

When light shines on a sandwich of two layers of silicon with different dopants, it drives electrons to the surface of one layer, where they can be collected by conducting wires. A set of wires connected to the other layer feeds electrons into the sandwich so a current can start to flow. Photocells in solar panels use this process.

Another class of semiconductors includes glassy compounds based on selenium and tellurium and phosphate glasses that contain transition metal ions. Both types have been used in the construction of semiconductor lasers.

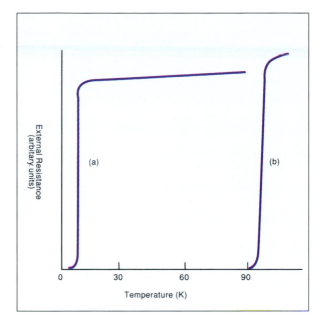

◀ These curves show the rapid change in electrical resistance at the critical temperatures (T_c) of two materials. Below T_c, the resistance falls to zero and the materials become superconducting. Material B remains superconducting at a much higher temperature than material A.

▶ A scanning tunneling microscope. This instrument has a special head unit that allows measurements to be made with atomic resolution down to within a few degrees of absolute zero. The microscope unit is housed in a small cryostat.

Superconductors

Some materials become superconductors below a well-defined transition temperature—that is, they completely lose their electrical resistance; thus superconducting materials are useful as the windings of powerful electromagnets, since their lack of resistance would prevent electrical power from being dissipated as heat. The practical problems lie in maintaining an adequately low temperature for superconductivity.

Early superconductors required temperatures near absolute zero (0 K, –460°F, –273°C). One of the highest transition temperatures was around 20 K (–424°F, –253°C) for an alloy of niobium,

aluminum, and germanium. Then in 1986, a German-Swiss team discovered a ceramic material, based on copper and oxygen, whose transition temperature was 30 K (–406°F, –243°C). Johannes Bednorz and Karl Müller shared the 1987 Nobel Prize in physics for this discovery. Subsequently, heat-treated materials composed primarily of copper and oxygen with metals such as barium, calcium, and mercury have given transition temperatures as high as 134 K (–218°F, –139°C). This temperature is well above the boiling point of readily available liquid nitrogen, which is 77 K (–321°F, –196°C).

The structures of these ceramics feature chains and sheets of copper and oxygen atoms, which are thought to play a crucial role in the superconducting properties of such materials.

Superfluids

The particles in a conventional liquid move in an uncoordinated manner. Collisions between the particles cause liquids to have viscosity—a type of internal friction—and place a lower limit on the size of hole through which a liquid can flow. Helium behaves in a different manner when its temperature approaches absolute zero. The atoms start to move in a coordinated manner, losing their viscosity and becoming able to pass through very small holes. This behavior is called superfluidity and is a consequence of quantum mechanical rules that allow many helium atoms to occupy the same quantum state under certain conditions.

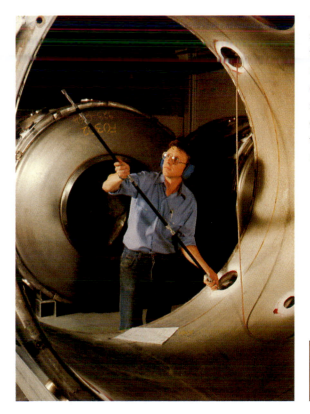

◀ A low-temperature superconducting magnet in the course of manufacture. The advent of high-temperature superconductors will enable such magnets to become much more compact.

SEE ALSO: Ceramics • Crystals and crystallography • Diffraction • Electronics • Insulator, electric • Semiconductor • Superconductivity

Conduction, Electrical

An electric current flows when charged particles move under the influence of an electric field. An electric field is a voltage gradient—a virtual "slope" down which current can flow—and the strength of an electric field is measured in volts per unit distance, typically, volts per meter.

If the terminals of a battery are connected by a conducting wire, the voltage across the terminals creates an electric field in that wire. A more exact term for this voltage is *potential difference*. The strength of the electric field in the wire increases if the potential difference increases or if a shorter wire is used. The increased electric-field strength encourages a stronger current to flow.

A conductor has electrically charged particles that are free to move under the influence of electric fields. Negatively charged particles may be electrons or they may be single or grouped atoms that have more electrons than protons. Such species are called anions. Positively charged particles include single or grouped atoms that have fewer electrons than protons. Under the extreme conditions of a hydrogen plasma—a hot, ionized gas—free protons can carry positive charge. Since the mass of a proton is some 1,800 times that of an electron, a proton will accelerate correspondingly less than an electron in an electric field.

If a conductor possesses both positively and negatively charged particles that are free to move, the positively charged particles will drift toward the negative electrode, or cathode, while the negatively charged particles drift toward the positively charged electrode, or anode. The total current is the sum of the individual currents of negatively and positively charged particles.

Mechanisms of conduction

Most materials, whether they are solids, liquids, or gases, consist of atoms and molecules that have no electrical charge. Each nucleus of protons and neutrons is surrounded by the correct complement of electrons to exactly balance the number of protons. Such structures would seem to preclude the conduction of electrical currents, which requires that electrically charged species are free to move under the influence of an electric field.

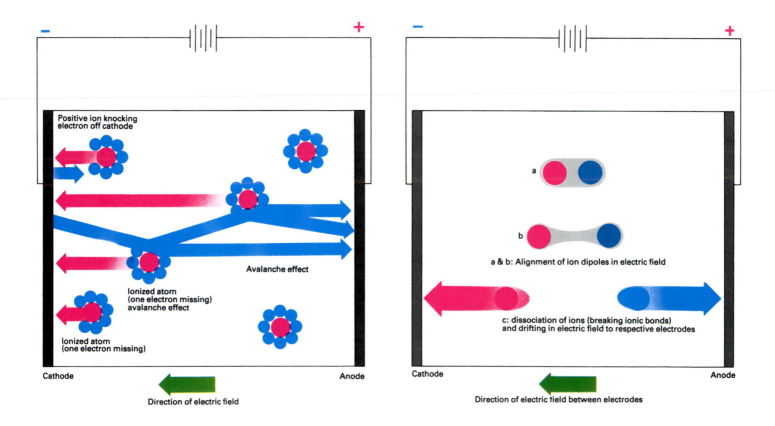

▲ The above diagram shows the flow of cations in an ionic solution placed between a cathode and an anode. A layer of water molecules surrounds each cation. When the cations reach the cathode, they accept electrons from it and form electrically neutral species. Anions, which are not shown here, drift toward the positively charged anode.

▲ When a nonconducting gas or liquid is subjected to an electric field, the electron distributions of its molecules shift to form an electric dipole that lines up with the field. A strong electric field can split a molecule into positive and negative fragments. The negative fragments are often free electrons. The fluid can then conduct a current.

In fact, there are three ways in which materials can conduct electricity. Some materials exist as positive and negative ions, whose charges balance each other. In the solid state, these ions form a rigid lattice and cannot conduct. If such a solid melts or dissolves in a solvent, its charged particles can move freely and conduct a current. In a second mechanism, an electric field can split the neutral molecules of a gas or liquid into charged fragments that can conduct electricity. Finally, the electrons of certain substances—metals and graphite among them—form electron "clouds" and are easily moved by an electric field.

Classes of conductors and insulators

Most materials are classified as conductors or insulators, depending on the relative ease with which they conduct currents. In fact, all common conductors have at least some resistance to the passage of a current, and most insulators conduct if subjected to a sufficiently strong field.

Certain materials become superconductors at low temperature: they provide no resistance to the flow of current. Semiconductors, on the other hand, are poor conductors whose conductivity increases if traces of impurities are added.

▲ This filament glows as the electrons passing through it collide with metal atoms and pass on some of their kinetic energy. The increased kinetic energy of the metal atoms then takes the forms of heat and light.

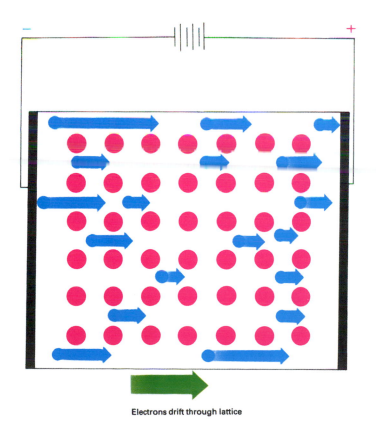

Electrons drift through lattice

▲ Some of the electrons in a metal take part in a delocalized bonding system that stretches throughout the sample of metal. If the sample is subjected to an electric field, these electrons are relatively free to move toward the positive electrode, carrying current as they do so. The nuclei and closely bonded electrons of the metal stay in a fixed lattice.

Conduction in gases

Lightning is a spectacular example of an electrical current passing through a gas, although a chain of invisible events precedes the formation of a lightning stroke.

Air consists of neutral gas atoms and molecules. Some of the molecules in air, notably water molecules, are polar, that is, they have regions of negative and positive charge that align with an electric field. Other atoms and molecules can become temporarily polarized as their electron clouds distort under the influence of an electric field. Where the electric field is particularly strong—at the pointed tip of a lightning conductor, for example—it can rip electrons out of molecules and atoms, forming free electrons and positive ions (positive because they have lost electrons).

Once a region of gas has ionized, its free electrons accelerate toward the positive pole of the field. Occasionally, fast-moving electrons bombard neutral atoms and molecules with enough energy to knock electrons out of those neutral species, forming further free electrons and positive ions. When the ionized region grows sufficiently to form a conducting path of ionized gas between the cloud and the ground, the current suddenly increases at an enormous rate. This current then causes the gas to get hot and emit light. What results is the lightning flash.

Lightning strokes can be simulated by causing a discharge between two electrodes through a sample of gas. The minimum electric field required to cause a discharge decreases as the pressure of gas between the two electrodes is reduced, since free electrons produced by ionization accelerate longer between collisions with neutral atoms or molecules—thus, more of them have sufficient energy to cause an ionization when they do collide. These ionizations produce a diffuse glow. This phenomenon is exploited in neon discharge tubes (in which neon is only one possible choice of filling gas), fluorescent lights, and lamps for street lighting.

Ionic materials and solutions

In a crystal of common salt (sodium chloride, NaCl), positively charged sodium ions (Na^+) and negatively charged chlorine ions (Cl^-) bond together in a rigid lattice. The application of an electric field across the crystal distorts the crystal lattice slightly, shifting the positive ions toward the cathode and the negative ions toward the anode. The strength of the crystal structure prevents these ions from moving from their lattice positions, however, and no current flows. Above the melting point of the salt, its ions become free to move, so the molten salt can conduct.

The ions of a salt also become free to move if the salt dissolves in a solvent such as water. Absolutely pure water is an extremely poor conductor, since its molecules resist dissociation into ions. Being polar, however, water encourages salts to dissociate into ions that are free to conduct.

Metals

Metals owe their characteristic conductivity to the type of bonding that holds them together. The atomic nuclei in a sample of solid metal occupy a regular crystalline structure. All but a few of the electrons in each atom are held closely to these nuclei and play no significant role in the bonding that holds the metal together. Those electrons that do take part in bonding—typically one or two electrons per atom—join a loosely bound system of electrons that permeate the whole structure. This type of bonding—known as a delocalized bonding system—is often described as a "cloud" or "sea" of electrons, since its electrons move readily under the influence of even the smallest electric fields. These electrons also interact with light and endow metals with their characteristic luster and opacity.

Electrons can move with little hindrance through a perfectly regular crystal of metal. Any irregularities in the structure, however, disrupt the flow of electrons, causing a corresponding reduction in conductivity. The most general irregularity is caused by thermal vibration of the atoms (owing to heat). As the temperature increases, so does the vibration; the electrons are scattered more frequently and the conductivity drops. The presence of impurities or the addition of alloying elements also reduces the regularity of the crystal and decreases conductivity.

Insulators and semiconductors

In an electrical insulator, each electron is strongly bound to its parent atom or molecule, and none is available to conducting an electrical current.

In the case of a pure semiconductor, a few of the bonding electrons will acquire enough energy from the random thermal motions of the atoms to break away from an electron-pair bond and participate in an electric current. Other bonding electrons can jump into the hole left behind, so that the hole appears to move like a positive charge. If the temperature is increased, both the

numbers of electrons and holes and the resulting conductivity goes up, unlike that of a metal.

Adding impurity atoms with more or fewer electrons than the semiconducting element provides an increase in conducting electrons or holes, respectively. The overall conductivity thus goes up as impurities are added, which again is unlike the usual behavior of metals.

Superconductors

Certain materials suddenly lose all electric resistance as their temperature decreases: once a current is started in a circuit of such a material, it will continue to flow indefinitely. This phenomenon, called superconductivity, has potential applications wherever a heavy current is required to flow. The electromagnets for MRI body scanners and magnetic-levitation trains are examples.

As yet, the use of superconductors has been limited by the expense and technical difficulty of maintaining the extremely low temperatures required for existing materials to superconduct. Materials scientists are working to develop materials that superconduct closer to room temperature. The best results to date have been for certain types of ceramic and polymeric materials.

▼ Electricity-supply companies use high-tension cables to transmit electrical power over great distances. Transmission voltages of 400,000 V or more reduce the amount of current that must flow to meet a given power demand (power = current x voltage), reducing the amount of power lost as heat, which increases with the square of current. The conductors in this power line are suspended from ceramic insulators, which prevent current from leaking into the ground through the transmission tower.

SEE ALSO: CABLE, POWER • ELECTRICITY • INSULATOR, ELECTRIC • MATERIALS SCIENCE • METAL • SUPERCONDUCTIVITY

Confectionery

Candy, or confectionery as it is known in many English-speaking countries, has different meanings in different countries, though the term usually covers all sweets, fancy cakes, and chocolates. Most confectionery is based on sugar and includes hard candies, toffees, fondants, nougat, gumdrops, jellybeans, and so on—all nonchocolate sweets.

The art of confectionery goes back thousands of years to ancient Egypt. The excavation of the ruins of Herculaneum, which was covered by lava when Vesuvius erupted in 79 C.E., revealed a complete confectionery workshop with utensils very similar to those used today. Confectionery was then based on honey, but in early times, sugar canes, crudely evaporated, were used in India and China. Sugar refineries first appeared in the seventh century in Persia. In the Middle Ages, the Venetians became the sugar brokers, but it was not until the 17th century that commercial refining was developed.

Ingredients

Modern confectionery, therefore, originated in the 17th century, and the development of beet sugar (1747) resulted in a dynamic growth of the confectionery trade. Sugar is the basic ingredient of all hard and soft candies, but in addition, syrups and invert sugars—glucose and fructose (both are found in honey)—are used. Invert sugar is added in small quantities where a soft (noncrystalline) end product is needed, such as in fondants and liqueur centers. Honey is still widely used for its delicate flavor in nougats and fondants. It has a soothing effect and is also used in cough drops. Vegetable fats are used in great quantities for making such products as caramels, fudges, pralines, and truffles. Milk is usually used in evaporated, powder, or block form. Other milk products used are butter, butter fat, lactose, and modified milk protein (egg albumen substitute). Egg albumen and other whipping (emulsifying) agents such as alginates, gums, gelatins, starches, nuts, fruit, artificial flavors, acids, and colors are also essential ingredients in many kinds of confectionery.

Making candy

Most candies fall into two main groups: hard boilings, such as toffee and caramel, and the softer fondants and pastes. Sugar solutions, when concentrated by boiling, cool into a sugar glass with an amorphous (noncrystalline) structure. If the cooling is accompanied by beating, a mass of tiny crystals suspended in syrup is formed. This solution is the basis of the manufacture of both hard and soft candy. To prevent the hard boilings from becoming cloudy and the fondants from becoming "grainy" with crystals, a small quantity of invert sugar is added to the syrup solution at the initial mixing stage.

Types of candy

Hard candies are made by boiling the sugar solutions as described and forming the sticky mass as it cools into separate candies in individual molds. A big breakthrough in confectionery technology occurred around 1960 when a continuous process was developed for making candy. Caramels, toffees, and butterscotch are made the same way, but their characteristics depend on the temperature to which the sugar is heated and on the addition of certain ingredients to the recipe such as milk, butter, and certain vegetable fats.

Fondants are creams and contain glucose syrup, which is beaten strongly during cooling. Since a great deal of heat is given out during crystallization, artificial cooling, usually by means of a water-cooled jacket around the beater, is necessary. The fondants are usually deposited into molds—basically impressions made in a bed of starch—a process known as starch molding.

Fudge, popular in the United States and Britain but hardly known in Europe, was probably invented because of an accident during the crystallization phase—that is, if a high-sugar soft caramel is beaten while cooling, it will tend to crystallize. The properties of fudge depend on the temperature of boiling, the amount of fat, and the beating at the time of crystallization. Commercially made fudge contains fondant, which aids the crystallization.

Nougat originated in the French town of Montélimar and was made from honey, eggs, and nuts. Today it is a high-boiled syrup to which is added a frappé made from egg albumen and gela-

▲ Sugar can be made into candies to tempt every sweet tooth, from caramels, fondants, and jellybeans to gumdrops, fudges, and marshmallows.

tin. Nuts, fruit, and so on, are added to taste. Marshmallows are basically the same as nougat but with a higher moisture content and no fat. Sugar syrups can be aerated with gelatin or egg albumen and beaten into a foam that sets into a resilient, aerated, gellike confection.

Gumdrops, jellybeans, and Turkish delight are all based on a sugar syrup to which various types of gum are added according to the end product required. The main types of gum used are gelatin and agar (for jellybeans), gum arabic (for gumdrops), starches (used as a gelling agent in Turkish delight), and pectin (used in acid-fruit jellybeans). The name dragee is applied to goods such as sugared almonds and soft-centered candies with a hard sugar coat. The coat is applied as successive layers of sugar sprayed into a metal pan in which the centers are rolled around.

Licorice is unique. It is the only known plant that contains glycyrrhizin, which is the sweetest chemical found in nature—50 times sweeter than cane sugar. All licorice products are prepared by grinding the root, leaching it with hot water, and evaporating the solution. The manufactured solution is then molded into the required shape.

Chocolate making

The Aztec Indians in Mexico were known to have made a beverage from cocoa beans, corn, honey, vanilla, and spices, which they called "chocolatl." On his fourth voyage in 1502, the Italian explorer Christopher Columbus took back cocoa beans on his return to Spain. The Spaniards improved it by the addition of sugar, and chocolate eventually became an expensive and fashionable drink in European society. In 1728, Dr. Joseph Fry built the first chocolate factory, and 100 years later Coenraad Van Houten in Holland patented a machine for pressing cocoa powder. This machine made possible the existence of today's black chocolate, which basically is chocolate mass (the

◄ Cocoa beans are ground to form a nib, a continuous process followed, after liquor production, by conching.

▼ Conching is a process that develops the flavor of the chocolate through agitation, heating, and aeration of the cocoa mass before it passes to the manufacturing stage.

crushed and ground inner part of a cocoa bean) with added cocoa butter, sugar, and in the case of milk chocolate, milk or milk crumb (dried milk).

Making the chocolate

The beans are first cleaned and blended (chocolate is normally made from a carefully blended selection of beans). After cleaning, the beans are roasted to liberate their full aroma—both the temperature and length of the roasting critically affect the flavor of the finished chocolate.

The next part of the process is winnowing the beans, where the object is to separate the nib (the inside of the bean) from the husk or shell. Various machines are designed for this process, some of which will extract a greater proportion of the nib than others. After the nibs have been broken into small particles, they are ground down (usually by rollers) to a soft mass from which all chocolate products are subsequently made.

The chocolate mass is carefully blended with extremely finely milled sugar and additional cocoa butter; the latter is produced by pressing some of the cocoa mass, leaving as a residue cocoa cake, which is made into cocoa powder. In the case of milk chocolate, milk (or milk crumb) is added at this stage. Excess acids and moisture are extracted. The mixture is then refined by passing it through fine rollers until the correct particle size is reached. Particle size determines the texture of the finished chocolate.

The next step in the process, conching, is an art that chocolatiers have differed over ever since chocolate was first invented. It consists of intense kneading, temperature treatment, and aeration, and here the chocolate takes on its smoothness, creaminess, and purity. The flavor becomes fully developed, and a completely homogeneous product is obtained. The word *conche* comes from the Latin word for "shell," and the original conche consisted of a flat granite bed on which heavy granite rollers attached to steel arms roll backward and forward. This old longitudinal conche looks like a shell, and many manufacturers believe that the best quality chocolate can only be made in this type of conche. Today, however, many manufactur-

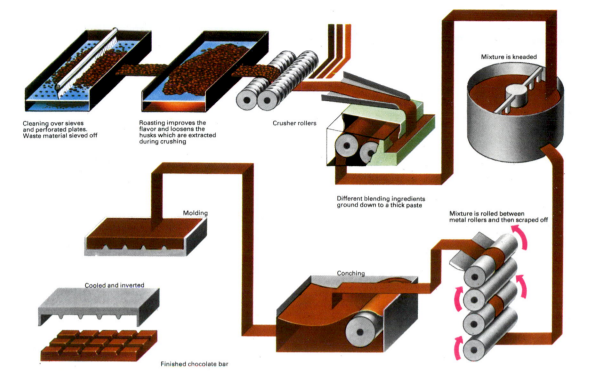

Cleaning over sieves and perforated plates. Waste material sieved off

Roasting improves the flavor and loosens the husks which are extracted during crushing

Crusher rollers

Mixture is kneaded

Different blending ingredients ground down to a thick paste

Mixture is rolled between metal rollers and then scraped off

Molding

Conching

Cooled and inverted

Finished chocolate bar

◀ The making of chocolate bars. After the cocoa beans are processed the liquid chocolate is poured into molds to form the top of the bars.

ers have changed to an upright steel conche, and most European chocolate is made this way. The length of the conching time and the conching temperature varies and is normally kept secret, but it is usually 10 to 24 hours for milk chocolate at around 150°F (65°C), with 24 to 96 hours for dark chocolate at up to 165°F (75°C), giving a slightly burned or high-roast flavor.

Types of chocolate

Next, the chocolate receives different kinds of treatment depending on its end use, the two main types of chocolate being chocolate couverture, that is, chocolate for enrobing or covering chocolates, cookies, and other centers and molding chocolate. The latter is poured into molds and allowed to set, and is used for plain and filled bars, Easter eggs, and chocolate novelties.

Other types of chocolate should be mentioned, although as food standards differ from country to country, they are not universally classed as chocolate. One of these is baker's covering, which normally uses hardened palm oil as the main fat, replacing cocoa butter and raising the melting point. There is also confectioners' coating, which is made from specially treated vegetable fats that are very similar to cocoa butter. Fats with a lower melting point than cocoa butter are used in a chocolate coating for ice cream.

Chocolate suitable for diabetics contains sorbitol, which sweetens and adds bulk, while replacing the sugar, dextrose, invert sugar, and starch-conversion products. It may include saccharin and nuts, which help with the cost, as sorbitol is several times the price of sugar. Low-calorie chocolates are low in fat content and contain substances that provide bulk but have no food value.

Chocolate couvertures are usually made by specialists and sold either in chip, slab, or liquid form direct to the manufacturer of confectionery products. The user first has to temper the couverture—that is, hold it at a certain temperature so that when it ultimately sets it does not bloom (have a cloudy appearance) but is smooth and glossy. The goods to be covered are passed through an enrober, which is a mesh conveyor belt that passes through a spray of chocolate. The completed chocolates are set in a cooling tunnel.

It is essential that molding chocolate is properly tempered, and a number of fully automatic tempering machines are now used in the modern continuous-molding plant. After tempering, the liquid chocolate is introduced into the molds by a depositor, and on cooling, the set chocolate is demolded. In the case of filled bars, molds are filled and then inverted so that the excess chocolate pours out. They then pass under the depositing head again, where the filling is introduced. There is then a further depositing of chocolate, which forms the back of the finished product.

For Easter eggs and novelties, the chocolate is poured into hinged molds, which are then spun while the chocolate sets. A recent invention is a foil mold that can also serve as the wrapper.

SEE ALSO: CARBOHYDRATE • COCOA MANUFACTURE • FOOD PRESERVATION AND PACKAGING • FOOD PROCESSING • SUGAR REFINING

Contact Lens

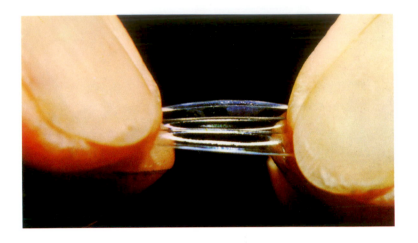

Contact lenses are used for correcting vision, but unlike glasses, which employ lenses mounted in a frame some distance in front of the eyes, they are fitted directly to the eyes. Strictly speaking, contact lenses do not make contact with the eye but float on a thin film of fluid.

There are two special types of contact lenses: corneal and scleral, or haptic, lenses. Scleral lenses fit over the entire front of the eyeball. (The sclera is the covering on the white part of the eye, and *haptic* means having to do with the sense of touch.) Corneal lenses fit on the cornea in front of the iris. Haptic lenses are thicker and are held in place by the eyelids and by capillary attraction, while corneal lenses, which are smaller and lighter, are located centrally by the steeper radius of the cornea. Haptic lenses are worn by people who participate in sporting events, because they do not pop out so easily, and by people who have diseased or damaged eyes or eyelids, to protect them from infection and promote healing. In cases where the wearer has a distorted cornea or a scar, the haptic lens can be designed with a tear lens underneath it to correct much of the corneal distortion. Corneal contact lenses, however, are the most common type today.

Most people who wear contact lenses rather than glasses do so for cosmetic reasons, but corneal contact lenses offer many advantages over glasses. Because they move with the eye, they do not restrict the field of vision. Certain types of visual correction can best be done with contacts. For people who have had surgery to remove cataracts, glasses produce distortion and contact lenses can go further toward restoring normal sight. Anisometropia is a condition in which the refracting ability of each eye is different. (Refraction is the bending of rays of light by a lens or by the cornea.) People who have anisometropia may have to be fitted with one convex

▲ Soft lenses are extremely flexible, which can make them vulnerable to rough handling.

▶ A contact lens in place is hardly visible. Hard and gas-permeable lenses sit over the pupil and iris of the eye. Soft lenses are slightly bigger. Both types follow the movement of the eyeball.

and one concave lens. If such patients wear glasses, they will have to move their head rather than just their eyes to look in another direction, or else they may see a double image. Contact lenses eliminate this problem; since they move with the eye, they are not subject to aberration. Keratoconus is a progressive disease causing a conical shape of the cornea; contact lenses may enable these patients to see well enough to carry on a normal life.

Development

The first refracting contact lens was made by E. A. Frick in 1887; in 1912, Carl Zeiss was making glass corneal lenses. In 1938, Obrig and Müller succeeded in molding scleral lenses in polymethyl methacrylate plastic (trade name Plexiglas in the United States, Perspex in Britain). Plastic is more rugged and considerably lighter, therefore, it will stay in place better. Until about 1950, most contact lenses were of the scleral type and required that an impression of the eyeball be taken for molding of the lenses.

In 1948, Kevin Touhy made the first plastic corneal lens. It was 0.4 in. (10.5 mm) in diameter, smaller than the iris; it neither covered up the sclera, depriving it of air and water, nor subjected it to pressure. The inside, or concave, surface was somewhat flatter than the cornea, allowing for circulation of air and water and minimizing pressure. In practice, however, the lens slipped, seeming too loose for the patient, and yet it was occasionally difficult to remove, at the same time paradoxically being too tight. It was soon discov-

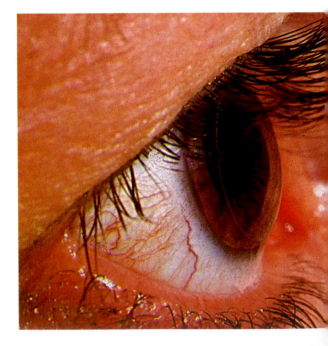

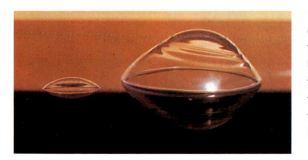

◀ Haptic lenses (right) cover more of the eyeball than ordinary contact lenses (left). They are held in place by the eyelids and the capillary attraction of the tear solution that keeps the eyeball moist.

ered that smaller lenses had better wearing qualities. In 1954, the diameter was reduced to 0.33 in. (9.5 mm), 17 percent smaller and covering 31 percent less corneal area. In 1957, the central posterior curve was redesigned to parallel the longest radius of curvature of the cornea, resulting in less variation of the fit and fewer refractive changes over a period of time.

Bifocal lenses became available in 1958. There are two types: annular, which have separately cut inner and out diameters and rotate on the eye, and segmented, which do not rotate and are shaped on the bottom edge so they rest on the eyelid.

Contact lenses can be made in different colors and different shapes for cosmetic or other reasons; they can be made shaded for use as sunglasses or with magnifying powers to enable people with poor eyesight to read small print. They have been fitted to children under three years old in cases of congenital poor eyesight. Compared with lenses for glasses, contacts must be very precisely made, because small errors in thickness or curvature will result in relatively large errors of refraction, but the machining and fitting of contact lenses is so highly developed that they can be custom-fitted to each patient.

Tolerance of contact lenses

The cornea requires oxygen, which it gets from dissolved air in tears. (Hence, the eyes normally blink several times a minute.) The cornea of contact lens wearers are said to be hypoxic, that is, they do not get enough air because the lens interferes with the amount of tears reaching them. It is this condition to which contact lens wearers must become accustomed, and therefore, the lenses can be worn only for a few hours each day at first until tolerance is built up. Older people generally have more tolerance for contact lenses than younger people, and people with diabetic or hypothyroid conditions or people who are taking oral contraceptives may have less tolerance. Wearing the lenses too long during the buildup period may cause a burning and itching sensation, which is called overwearing syndrome.

Since the early 1970s, hydrophilic, or soft, lenses have been increasingly available. These

▶ The fit of contact lenses can be checked by dropping a special fluid into the eyes. Shining ultraviolet light onto them makes the fluid glow, showing any irregularities in the fit.

lenses were first made in Prague, when a Czechoslovakian scientist discovered the unusual properties of a plastic called polyhydroxyethylmethacrylate. Lenses made of this material are hydrated by placing them in a saline solution; they soak up water from the solution and become soft. More hydrophilic lenses are now being used, including a variety of ultrathin lenses and lenses with high water content. Allowance must be made in the manufacture for expansion because, depending on the type of plastic used, the lens may double in weight during hydration. The more water the lens soaks up, the softer and more comfortable to wear it becomes.

Depending on the tolerance of the individual, soft lenses will cut down the buildup period or even eliminate it entirely. High-water-content lenses are used for extended wear, with the early lenses enabling five to six days wear without removal. In the 1980s, extended-wear soft lenses, which can be worn without removal for several weeks at a time, were introduced. In cases where lenses are needed for therapeutic reasons, they may be worn constantly for months. Newer types include disposables—low-cost soft lenses that can be worn for extended periods and then disposed of at the end of the week or month.

The disadvantages of soft lenses are that they are not as durable as hard lenses (they can be torn by rough handling) and they must be sterilized

◀ The refracting curves are cut on this small, specially designed lathe. A blue plastic blank is held in the machine by a drop of wax.

before each insertion, because the water may be a carrier of bacteria. They are also less effective than hard lenses in treating astigmatism because they follow the corneal curvature more closely.

There are two methods of sterilization: the lenses can either be boiled or, more commonly, kept in a special germicidal solution between wearings. Research is continuing to make the soft lenses even more convenient, with many new variations on existing types and new materials appearing, and increasing numbers of them are fitted to new users each year.

Gas-permeable hard lenses are similar in construction to corneal lenses but allow gases to pass through to the eye below to improve the corneal metabolism and ease some of the discomfort sometimes experienced with prolonged use. Cosmetic hard and soft lenses have been produced to supplement the use of scleral lenses in damaged and unsightly eyes.

Manufacture

Contact lenses can be furnished to the practitioner by the manufacturer in either a finished state or, if the practitioner prefers to do the fitting personally, a semifinished state. The semifinished lens has only the refracting curves, that is, the central anterior curve, CAC, and central posterior curve, CPC. These lenses are produced either by molding them or by cutting (or generating) them on a specially built lathe.

There are four different molding processes. Injection molding is done by injecting the melted plastic into the mold under pressure. Casting the lens involves free pouring of the melted plastic into the mold. In compression molding, a plastic pow-

der is pressed between dies under heat and pressure. Sheet forming is done by pressing a sheet of plastic between dies under pressure and heat. Since all the molding processes involve the application of heat, allowance must be made for the shrinkage of the lens as it cools. A disadvantage of sheet molding is that the lens may tend to flatten out because of a property known as plastic memory.

Molded lenses are mass produced on automatic machinery by some manufacturers in the most common prescriptions, but the more usual method of producing semifinished lenses is still cutting them on a lathe. Computerized lathe technology is now available for this purpose.

The blank for the semifinished lens is made by cutting it off the end of a plastic rod or by stamping it out of a sheet of plastic. (Sheet plastic can be more uniformly annealed in the manufacture; the refraction qualities of a plastic rod may not be the same from one end to the other.) The blank is fastened to a steel button by means of a drop of melted wax. The button is then installed in the lathe and centered magnetically. While the blank spins at high speed, a diamond cutting tool takes several concave cuts until the desired CPC is formed. With each cut, the operator removes less plastic until the final cut is a very fine one. There are dial indicators on the machine to tell the operator exactly how deep a cut is being taken.

Next, a lapper made of wax is trimmed with a template to match the curve of the CPC. The button with the blank on it is installed in the top half of a lapping machine, which holds the blank against the lapper. The blank turns in one direction and the

▶ The semifinished lens is polished with a mildly abrasive solution.

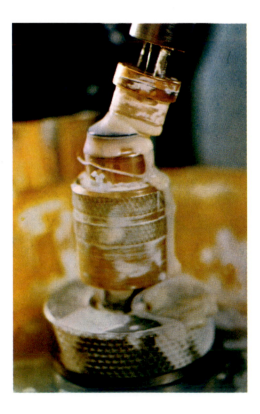

lapper turns in the other. In addition, the top part of the machine moves the blank around on the lapper in a small figure-of-eight motion. Lapping compound on the lapper polishes the machined surface of the blank in two to four minutes.

The blank is removed from the button and carefully inspected for the quality of the surface and the accuracy of the curve. Next, the finished surface of the blank is mounted on the end of a steel arbor, which is ground to match the CPC. The arbor is installed in a lathe, and a series of convex cuts are taken. This time, the operator has to read the dials to pay special attention to the

▲ A diamond-tipped cutting tool grinding the central refracting curve of a lens. The plastic blank is spinning at very high speed.

◀ A contact lens and its alignment with the eye. The main refracting curves are in the middle of the lens; they must blend smoothly into the next curves. The entire lens must be free enough not to obstruct the circulation of fluid over the cornea.

thickness of the lens being formed as well as the accuracy of the central anterior curve (CAC). The lathe can also trim the diameter of the lens, but trimming is usually left until the edging process.

Next the anterior side of the lens is lapped in a similar way to the lapping of the other side, except that the lapper is trimmed to a concave shape instead of a convex shape, and the figure-of-eight motion is not made by the lapping machine. The blank is now in a semifinished state.

Whether the finishing is done by the manufacturer or the practitioner, the important elements remaining to be finished are the edge, the peripheral posterior curve (PPC), and the intermediate posterior curve (IPC). These are all concerned with the custom fit of the lens. Each curve must blend into the one next to it, and there may even be several intermediate curves. The edge must be shaped so that the lens can move on the wearer's eye each time he or she blinks and to allow circulation of tears beneath it.

Standard edges can be ground on lenses with the use of conical tools having emery paper fastened to the shaping surfaces. Razor blades, grinding stones, and lathes may also be used in the finishing process. The lenses are held on the ends of arbors by means of double-sided tape or on suction cups. An experienced operator can grind the right finishing curves in a matter of minutes.

Conjunctiva

Aqueous humor

Pac

Iac

Ppc

Cornea

Iris

Vitreous body

Cac

Pupil

Lens

Cpc

Ipc

Sclera

Suspensory ligament

SEE ALSO: Eye • Lens • Light and optics • Ophthalmology • Ophthalmoscope • Optometry • Plastics • Spectacles • Stereoscopy • Surgery

Conveyor

◀ A belt conveyor in use at an opencast lignite mine near Cologne, Germany.

Conveyors are extremely useful devices for transporting a wide variety of objects. They are used in luggage handling systems, the transport of raw materials such as mineral ores, coal, or grain, the movement of components along assembly lines, and the handling of packages. They may have fixed or selective loading or discharge points, while the actuating power for a conveyor may be human muscle power, the force of gravity, air, vibration, or belts, chains, or cables operated by motors.

Unpowered conveyor

The simplest type of conveyor is a slide, often used where a downward incline will allow the force of gravity to pull boxes or packages. Usually a lower coefficient of friction is desired, and the conveyor takes the form of a frame with wheels or rollers installed between its sides. In a level or slightly inclined plane, the goods are simply pushed; in a downward plane, they will roll under their own momentum.

Several wheels across the width of the conveyor arranged in rows along its length or single rollers, each as wide as the frame, often have roller bearings inside them to achieve the low friction. The rollers or wheels may be made of steel, aluminum, or nylon and will be from 1 in. (25 mm) to 3 in. (76 mm) in diameter. This type of conveyor is also called a roller, or gravity, conveyor. It is often fitted with casters to enable it to be pushed from place to place and is typically used for the unloading of goods vehicles at warehouses and supermarkets. When the

angle of inclination is greater or more control over the flow is desired a powered conveyor must be used.

Belt conveyor

Loads may be moved on a level plane or an incline of up to 30 degrees by means of power-driven belts, which are made of rubber, canvas, steel, or wire mesh. The belt fills the width of the frame, and the unit includes a device for adjusting tension on the belt and an electric motor. The motor is connected to the head roller by means of a gear or a chain and sprocket. The head roller is at the destination end of the conveyor, and therefore the loaded section of the belt is pulled. The power unit usually provides a fixed or variable speed of from a few feet per minute to 50 ft. (15 m) per minute. Normally ¼ horsepower motors are used, but they can be larger for heavier duties. Belt conveyors are often used in warehouses to move goods from one point to another.

▶ A sheet of float glass on a conveyor. The float glass process produces high-quality, distortion-free glass sheets that do not require grinding and polishing.

Chain conveyor

Chain conveyors are those in which an endless chain or chains travel the entire length of the conveyor, transmitting the pull from the driving unit. They may be divided into two basic groups: those in which the weight of the material is carried by the chain (overhead chain conveyors, pan conveyors, chain and bucket elevators) and those in which the material is pushed, dragged, or scraped along in a trough (scraper conveyor, drag-link conveyor).

In an automobile factory, overhead chain-hook conveyors may be thousands of feet long and carry parts from one end of the plant to the other. Such a conveyor may carry body panels on hooks past the spray booths, where they are painted and thence directly through an oven where the paint is baked dry. Several chain-hook conveyors are loaded with parts in such a way that the parts arrive at the assembly line as they are needed. The assembly line itself is usually a heavy-duty chain conveyor, carrying the cars down the line as they are assembled.

A chain conveyor is sometimes installed in a trough in the floor so that hooks connected to carts, barrows, or fixtures on wheels can be attached to it. Such a chain conveyor is called a tow conveyor. Tow conveyors may be used in a coal mine to haul loads of coal up an inclined shaft or on a car assembly line to pull fixtures around in a circle on a subassembly line. At one point in the circle, the finished subassembly will be removed from the fixture and new parts put on it to be welded or bolted together as the fixture goes around again.

Pneumatic conveyor

One of the more recent innovations in the field of bulk materials handling is the pneumatic conveyor. This type uses air pressure to push or vacuum pressure to pull almost all free-flowing bulk materials (granulated or pulverized chemicals, ores, pulps, and so on) in an enclosed system, with conveying speeds much higher than achieved using mechanical conveyors. The pneumatic conveyor uses far more power per ton of material moved; the air or gas velocity used will be in the range of 6,000 to 7,000 ft. per min. (30–36 m/s) with the material traveling at 70 to 80 percent of these speeds. The resulting capacity may be 2,000 tons (1,800 tonnes) an hour or more.

A large modern bakery, for example, may have a pneumatic conveyor that can suck a truckload of

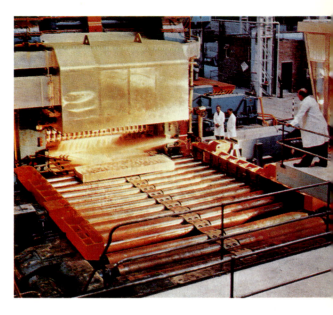

▶ Aluminum alloy is rolled on a conveyor at a modern mill.

flour into a tank for distribution to the dough mixing machines. In this way, the conveying operation can be entirely enclosed, preventing the loss of any of the flour.

Vibrating conveyor

A vibrating conveyor moves material down a slope through high-frequency vibrations induced by either electric or mechanical means. The vibrations are sufficient to dislodge the material from the bed of the conveyor, thus causing movement down even a shallow slope. The biggest application of this type of conveyor is in grading or screening operations for bulk granular materials such as sand, beans, coal ores, and so on.

Mechanically produced vibrations are generated by an eccentrically machined rotary shaft with counterweights independently supported on the frame, which make the frame vibrate at speed. Electrically produced vibrations are achieved by passing an alternating current through a winding, creating a series of intermittent magnetic pulses on an armature attached to the frame.

Screw conveyor

An Archimedes' screw, or helical auger, inside a pipe or a chute conveys the material in its thread, or pitch, as it turns. Screw conveyors are used for moving bulk materials in certain applications. The material is moved in the same way as a chip is removed by a drill bit when drilling a hole. An example of a screw conveyor can be found in the combine harvester, which may use such a device to move the harvested grain from the bottom of the machine to the storage tank.

◀ A factory worker checks finished cigarette packs as they move along on a conveyor belt. The speed of the conveyor must be controlled to match the working speed.

SEE ALSO: AIRPORT • ESCALATOR AND MOVING WALKWAY • FREIGHT HANDLING • MASS PRODUCTION

Copper

Next to aluminum, copper is one of the most-important nonferrous metals. It is a red, ductile, and malleable metal with good resistance to corrosion, but its most outstanding property is high electrical conductivity. After silver, it is the best conductor of electricity and is used widely in the electricity industry for a wide range of applications from overhead power lines carrying megawatts of power (although aluminum is being used increasingly for this purpose) to domestic wiring. As a structural alloy, copper is an important component of brass and bronze.

Chemistry of copper

Copper is one of the transition elements and comes in Group 1b of the periodic table together with silver and gold. It has a melting point of 1985°F (1085°C) and is only soluble in strong oxidizing acids, such as nitric acid and hot concentrated sulfuric acid.

The majority of copper compounds are divided into cuprous (with a valency of 1, Cu^+), which are the most stable in the solid state, and cupric (with a valency of 2, Cu^{2+}). In solution, however, only the cupric ion is stable. Well-known compounds include copper (cupric) sulfate, $CuSO_4 \cdot 5H_2O$, known as blue vitriol, a blue crystalline salt used as a mordant in dyeing and a fungicide; cupric oxide, CuO, a black powder used to give glass a green color; and cuprous oxide, Cu_2O, a red insoluble powder used to give a red color to glass.

Extraction

The metal that heralded the Bronze Age can be found in the natural state. Commercially all copper is extracted from either sulfide (copper glance, Cu_2S, and copper pyrites, $CuFeS_2$) or oxide (cuprite, Cu_2O) ores. Principal sources are the United States, Russia, Canada, Chile, and Zambia. Much of the ore occurs mixed up with rock in what is known as a porphyry deposit.

Sulfide ores, which are the more common, are reduced and purified by high-temperature pyrometallurgical (involving strong heating) processes, whereas the metal is extracted from its oxide ores by hydrometallurgical (extraction by aqueous solution) methods involving dissolution.

The first stage in the extraction of the sulfide ores is the removal of as much crushed rock as possible by using a froth flotation method. The mined material is put in a water bath together with specific surface-active agents, and air is blown through. Helped by the surface-active agent, the

▶ Naturally occurring copper crystals embedded in marble. Most copper is extracted from ores where it is combined with sulfur or oxygen.

small particles of copper-bearing ore cling to the air bubbles and are brought to the surface, where they are removed by skimming off the froth.

Copper sulfide is invariably found in association with iron sulfide, and the initial extraction processes are designed to remove as much iron as possible. They exploit the fact that at high temperatures copper has a lower affinity for oxygen than either iron or sulfur. The first process is known as matte smelting. The ore is melted in a furnace and some oxidation of the iron sulfide takes place. The iron oxide produced dissolves preferentially in the silicate-rich slag, which floats on the surface, leaving the melt enriched in copper sulfide.

At completion, the melt, or matte as it is called, is then placed into a converter-type furnace designed to enable a blast of air to be blown through the molten charge. The forced air completes the oxidation of iron sulfide to iron oxide, which is absorbed into the slag and periodically poured off by tilting the converter. When most of the iron has been removed as oxide, the air blast is

▶ After refining, copper is cast into ingots, from which it can be drawn into wires for use in electric power cables.

continued, and the chemical reaction in which copper sulfide is reduced to copper metal commences. When the reaction is complete, the metal is cast. During solidification, much of the dissolved sulfur dioxide is released, but some of the bubbles are caught in the cooling metal, giving it a blistered appearance. It is called blister copper.

The extraction of copper from oxide ores starts by dissolving the ore in sulfuric acid. The iron content of the solution is reduced by adding other chemicals and the copper extracted by electrodeposition (electrolysis). In comparison with the smelting of sulfide ores, hydrometallurgical extraction from oxide ores is much less used.

Refining
The exact type of refining procedure adopted depends on the types of impurities present in the blister copper and the final purity required. Refining is centered on two important processes: fire refining and electrolytic refining.

In fire refining, the blister copper is purified by remelting in an oil-fired furnace and again blowing air through the liquid metal. The process of removing impurities by oxidation is then continued, but in a much more controlled fashion than was possible in the converter, and the oxides skimmed from the surface of the melt. It is, however, impossible to reduce the sulfur content to the required level without leaving a significant amount of oxygen dissolved in the copper. An acceptably low sulfur content means nearly 1 percent dissolved oxygen, which forms about 5 percent copper oxide on cooling. This amount of oxide renders the metal brittle and useless.

In practice, the oxidation is continued until virtually all the sulfur has been removed. A large green tree trunk is then suspended from a crane and pushed into the melt, which is also covered with coke. The hot copper liberates a lot of hydrocarbon gases from the wood. These gases combine with the dissolved oxygen to form steam, which bubbles out of the melt. The operation is known as poling, and its control is critical. The progress of the reaction is monitored continuously by taking samples from the melt and casting them in small molds.

A casting after insufficient poling has a characteristic sunken surface and will contain an unacceptably high amount of oxide. Continued poling further reduces the oxygen content of the melt, resulting in an increase in the concentration of dissolved hydrogen and hydrocarbon gas. As a cast sample cools, this high hydrogen content reacts with the remaining oxygen and removes it as steam before the copper oxide is able to form. The metal no longer contains embrittling

oxide, but it is now full of steam bubbles and the sample casting has a convex domed surface. In practice, the poling operation is stopped before this stage is reached and when just enough bubbles are produced to exactly balance the sample shrinkage on solidification. The sample casting has a flat top, the copper is not too porous, fairly tough, and contains less than 0.05 percent dissolved oxygen. In this condition, it is called tough-pitch copper. Blister copper is not very suitable for electrolytic refining, and the electrolytic process is used mainly in the further refinement of tough-pitch copper.

Anodes about 3 ft. (1 m) square and weighing 440 lbs. (200 kg) are cast from already (roughly) refined copper and arranged in a lead-lined tank of acidified copper sulfate solution. Between each pair of anodes, there is a thin, very pure copper cathode onto which the copper, which dissolves off the impure anodes, is electrodeposited. The electrolyte is continuously circulated and maintained at a temperature of 122°F (50°C). The electrodeposition is completed in about four weeks, when the remains of the anodes are removed and remelted. The electrolyte is periodically changed during each run so as to keep the concentration of other soluble elements as low as possible. An important economic factor in this process is the recovery of precious metals from anode slimes, and if the blister copper happens to be rich in silver, gold, or platinum, it will certainly be electrolytically refined.

Refined copper
The small amount of oxide present in tough-pitch copper does not itself adversely affect electrical conductivity or mechanical working properties,

◀ In the process to extract the metal from copper ore, molten matte is poured into a converter.

although other soluble impurities can substantially reduce the conductivity. Gas welding of tough-pitch copper is not recommended because hydrogen entering the metal reacts with the oxide to produce steam-filled cavities that can lead to cracking of the weld. Similarly, the possibility of gas reactions means that tough-pitch copper is not particularly suitable for making castings.

High-grade tough-pitch copper is made from selected blister copper that is low in those impurities that cannot be removed by fire refining. It can be better than 99.93 percent pure and is suitable for electrical applications. Oxygen-free copper is made by heating tough pitch with phosphorus. Its electrical conductivity is much reduced by residual phosphorus, but the low oxide content means that it is suitable for both welding and casting.

Electrolytic copper is made by electrolytically refining tough-pitch. It is very pure, better than 99.98 percent, but is quite unsuitable for direct working on account of its very fine grain size. It is, however, used for making copper alloys. Further fire refinement of electrolytic copper creates electrolytic tough-pitch copper that can be drawn into wire and has a high conductivity. In electrical applications where an especially low oxygen content is desirable, the electrolytic tough pitch is deoxidized with carbon to make oxygen-free high-conductivity material. For special purposes, even purer metal can be prepared, and copper purity better than 99.999 percent is commercially available, but at a high price.

Electrical properties

Completely pure copper has a very low electrical resistivity. The presence of a very small amount of some impurities can drastically increase the resistivity of the metal. Phosphorus, silicon, arsenic, and iron are the worst offenders in this respect. Other elements have a much less drastic effect—for example, as much as 1 percent cadmium can be added before the resistivity is increased by 10 percent—and they are used when it is necessary to strengthen the metal without destroying its good electrical properties. Overhead power lines have to be good conductors but also strong in tension so that the pylons can be economically spaced. The copper used has 0.9 percent cadmium added to it and is cold worked. This process raises the tensile strength from 15 to 40 tons per sq. in. (232×10^6–618×10^6 N/m^2), while increasing the resistivity very little.

Aluminum has now become cheaper than copper and is challenging copper in some applications, such as overhead power lines, but it will never completely replace copper as an electrical

▲ Easily hammered and shaped, copper has been in use since the Stone Age. These attractive utensils are on sale in a Turkish market. Copper conducts heat very well, making it ideal for cooking pots.

material for applications where space is limited, such as motor windings, and conductivity per unit volume is the important criterion. Copper has the further advantage that it can be readily soldered, and its good oxidation resistance means that electric switches can be made satisfactorily using copper contacts.

Alloys

Copper is widely used as a base for alloys. Brasses and bronzes are the two most important groups. Originally the term bronze meant a copper–tin alloy, but it is now applied to many other copper alloy systems with the exception of the brasses and cupronickel alloys.

The addition of up to 45 percent nickel to copper increases its strength and high-temperature corrosion resistance, with maximum ductility being obtained at about 20 percent nickel. Many silver coins are alloys of copper and nickel. Cupronickels find application in condenser tubes and other situations where a high-temperature corrosive environment is encountered. As with electrical conductivity, the thermal conductivity of copper is reduced by alloy additions. The thermal conductivity of a 40 percent nickel alloy will be only about 5 percent that of pure copper, and therefore cupronickels are not selected for service in heat exchangers, car radiators, or cooking utensils. In these cases, pure copper hardened with 0.5 percent arsenic or chromium is used.

There are two particular cupronickel alloys worthy of note. Constantan (60 percent copper, 40 percent nickel) has a high electrical resistivity that is remarkably insensitive to temperature, and finds application in electrical resistors and thermocouples. Nickel silver (German silver) contains 25 to 50 percent copper, 5 to 35 percent nickel, and 10 to 35 percent zinc. It has an attractive appearance and is used as a base for silver plating in tableware and costume jewelry.

SEE ALSO: ALLOY • BRASS • BRONZE • CABLE, POWER • COINS AND MINTING • ELECTROLYSIS • FURNACE • METALWORKING

Corrosion Prevention

Corrosion is a continuous destructive attack—usually on a metal—that causes a gradual wasting of material and can lead to the eventual failure of structural elements or components of machines. It has been estimated that corrosion damage costs industrialized nations around 3 percent of their gross national product—the profits from all commercial and industrial activity—so corrosion prevention is an important task.

The most common form of corrosion is the surface attack on iron and steel that leads to the formation of hydrated iron oxide, better known as rust. These materials—particularly steel—are very widely used, and they are prone to attack by everyday atmospheric conditions, such as moisture and polluted air.

Iron and steel are not the only materials to suffer from corrosion. The degradation of concrete by so-called concrete cancer is of growing concern, and materials such as aluminum, brass, copper, stainless steel, and even glass can corrode in appropriately hostile environments.

Corrosion science attempts to understand the fundamental mechanisms of corrosion processes and to discover means by which those mechanisms can be controlled or even halted. It draws on knowledge from many other fields, including metallurgy, electrochemistry, and microbiology.

Corrosion engineering uses the findings of corrosion science in diverse applications, such as prevention of corrosion in automobiles, aircraft, armaments, heating systems, oil rigs, pipelines, power plants, and surgical implants. Corrosion engineering also helps in the conservation of important archaeological finds.

Forms of corrosion

Corrosion sometimes happens rapidly and in a manner that is not easily detected, with the consequent danger of unpredictable failure. Common forms of localized corrosion include pitting, which is the formation of small holes; crevice corrosion, which occurs in fissures where there is a break in a protective coating; corrosion fatigue, which occurs when alternating stresses act; and corrosion cracking, which occurs in the presence of a tensile stress or stretching force.

Corrosion may be further classified as high-temperature oxidation, where a combination of heat and air causes damage to a metal or alloy; wet corrosion, where the damage is caused by a corrosive liquid; atmospheric corrosion, which is caused by airborne moisture and pollutants; and microbially influenced corrosion.

◀ This chain has rusted through exposure to sea spray. The combination of air, salt, and water in a marine environment promotes corrosion. Corrosion prevention aims to minimize the loss of valuable equipment to damage such as this.

High-temperature oxidation

High-temperature oxidation is a potential problem for the metal used to build furnaces and other equipment that is designed to operate at elevated temperature over prolonged periods. Most metals are covered by thin layer of metal oxide, which forms through contact with air at room temperature. At elevated temperatures—roughly 1800°F (1000°C) or more, depending on the metal—further oxidation of the metal can thicken the oxide layer until it becomes a scale and flakes off, causing a loss of material.

The growth of the oxide layer occurs by migration of metal ions. Nickel, for example, is coated by a thin layer of nickel oxide (NiO) under normal circumstances. At high temperatures, nickel atoms lose two electrons each and form nickel ions (Ni^{2+}). These ions migrate through defects in the nickel oxide layer where metal ions are absent from some sites in an otherwise regular lattice. The electrons also migrate through the oxide layer, forming oxide ions from oxygen molecules at the surface. These oxide ions then combine with nickel ions to form nickel oxide.

▶ The greater part of this rig will be submerged in saltwater when it reaches its planned location. Its steel structure will be protected from corrosion by several magnesium bars, visible as white strips against the darker steel. When the bars have corroded, divers will replace them to ensure continued protection.

Oxide formation is also a problem when hot steel is rolled to form plates or sheets. The thick layers of iron oxides must subsequently be removed either mechanically—by sandblasting, for example, or by pickling with acid, which converts the oxide into soluble salts that wash away.

Some metals form oxides whose lattices are highly coherent—they have few vacancy defects. Aluminum, chromium, and silicon are notable examples of metals that are resistant to oxide thickening by high-temperature oxidation, since their oxide layers block the migration of metal ions. They also contribute to the protection of alloys that contain them, as their oxides form at the surface of the metal, sealing the surface from metal ion migration. Thus, stainless steel, which contains chromium, is more resistant to high-temperature oxidation than is mild steel.

Aluminum and chromium can be used as protective coatings for metal objects. Chromium-plated exhaust tailpipes resist tarnishing at the high temperatures of exhaust gases.

The protective action of a coherent oxide layer can be enhanced by the inclusion of cerium or yttrium in an alloy. These metals inhibit the formation of cracks in the protective oxide layer.

Some hot industrial gases can form chlorides, nitrides, or sulfides on the metal surface. These compounds are usually less protective than oxides. Substances that can accelerate oxidation include salt (NaCl) and the vanadium compounds that commonly occur in solid-fuel ash.

Wet corrosion

When a metal is immersed in aerated water, a destructive electrochemical reaction can occur where there are breaks in the superficial oxide layer. In the case of iron, the equation for this reaction is as follows:

$$Fe \rightarrow Fe^{2+} + 2e^-$$

This reaction, called the anodic reaction, converts insoluble iron atoms into soluble iron (II) ions and feeds electrons into the metal.

Elsewhere on the metal surface, another reaction, the cathodic reaction, converts oxygen and water molecules into hydroxide ions:

$$O_2 + 2H_2O + 4e^- \rightarrow 4OH^-$$

This reaction absorbs electrons, establishing a flow of electrons from anodic regions to cathodic regions. At the same time, hydroxide ions migrate through the liquid to form solid iron (II) hydroxide ($Fe(OH)_2$) where they meet iron (II) ions. Oxygen rapidly reacts with iron (II) oxide to form a complex compound that is essentially hydrated iron (III) oxide (Fe_2O_3).

The mechanism of corrosion changes slightly in acidic environments. The anodic reaction is unchanged, but the cathodic reaction is between hydrogen ions from the acid and electrons:

$$2H^+ + 2e^- \rightarrow H_2$$

No hydroxide ions form, so the corrosion product is not rust but an iron salt. Whereas rust forms an insoluble layer that hinders further corrosion, the salts formed with acid wash away from the surface, thereby promoting rapid corrosion.

Wet corrosion is also promoted when the metal under attack is connected electrically to a less reactive metal because less reactive metals, such as tin, act as good cathodic regions, providing a demand for electrons and thereby encouraging the anodic reaction.

Preventing wet corrosion

Techniques for preventing wet corrosion focus on suppressing the anodic reaction, the cathodic reaction, or both. In many cases, this is done by physically excluding the corrosive medium from the metal surface, for example, by covering the surface with an inert film such as grease or paint. Grease has the advantage that it can be removed by solvent to reveal a clean surface at any time; paint has the advantage of being more durable. Other inert coatings include plastic, rubber, enamel, glass, and concrete. In order to be effective, a protective coating must cover the metal surface without interruption, otherwise corrosion will occur where there are breaks in the film.

Aluminum surfaces can be protected by stimulating the thickening of an inert oxide layer, that is, by anodizing—making the aluminum object the anode in an electrolytic bath that contains sulfuric acid. If a dye is included in the bath, it becomes trapped in the oxide film, giving a permanent color to the surface.

◄ Hollow panels of a car body are injected with wax to prevent corrosion. The wax forms a protective coating that repels water and so prevents road spray from collecting where it could cause rusting.

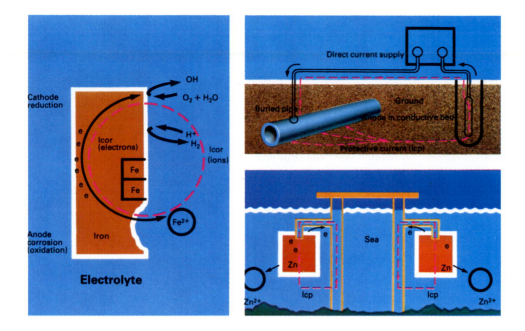

◄ When unprotected iron or steel corrodes, electrons are fed into the body of the metal where the surface is under attack (left). The process of corrosion can be halted by connecting the metal object to the negative terminal of a direct-current supply (top right). The excess of electrons at the metal surface discourages the formation of iron ions. This method of corrosion prevention is called cathodic protection. A similar effect occurs in sacrificial protection (bottom right). In this case, the supply of electrons comes from the corrosion of a metal, such as zinc or magnesium, that is more reactive than iron. The sacrificial anodes are attached where they are easy to access and replace.

Steel can be protected by electrolytically coating it with a thin layer of tin. Tin is less reactive than steel, so it corrodes more slowly, which is why tin-plated steel is used to make food cans. Unfortunately, if the tin layer is scratched through to the steel, it encourages corrosion of the steel by acting as a good anode.

Steel objects can be protected by galvanizing them (dipping them in molten zinc). The zinc layer corrodes more rapidly than steel so that steel exposed by a scratch in the zinc will not corrode. This is an example of sacrificial protection, whereby one metal is protected at the expense of a more reactive metal. Steel structures and pipelines can be protected by attaching blocks of zinc or magnesium, which are reactive metals.

Closed heating and cooling systems can be protected by adding chemical compounds called inhibitors to the fluid in the system. Typical inhibitors are chromate, phosphate, and bicarbonate salts, which act by slowing either the anodic or cathodic reaction of the corrosion process.

Atmospheric corrosion

Atmospheric corrosion is a problem that mainly occurs in regions with humid or rainy climates. Above a certain relative humidity, known as the critical humidity, the corrosion of metals such as iron and nickel accelerates rapidly owing to an electrochemical corrosion process that occurs in a fine layer of moisture on the metal surface. The corrosion reactions are essentially the same as those that occur in wet corrosion.

Atmospheric corrosion is promoted by oxides of nitrogen and sulfur—present as a consequence of pollution—which acidify the moisture layer. Sodium chloride—present in sea spray and as a consequence of deicing roads with rock salt—

breaks down protective oxide films and accelerates corrosion. Soot and other solid particles deposited on metal surfaces promote corrosion by holding acidic solutions in contact with metal.

Prevention of corrosion in the atmosphere naturally includes the coating methods already mentioned as well as specialized techniques such as cocooning (enclosure in a dry, clean atmosphere), special inhibitive paper wrappings, and vapor phase inhibitors, such as dihexylamine nitrate, which deposit themselves and inhibit corrosion at active sites. The green patina formed by the corrosion of copper is sometimes used to decorative effect for the roofs of buildings.

Microbially influenced corrosion

Microbially influenced corrosion, or MIC, is any form of corrosion that is promoted or initiated by the action of microorganisms. Although MIC was overlooked for many years, some corrosion scientists now believe that up to 40 percent of all corrosion damage might be influenced by bacteria. Typical targets for MIC include heating and drainage systems and underground structures.

In certain oxygen-free environments, such as waterlogged clay, sulfate-reducing bacteria boost the cathodic reaction by converting sulfates in the soil into acidic hydrogen sulfide and precipitating corroded metal as insoluble sulfides.

Certain types of bacteria oxidize nitrogen and sulfur compounds in soil and sewage to form nitric and sulfuric acids. These acids can cause extensive damage to concrete sewer pipes and other concrete-based structures.

SEE ALSO: ACID AND ALKALI • CIVIL ENGINEERING • ELECTROLYSIS • IRON AND STEEL • METAL • OXIDATION AND REDUCTION

Cosmology

Cosmology is the study of the origin of the Universe and how it changes as time passes. Study involves trying to explain the structure of the Universe as we see it today, to describe how it was in the past, and to predict what might happen in the distant future. Attempts to answer these questions have led to the proposal of many different cosmological models, or theories. New instruments, such as the Hubble Space Telescope and the Cosmic Background Explorer are providing information that may change our ideas radically. Key to the process has been determining a value for the Hubble constant. From this, astronomers have been able to estimate how old the Universe is, and its likely fate.

The Big Bang

The most favored cosmological model is the Big Bang scenario. According to this theory, the Universe began as an unbelievably hot, super-dense state in a single instant between 10 and 15 billion years ago and is presently expanding.

There is plenty of evidence that the Big Bang did take place, but scientists are unsure about why it did or what happened in the Universe during the first few instants of time as we know it. Scientists agree that this period involved pressures and temperatures and densities of matter far greater than any that can be created in laboratories on Earth or seen through astronomical observations. Since we cannot know what the laws of physics would be like under such extreme conditions, some theorists have tried to guess the form such laws would take in a way consistent with what we know about the behavior of matter under less extreme conditions, but identifying an overall symmetry or simplicity. This is the origin of current interest in superstring theory, which attempts to treat all particles and all forces within a unified framework.

While the name suggests an explosion, the Big Bang is probably better thought of as an expansion of space itself. According to the general theory of relativity introduced by U.S. physicist Albert Einstein, the Universe as a whole could be expanding or contracting or in a steady state. Einstein at first found the notion of a nonsteady Universe so disagreeable that he introduced a special term, a "cosmological" constant, into his equations to ensure a steady state. He later described this as the biggest mistake he had ever made. Most scientists now consider the current state of the Universe to represent an expansion of the Universe, with the distance between galaxies expanding due to the expansion of space itself.

The Hubble constant

In the 1920s, the U.S. astronomer Edwin Hubble found that in all distant galaxies the emission lines in their optical spectra were shifted toward the red end of the spectrum. This finding is consistent with objects moving away from Earth: if they

▲ This cluster of galaxies, called Abell 2218, was found in the constellation of Draco by the Hubble Space Telescope. The cluster is so massive that light rays passing through its enormous gravitational field are bent in the same way as if they were traveling through an optical lens, forming arc-shaped patterns. This phenomenon, called gravitational lensing, enables astronomers to view extremely distant galaxies in more detail, as if they were using a magnifying glass. The galaxies in this cluster existed when the Universe was one-quarter its present age, giving scientists a glimpse of how star-forming regions are distributed in remote galaxies.

were moving toward Earth, the shift would appear blue. Today most astronomers support Hubble's interpretation that each galaxy or cluster of galaxies is receding from every other one at speeds proportional to their distances. If the galaxies are moving apart now, they must have been very close together at some time in the past. This idea is at the center of the Big Bang theory. The relationship between the speed of recession and distance is known as Hubble's Law, and the factor linking the two is called the Hubble constant.

The cosmological distance scale

All methods of distance measurement rely on knowing the true brightness or size of a standard object, assuming that all similar objects throughout the Universe have the same properties. For comparatively close galaxies, these standard objects are either the size of clouds of hydrogen gas where stars are forming or the brightness of Cepheid variable stars, which are easily recognized by their rhythmic pulsations. At greater distances, astronomers use the brightness of Type Ia supernovae for distance measurement. These exploding stars should always reach the same peak

▶ Variations in the cosmic microwave background of only 0.01 percent are shown on this map made by the COBE spacecraft. Most of the variations are caused by instrumental noise, but the slight effect remaining reveals a lumpiness in the early Universe that is thought to be the origin of stars and galaxies.

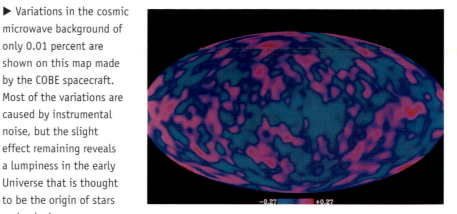

of brightness. Type Ia supernovae can be seen 1,000 times farther away than Cepheid variables.

In 1992, using the Hubble Space Telescope, astronomers began observing Cepheid variables in galaxy IC 4182, 16 million light-years away. A type Ia supernova occurred in this galaxy in 1937. The observations enabled a tying together of the Cepheid and Type Ia supernova cosmological distance "ladders." They indicated a value for the Hubble constant of about 45 kilometers per second per megaparsec (km/s/Mpc), implying that the Universe is between 14 and 20 billion years old. This calculation was somewhat greater than the ages of the oldest known stars, but it contradicted work involving the same galaxy that favored a higher value for the Hubble constant, about 80 km/s/Mpc, indicating that the Universe is younger.

The Hubble constant is not known as precisely as astronomers would like, but after eight years of measurements of distant stars and galaxies by the Hubble Space Telescope, they have refined estimates of its value to approximately 70 kilometers per second per megaparsec—that is, a galaxy one million parsecs (3.26 million light-years) away has a redshift of 70 km/s. This reckoning implies that the age of the Universe is about 12 billion years old. The reason these figures are so uncertain is that it is hard to measure the distances of remote galaxies accurately, and different methods give different results.

Elemental evidence

Further support for the Big Bang theory comes from measurements that show that helium is the second most abundant element in the Universe after hydrogen. The amount seems too great to have been produced by the nuclear processes occurring in stars that transform hydrogen into helium. There is a solution to this problem if most of the helium was made in the Big Bang.

Theory tells us that a few minutes after the Big Bang, the Universe consisted almost entirely of hydrogen nuclei (single protons) and helium

CEPHEID VARIABLES

Cepheid variables are a class of stars that have a variable luminosity because they oscillate between two states—expansion and contraction. By using the relation between the Cepheid's brightness and pulsation rate, astronomers can determine how far away they are. Using the Hubble Space Telescope, the distances to 800 Cepheids were measured in galaxies as far out as 65 million light-years. The data were plotted on a graph of galaxy distance against the velocity that the galaxy appears to be receding from Earth (below). The best fit to the data indicates that the expansion rate of the Universe (the Hubble constant) is 70 kilometers per second per megaparsec. Hubble constants of 63 and 77 do not fit the data so well.

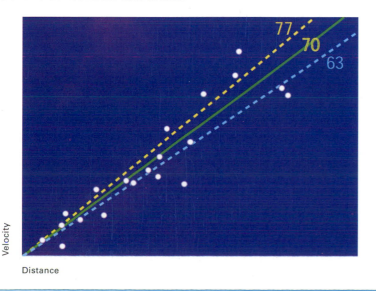

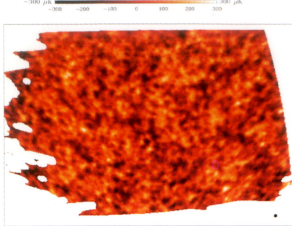

nuclei in a ratio, by mass, of 70 to 75 percent hydrogen to 30 to 25 percent helium. The fact that hydrogen and helium exist today in just these proportions in the observable Universe together with a few parts per billion of lithium, the third lightest element, strongly supports the theory.

Using the Hubble Space Telescope in 1990, scientists observed the spectral signature of helium in the light of the quasar UM675. This object is 12 billion light-years away, and its light began its journey to us at an early stage in the Universe. The observations therefore suggest that the helium was produced in the Big Bang rather than comparatively recently in stars.

Background radiation

A vital piece of evidence for the Big Bang is the weak background of cosmic microwave and infrared radiation found throughout the Universe that is thought to be a relic of the initial expansion. This radiation was first observed by a ground-based telescope in 1965 and confirmed by the Cosmic Background Explorer (COBE) satellite in 1991. At the time of the Big Bang, the Universe was a dense plasma soup of photons and subatomic particles. About 300,000 years after the Big Bang, when the superhot matter had cooled to a few thousand degrees, the subatomic particles joined together to form atoms, making space more transparent. The photons could then travel through it without being scattered or absorbed by matter. It is these photons that form the background radiation. The Universe has since expanded a thousandfold, and the original radiation has been diluted and cooled to a temperature of just 2.736 K.

As the subatomic plasma began to cool, small variations in density began to appear. Though weak, these variations were strong enough to affect the temperature of the photons. The more dense regions observed by COBE correspond to hot spots in the microwave background, the less

◀ This picture of the early Universe was taken by the Boomerang telescope. The color scale of the image has been enhanced to show the 100 ppm variations in the temperature of the subatomic plasma. The relative size of the Moon is depicted in the bottom right corner of the image to indicate the size of these regions, which eventually formed into galactic clusters and voids.

▼ Astronomers are still trying to determine the fate of the Universe and have a number of scenarios based on the mass and density of matter within it. While they have ruled out the likelihood of the Universe collapsing in a "big crunch," until a definite age can be determined, it is unclear whether the expansion rate of the Universe is steady or accelerating.

dense regions to cold spots. These structures are believed to be the earliest signs of the development of clusters of galaxies.

Confirmation of this theory came in 2000 with the results from two balloon-based telescopes, Boomerang and Maxima. Between them, these instruments covered a wider region of the sky at a higher resolution than was possible with COBE. Images revealed even smaller temperature variations than COBE of 100 parts per million. The patterns seen in the Boomerang and Maxima plots confirm predictions of the patterns that would result from sound waves and gravitational forces sculpting the structures that would form galaxies and clusters. Though the Universe is silent today, oscillations in the denser regions of the plasma would have caused it to alternate between compression and rarefaction, producing sound waves. As the Universe aged, the sound became louder until the plasma cooled to form hydrogen, when the noise suddenly stopped. The patterns seen in the microwave background reflect this moment.

Analyzing the data, the scientists expected to find a range of spot sizes corresponding to the length of oscillation. A peak was found that confirmed that sound must have once been heard in the Universe, as predicted by the Big Bang scenario. This finding also reinforced the idea that the expansion of the Universe was inflationary.

The shape of the Universe

A key area of debate since the Boomerang and Maxima flights has been the shape of space. Einstein's general theory of relativity tells us that gravity is the result of the way mass and energy curve space. If there is enough mass and energy in the Universe to counteract its expansion, it will

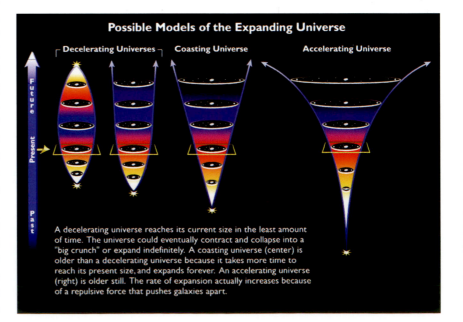

Possible Models of the Expanding Universe

A decelerating universe reaches its current size in the least amount of time. The universe could eventually contract and collapse into a "big crunch" or expand indefinitely. A coasting universe (center) is older than a decelerating universe because it takes more time to reach its present size, and expands forever. An accelerating universe (right) is older still. The rate of expansion actually increases because of a repulsive force that pushes galaxies apart.

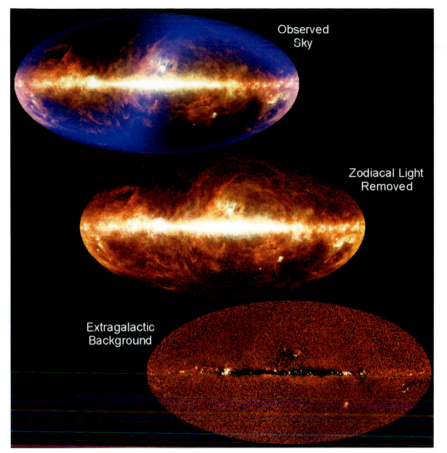

Observed Sky

Zodiacal Light Removed

Extragalactic Background

will expand forever. If it is closed, the Universe will eventually collapse back on itself, as matter, under the influence of gravity, comes together. If the Universe is neither open nor closed, it is said to be flat.

If the actual mean density of all matter in the Universe is greater than a critical value, equivalent to about three hydrogen atoms per cubic meter averaged over the whole of space, then the Universe would eventually contract. A value equal to the critical density marks the boundary between the open and closed universes. There is some theoretical prejudice in favor of a universe where the average density of matter is very nearly equal to the critical value.

Cosmologists have been thinking about what form this dark matter might take. Suggestions have included old dead stars, very low-mass stars called brown dwarfs, rocky bodies the size of planets or asteroids, black holes, and exotic particles, all of which hardly ever interact with ordinary matter and, consequently, have never been observed. One dark-matter candidate is the mysterious particle called the neutrino. A neutrino is a form of hot dark matter—described as hot because neutrinos would have been rushing around at high speeds relative to ordinary matter when the Universe was young. Slower-moving particles are called cold dark matter. They have exotic names such as axions, photinos, gravitinos, and WIMPS (weakly interacting massive particles). None of these forms of cold dark matter has yet been detected.

A more pressing problem for astronomers has been locating the rest of the known mass of the Universe. Less than half of the hydrogen gas that formed in the early days of the Universe became

eventually collapse. If there is less, the Universe will expand indefinitely. If space is curved, light traveling from distant objects will follow the curve, giving a wider angle than if space were flat. When this principle is applied to the plots of the microwave background, if the dominant spots covered an angle of roughly one degree, space would be flat. If they were larger, space would be spherical; if smaller, space would be curved like a saddle. Early assessment of both sets of data put the angle at 0.9 degrees—close enough for researchers to declare that space was flat. However, there was sufficient discrepancy in the results for later analysis to indicate that space may after all be spherical. Yet this sphericity could arise only if the early Universe was infinitesimally close to being flat. Finding the reasons for these apparent contradictions has posed new problems for cosmologists. What has become more evident, however, is that there is probably not enough matter to make the Universe contract again, and it will continue to expand.

Dark matter

There is abundant evidence that there is a large amount of hidden mass, or dark matter, in the Universe, possibly ten times as much as visible mass. The amount of dark matter is crucial to answering the question of whether the Universe is open or closed. If it is open, then the Universe

▲ Infrared background radiation is another cosmic fossil, found by COBE, thought to originate from millions of stars hidden by dust or to be too faint or far away to be seen. Removing the glow from solar system dust (top) and intergalactic dust (middle) reveals a uniform glow throughout the Universe.

▶ History of the Universe. After a rapid early inflation, the Universe formed a hot plasma soup of elementary particles, which converted into hydrogen and helium atoms as it cooled. It then took at least 11 billion years to form the galaxies we see today.

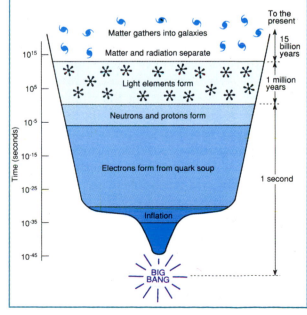

Time (seconds)

10^{15} — Matter gathers into galaxies / Matter and radiation separate — To the present / 15 billion years

10^5 — Light elements form — 1 million years

10^{-5} — Neutrons and protons form

10^{-15} — Electrons form from quark soup — 1 second

10^{-25}

10^{-35} — Inflation

10^{-45} — BIG BANG

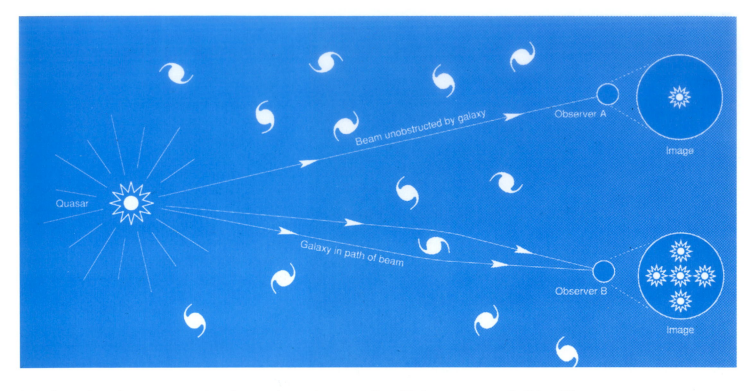

Quasar

Beam unobstructed by galaxy

Observer A

Image

Galaxy in path of beam

Observer B

Image

locked into the galaxies we see today; the rest simply vanished. However, astronomers now believe they have located vast intergalactic clouds of hydrogen, which are so hot that the hydrogen atoms have lost their electrons, rendering them invisible to normal detection methods. Instead, astronomers used the Hubble telescope to look for traces of ionized oxygen between galaxies. The presence of ionized oxygen is indicative of huge quantities of very hot hydrogen, and researchers have found enough oxygen to extrapolate the results to the whole Universe, solving the mystery of the missing mass.

The lumpy Universe

One of the greatest unsolved problems of cosmology is the origin of galaxies, clusters, and voids. The development of this "lumpiness" contrasts with the smoothness of the subatomic plasma. Most astronomers believe that gravity played a key part in the initial clumping of material. However, it would take a great deal of time for this clumping to happen, and the Universe is thought to be too young to have reached this stage of development if gravity had acted alone.

One hypothesis suggests this clumping could have happened only if dark matter, which behaves in a different way to the visible mass, had combined with gravity to pull material into clumps. Another puts forth a case for a less dense Universe, where protons and electrons had more influence than dark matter. When they combined to form atoms, sound waves swept through the plasma, giving a boost to the attempts by gravity to form clumps. A third possibility is that when

the expanding Universe measured 600 million light-years radius, the average density of matter overtook that of radiation and affected the pressure fluctuations (known as the power spectrum) within the plasma. Whichever hypothesis is eventually proved correct, this lumpiness shows that the distribution of galaxies in the Universe is not uniform as was once believed but has been subject to the effects of random processes.

Gravitational lenses

Another development is the successful use by astronomers of natural "gravitational lenses" to study the faint light from remote galaxies and quasars that would otherwise have been beyond the reach of even the most powerful telescopes. If a faint, distant galaxy or quasar lies behind a nearer cluster of galaxies, then, if the cluster is sufficiently massive, light rays from the distant object will be bent by the strong gravitational pull of the cluster. The overall effect is that the cluster acts like a lens, magnifying and distorting the image of the faint galaxy or quasar behind it, producing arcs or multiple images.

Observations of lensing can be used to "weigh" clusters of galaxies, and help us to understand the distribution of dark matter within them. Gravitational lenses are also being used to investigate star formation in distant galaxies, the size and structure of distant quasars, and the scale of the Universe.

▲ Gravitational lensing occurs when light from a distant quasar passes close by a galaxy. In position A, unobstructed, the observer sees a single image. In position B, beams are bent by the galaxy, yielding a distorted image.

SEE ALSO: ASTRONOMY • ASTROPHYSICS • ELEMENTARY PARTICLE • GRAVITY • LIGHT AND OPTICS • PLASMA PHYSICS • RELATIVITY

Index

Page numbers in **bold** refer to main articles; those in *italics* refer to picture captions.

A

accelerated graphics port (AGP) 534–5
acetylcholinesterase 437
Ada, Countess of Lovelace 523
Agents Blue, Orange, and White 438
aggregate 546, 549
alchemy 449
aldehydes 456
alicyclic compounds 455
alkali industry 450
alkanes (paraffins) 454, 456
alkenes (olefins) 454–5, 456
alkoxide ions 456
alkynes 454, 455, 456
alloys, for coins *507*
aluminum 449, 570
aluminum chloride, anhydrous *449*
ALUs (arithmetic and logic units) 528
amides 457
amino acids 458
ammonia, manufacture 451
ammonium nitrate, fertilizer *450*
analog audio 513–14
aniline (phenylamine; aminobenzene) 453, 457, 498
animation 536
anisometropia 560
annealing *507*
Antarctic, ozone layer over 480
anthracene 498
anthracite (hard coal) 494
anthrax *437*, 438, 441
Archimedes' screw 565
arithmetic and logic units (ALUs) 528
aromatic compounds 455
  aromatic rings as functional groups 456
  from petroleum 453
artificial intelligence, and personal computers 531
ASCII 529
assembler programs 530
assembly language 530
atmosphere, corrosion in 571
atomic structure
  Dalton's atomic theory 461
  electron orbitals (shells; quantum energy levels) 442, 461, 462
audio and video recording 513–15
augers, in screw conveyers 565
automobile factories, conveyors 564–5
automobiles
  chromium-plated tailpipes 570
  corrosion resistance *570*
  engine, pumps 521
  transmission 491–2
  trim *472*, 473

B

Babbage, Charles 523
bacteria
  corrosion-inducing 571
  used as biological weapons 438
baud rate 541
beetles, and past climates 477, *478*
bellows 518
Belusov-Zhabotinski reaction *463*
beneficiation 497
benzene 444, 455, 498
benzol 498
bicycle pumps 518
Big Bang 572, 573–4
binary system 514–15, 524, 529

bioinorganic chemistry 452
bipolar disorder 452
bitmaps 533
bits (computer), check 541–2
blood pumps, external *520*
body scanners, MRI 448
Bohr, Niels 461
Boltzmann distribution 463
bond polarization 459
bonds, chemical *see* chemical bonding and valency
bone ash (calcium phosphate) 465
boranes 451
boron hydrides 451
Boyle, Robert 449
bridges 474–5, 476, 549
bromoethane 459
brucellosis 438
buckminsterfullerenes (buckyballs) 451
butadiene 460
butane 454

C

cables
  between computers 539
  coaxial 539
  power *556*
caesium, in atomic clocks 485, 488
calcium phosphate (bone ash) 465
calorimetry 462–3
carbolic oil 498
carbon
  activated 476
  bonds 454
  inorganic compounds 449
carbon dioxide *477*, 479
carbon disulfide 464
carbon monoxide, molecules 462
carbonyl chloride *see* phosgene
carboxylic acids 457
cards
  CD business cards 515
  plug-in 539
casting, slip 466–7
catalysts 452, 464
  chiral 458
cathode-ray tubes (CRTs) *533*
cathodic protection *571*
CDs *see* compact discs
cellular telephones (cell phones), Internet access via 540
central processing units (CPUs), computer 527, 528, 529, 530
Cepheid variables 573
CFCs (chlorofluorocarbons) 480
chamber process 452
Channel Tunnel 475, 476
chemical and biological warfare 437–41
chemical bonding and valency 442–4
  coordinate bonds 444
  covalent bonds *442*, 443
  hydrogen bonds 444
  ionic bonds 442–3
  metallic bonding 442, 444
  polar bonds 444
  valency 442
chemical reactions 464
Chemical Weapons Convention (CWC) 437, 439
chemistry
  analytical 445–8
  inorganic 449–52
  organic 453–8
  organometallic 459–60
  physical 461–4

Chek Lap Kok Airport 474
china clay (kaolin) 466
china and porcelain 465–8
chirality (optical activity) 457
chiral synthesis 458
chlorine
  as a chemical weapon 437, 438
  manufacture *452*
  in the water supply 476
chlorofluorocarbons (CFCs) 480
chloromethane 459
chocolate 499, 558–9
chromatography 446, 469–71
  column 469
  gas chromatography and mass spectrometry (GCMS) 471
  gas or gas-liquid (GC; GLC) 448, 470–1
  gel-permeation (GPC) 471
  ion-exchange 471
  liquid *470*
    high-performance (HPLC) 471
  paper 470, *471*
  thin-layer (TLC) *469*, 470
chromic oxide 472
chromite ore, extraction 472
chromium 472–3
chronometers 484
civil engineering 474–6
clepsydrae (water clocks) 481, 488
climatology 477–80
clip art *533*
clocks 481–8
  alarm 481, 486
  atomic 485, 488
  electric 486
  mechanical 481–6
  quartz 486–8
  radio-controlled 488
  water 481, 488
clothing
  against chemical weapons *439*, *440*
  manufacture 489–90
clutches 491–2
coal
  mining 493–7
  types 494
coal tar 453, 498
cocoa manufacture 499–500
coffee 501–3
coffee-making equipment 504–5
cog railways 506
coins and minting 507–9
coin-validating machines *509*
coke 494
color 510, *511*, *512*
color blindness 510
colorimetry 447, 510–12
color mapping 533–4
color-register encoding 534
compact discs (CDs)
  audio 513–17
  CD-ROMs, drives 527
compression techniques, computer 533, 534
compressors and pumps 518–22
  compressors 518, 519–20
  pumps 520
    bicycle 518
    Bolsena 520, 521
    centrifugal 521
    double-action 520–1
    electromagnetic 522
    high-pressure 522
    hydraulic 521
    jet 522
    peristaltic 521, *522*

positive-displacement 520–1, *522*
  reciprocating 520–1
  rotary *520*, 521
  self-priming 521–2
  vacuum 522
computer-aided design (CAD) 489, 532
computer-aided manufacture (CAM) 532
computer graphics *464*, 532–6
computer printers 528, 543–5
  ink-jet 544–5
    bubble-jet 544
  laser 528, 543
  line 545
  plotters 528
computers 523–31
  analog and digital 523
  and the binary system 524, 529
  components *527*, 528
  development of 523–4
  future of computing 531
  graphical user interfaces (GUIs) 531
  graphics cards (video cards; adapters) 527
  languages 530
  laptop 526
  mainframe 526
  minicomputers 525, 526
  monitors (VDUs; visual display units) 527, 532, 533
  multimedia 525, 534–5
  networks 526, 537–42
    local-area (LANs) 526, 537, 538–9, 541
    peer-to-peer 538
    wide-area (WANs) 537, 539–40, 542
  operating systems 525, 530
  output devices 527–8
  palmtop 526
  personal organizers *530*
  personal (PCs) *523*, 525, 526–7
    future developments 531
    input devices 527
    output devices 527–8
    parity-bit checking 542
  programming and software 523, 529–30, 534
  security 530–1
conching 558–9
concrete 546–9
  corrosion 571
  lightweight 549
  polymer-impregnated (PIC) 549
  precast 547–8
  prestressed 548–9
  reinforced 547
condensed-matter physics 550–3
conduction, electrical 554–6
confectionary 557–9
contact lenses 560–3
contact process 452
continental drift 478
conveyors 564–5
copper 566–8
  alloys 568
  blister 567
  electrical properties 568
  electrolytic 568
  extraction 566–7
  oxygen-free 568
  patina 571
  refined 567–8
  tough-pitch 568

copper sulfate (blue vitriol) 566
copper sulfide 566
corrosion, prevention **569–71**
Cosmic Background Explorer
  (COBE) satellite *573*
cosmology **572–6**
cracking 453
  catalytic *459*
creosote oil 498
crops, biowarfare against 441
crystals and crystallography 550
  ionic crystals 443
  liquid crystals 551
  X-ray diffraction 462, 551
CS gas 437
cupronickels 568
cycloalkenes 455
cycloalkynes 455
cyclohexane 455
cyclopropane 455

D
Dalton, John 461
DAM-ATOLL ocean energy conversion system 549
dark matter 575–6
data storage
  using scanning tunneling micro-
    scopes (STMs) 552
  Zip drives and disks 527
Davy, Sir Humphry 449
decibels (dB) 513–14
defoliating agents 438
dendrochronology 478
densitometers, reflection *512*
diamonds, covalent crystals 443
diethylamine 456
Difference Engine 523
diffraction, X-ray 462, 551
digitally-encoded sound, on CDs
  514–15
digital subscriber lines (DSLs) 540
dioxins 438
dipoles (electrical) *554*
discharge tubes, neon 555
distillation 445
distributed processing 538
dithering 533–4
dopants 552
drives, computer 527, 528
dyes 464, *498*

E
earthenware 465
Ebola virus 440–1
Edison, Thomas 513
Einstein, Albert, general theory of
  relativity (theory of gravity) 572,
  574–5
ejectors, air 522
electrical circuits, bistable 487
electrochemistry 464
electrolysis, of sodium chloride 450,
  452
electrons, orbitals (shells; quantum
  energy levels) 442, 461, 462
electroplating 473
electrum 507
elements, chemical 449
El Niño 478–9
e-mail 531, 537
emeralds 472
enantiomers 457, 458
entropy 463
escapement, deadbeat 484
Essen rings 487–8
esters 457
ethanamide 457
ethane 454
ethanoic acid (acetic acid) 457
ethanol (ethyl alcohol) 456, 458
Ethernet 539, 541

ethers, crown 458
ethylamine 456
ethylene (ethene) 454, 456
ethyne (acetylene) 455
eyes
  and color vision 510
  contact lenses **560–3**

F
fat(s) 457
FDDI (fiber-optic digital device
  interface) 539
ferrocene *459*, 460
fertilizers, ammonium nitrate *450*
fiber optics, in cable networks 539,
  542
fibers, synthetic 490
firing
  china and porcelain 467
  glost 468
fishing, and suction pumps 522
fluorine 442
fondants 557
food processing
  cocoa manufacture **499–500**
  coffee **501–3**
fractals 535
freeze drying, coffee 503
fudge 557
fullerenes 451, *455*
  buckminsterfullerenes (buckyballs)
    451
functional groups 456–7
fusain (mineral charcoal; mother-of-
  coal) 497
fusion, latent energy of 463

G
galaxies *572*, 573
galvanizing 571
games, computer 536
gases
  conduction in 555
  gas laws 464
gasoline, tetraethyl lead additive 459
gateways 541
gemstones, coloration 472
genetic engineering, and biological
  weapons 440
GIF (graphics image format) 534
glass 493
glazing 467
Global Climate Observing System
  (GCOS) 479
global warming 479–80
glycerol (glycerine) 457
goggles, virtual-reality 532
grabs, cactus 496
graphical user interfaces (GUIs) *531*
graphics cards (video cards; adapters)
  527
graphics image format (GIF) 534
graphics tablets (digitizers) 535
gravimetric analysis 446
gravity, Einstein's theory of (general
  theory of relativity) 572, 574–5
gray-scale imaging 533
greenhouse gases *477*, 479
grenades, chemical *438*
gunpowder 449

H
Haber (Haber-Bosch) process 451
haloalkanes 456, 459
handshaking 541
hapticity 460
heat capacity 463
helium
  produced by the Big Bang 573–4
  superfluidity 553
hexane *454*, 459
honey 557

Hong Kong, airport 474
horologiums 481
hours 481
Hubble constant 572–3
Hubble's Law 573
hubs, computer-network *539*
Huygens, Christiaan *482*, 483, 486
hydraulic pumps 521
hydrogen, bonds 443, 444

I
IBM System 360 computers 525
ibuprofen 458
ice, humans preserved in 477, *478*
ice ages 478
images, 3-D, and computer graphics
  536
impellers 521
incineration, of chemical weapons
  440
infrared radiation, cosmic 574, *575*
insulators, electric 555, 556
integrated circuits (silicon chips;
  microchips) *524*, 525
  switches 552
Internet 537, 539–40
  and viruses 531
Internet service providers (ISPs) 526
ion exchange, chromatography 471
ionic materials
  solids 443, 555–6
  solutions 556
ionization, of gases 555
ions, molecular 448
Iran-Iraq War, chemical weapons 439
iron (III) oxide (ferric oxide),
  hydrated (rust) 570
iron and steel
  corrosion 569, 570
    prevention 571
  steel
    chromium 473
    for reinforced concrete 547
    stainless 473, 570
    tin-plated 571
    tool 507–8
ISDN 540
isomerism, geometric 455

J
joysticks, computer 535
JPEG (Joint Photographic Experts
  Group) 534

K
keratoconus 560
ketones 456
keyboards, computer 527, 535
kilns, for china and porcelain manufacture 467
kinetics, chemical reaction 464
Kismet (robot) *529*
Korean War, defoliants used in 438

L
lactic acid, chirality 457
lamps (lights), neon 555
La Niña 479
LANs (local-area networks) 526, 537,
  538–9, 541
laptops (laptop computers) 526
lasers
  and chemical bonds *461*
  and compact discs (CDs) 515–16
  and fiber optics 542
Lavoisier, Antoine 449
LCDs *see* liquid crystal displays
leather, tanning *473*
leaving groups 459
Leblanc process 450
lecithin 500
Leclanché cells 486

lenses
  contact **560–3**
  "gravitational" *572*, 576
lever escapement mechanism 483
licorice 558
light 510
lightning 555
light pens 535
lignite 494
Lindow Man 477
liquid crystal displays (LCDs) 532
liquid crystals 551
liquids 550
lithium carbonate 452
lithium fluoride *442*
lithos 468
local-area networks (LANs) 526, 537,
  538–9, 541
locomotives, trolley, in coal mines
  494
London dispersion forces 444
longitude *488*
longwall working 496–7
looms, Jacquard 523
LSD (lysergic acid diethylamide) 437

M
machine tools, clutches in 492
magnetic resonance imaging (MRI)
  448
manganate (VII) salts 443
mass production 486, 489–90, 493
mass spectrometry *445*, 448
  gas chromatography and mass
    spectrometry (GCMS) 471
  ion-trap 441
matter
  dark 575–6
  law of conservation of 449
mauveine (dye) 453
mechanics, statistical 463
Mendeleyev, Dmitri 449
mescaline 437
metallocene 460
metals
  bonds 442, 444
  electrical conduction 550, 556
  tests for 446
meteorology
  virtual reality weather *534*
  weather records 477
methane 454, 494
  bonding in *442*, 455
methanol (methyl alcohol; wood
  alcohol) 458
mice and pointing devices 527, 535
microchips *see* integrated circuits
microphones, as computer input
  devices 527
microscopes 551–2, *553*
Microsoft operating systems
  MS-DOS 525
  Windows 525, 539
microwaves
  cosmic 574
  used in computer networks 542
Milankovitch cycles 478
mineral charcoal (fusain) 497
minicomputers 525, 526
mining
  surface (opencast mining; strip
    mining) 495–6, 564
  underground, for coal 496–7
modems 540
molding, contact lenses 562
molecules
  computer graphics *534*
  structure established 462
monochromatism 510
movie production, animation 536
multiplexing 535, 542
mustard gas 437, 438

N

naphthalene 455, 498
neon 442
neon tubes (neon lamps) 555
nerve gases 437, 438–9
neutrinos 575
nickel
  alloys 473, 568
  corrosion 569
nickel oxide 569
Nimonic alloys (superalloys) 473
nitric acid *444*, 451
nitrogen, bonds in 442
nitrous oxide, bonds in 444
noble-gas configurations 442
noble gases 442
no-fines concrete 549
nonlethal weapons, tear gases 437
nougat 557–8
nuclear magnetic resonance (NMR)
  448

O

obelisks 481
oil drilling rigs *548*
oil refining
  cracking 453, *459*
  products from 453
olefins *see* alkenes
operating systems, computer 525,
  530
optical character recognition (OCR)
  systems 527
optical scanners 527, 535
overlock machines 490
oxidation state 443
ozone layer 479, 480

P

packet switching 541
paraffins *see* alkanes
parallel processing 526
parity checking 541–2
passwords, computer 530–1
patina, of copper 571
peat, preservation in 477
pendulums, in clocks *482*, 483–4
pentane 454
periodic table 449
personal organizers *530*
Perspex 560
petroleum (crude oil) 453
  alternatives to 450
pH, titration and 446
pharmaceuticals, design *534*
phenol 457, 498
phonographs 513
phonography (records and vinyl
  discs) 513–14
phosgene (carbonyl chloride) 437,
  438
photochemistry 464
photographic editing software 534
photons (quanta), X-ray 461–2, 551
photovoltaic (PV) cells 552
physics
  condensed-matter **550–3**
  solid-state 550
piezoelectric material 487, 545
pilot plants *449*
pitch (material) 498
pitting 569
pixels 532, 533
planets, and extraterrestrial life *446*
plastics, uses, contact lenses 560
Plexiglas 560
plotters 528
poison gas 437
poling 567
pollution
  and corrosion 571
  in the water supply 476

polybutadiene 460
polymers, "living" 460
polymethylmethacrylate 560
polypropylene (polypropene) *546*
polyvinyl acetate (PVA) *546*
porcelain 468
potential difference 554
power supply units (PSUs) 529
pozzolana 546
precipitates 446
pressing, clothes 490
pressure, dynamic 521
printers, computer *see* computer
  printers
printing, colorimeters used in *512*
propane 454
propanone (acetone) 456
propene (propylene) 454
propyne 455
proteins, chiral 458
protocols 537
PSUs (power supply units) 529
psychochemicals 437
pumps *see* compressors and pumps
pyridine 455

Q

Q fever 438
quantum mechanics, and electron
  orbitals 442, 461
quartz 486–8, 529
quinuclidinyl benzilate (BZ) 437

R

rack-and-pinion systems 506
railroad systems 475–6
railways, cog **506**
RAM (random-access memory) 528,
  529
raytracing 536
recrystallization 445
reduced-instruction-set computer
  (RISC) processors 526
reducing machines 507
reforming 453
relativity, general theory of (theory of
  gravity) 572, 574–5
resonance (in chemical bonding) 444
retina 510
retrosynthesis 458
ricin 438
RISC (reduced-instruction-set
  computer) processors 526
roadways, world's oldest 477, *478*
robots, with facial expressions *529*
routers 541
rubidium, in atomic clocks 485
rubies 472
rust 569, 570

S

sacrificial protection 571
Sarin 437, 439, *441*
satellites, artificial
  astronomical *573*
  communications 540, *541*, 542
  weather and climate *479*
saxitoxin 438
Schrödinger, Erwin 461
Schrödinger equation 462
screws, Archimedes' 565
sea levels, and global warming 480
sediment cores 478
semiconductors 552, 555, 556
servers (in computer networks) 526,
  537, 538
service providers, Internet 540
sewing machines 490
sheet forming 562
silicon 449
  a semiconductor 552
silicon chips *see* integrated circuits

silicon-tellurium-arsenic-germanium
  (STAG) 552
slopers 489
smallpox 437
soaps 457
sodium 442
sodium carbonate (soda; soda ash)
  450
sodium chloride (salt)
  bonds 442–3
  and corrosion 570, 571
  electrical conduction 555–6
  electrolysis 450, *452*
solar panels 552
solids
  amorphous *550*, 551
  ionic 443, 555–6
Solvay process 450
solvent extraction 446
soot, and corrosion 571
spam 531
spectrometry 447, 448
spectrophotometry 512
spectroscopy
  and electron orbitals 461
  laser-induced breakdown spec-
    troscopy 441
  molecular 462
  spectrophotometry 512
  X-ray fluorescence (XRF) 447
stars, Cepheid variables 573
statistical mechanics 463
steel *see* iron and steel
Store Baelt Bridge (Great Belt) 474
"subcode data" 516
submarines, concrete used in 549
sugar 557
sulfuric acid, manufacture 452
sundials *481*
"superbugs" 440–1
supercomputers *525*, 526
superconductivity 550
  superconductors 553, *555*, 556
superfluids 550, 553
supernovas, for distance measurement 573
super video graphics arrays (SVGAs)
  532
Sweet Track roadway 477, *478*
switches, glass memory 552
switches (intelligent hubs) 539

T

tabun 437
tanning *473*
tartaric acid *447*
tear gases 437
telecommunications
  fiber optics 539, 542
  satellite links 540, *541*, 542
teleconferencing 525
telephones, cellular (cell phones),
  Internet access via 540
television receivers, color *511*
temperature, transition 553
terracotta 467
tetrachloromethane 462
tetraethyl lead 459
textiles, for the clothing industry 490
TGV (Train á Grand Vitesse) 476
thermodynamics 463–4
thiophene 455
thunderstorms
  lightning 555
  virtual reality simulations *534*
tin, tin-plated steel 571
titration 446–7
Tollund Man 477
toluene 498
total color transfer process 468
trackballs 535
trackpads 535

Train á Grand Vitesse (TGV) 476
transistors, in computers 524
transition elements 452
  compounds *443*
tree rings, study of 478
triethylamine 456
trihalomethanes 476
trolley locomotives, in coal mines *494*
tularemia 438
tunneling 475
typhoid, as a biological weapon *437*

U

UNIVAC machines 524
Universe 573–6
urea 453

V

vaccines, against biological weapons
  440
vacuum pumps 522
vacuum tubes, in computers 524
V agents 437
valency 442
vanadium pentoxide 452
vaporization, latent heat of 463
vending machines, coin validation
  509
Vietnam War, chemical weapons 438
Viking space missions *446*
virtual reality (VR)
  goggles 532
  weather processes *534*
viruses (computer) 530, 531
viruses (microorganisms), as biological weapons 438
vitalism 453
vitrification 467
voltage 554

W

WANs (wide area networks) 537,
  539–40, 542
watches, mechanical 483
water, bonds in 444
water supply 476
wave power 549
wax, corrosion-prevention by *570*
weather
  records 477
  virtual reality *534*
wide area networks (WANs) 537,
  539–40, 542
wide band code division multiple
  access (WCDMA) 540
winding mechanisms, at pit heads *494*
Windows (operating system) 525,
  539
wireframes 536
workstations 526
World War I, chemical weapons 437,
  438
World War II
  chemical weapons 437, 438
  computers 523

X

X-ray diffraction 462, 551
X-ray fluorescence (XRF) 447
xylene (dimethylbenzene) 498

Y

yellow fever, as a biological weapon
  438

Z

zeolites *464*, 471
Ziegler-Natta polymerization
  catalysts 460
zinc, galvanizing with 571
Zip drives and disks 527
zippers, insertion of 490